The essays in *An Interrupted Past* describe the fate of those German-speaking historians who fled from Nazi Europe to the United States. Their story is set into several contexts: the traditional relationship between German and American historiography, the evolution of the German historical profession in the twentieth century, the onset of Nazi persecution after 1933, the special situation in Austria, and the difficulty of settling the refugees in their new homeland. In addition to articles on prominent scholars, there are accounts of the group as a whole, including information on more than ninety individuals, and of their family lives. Felix Gilbert recalls what it was like to study history in Berlin during the twenties, while Carl Schorske gives his reflections on the relationship between the refugees and their American colleagues in the wartime Office of Strategic Services. The volume concludes with analyses of the refugee scholars' impact on postwar American and German historiography, with special emphasis on four key individuals – the modern historians Hajo Holborn and Hans Rosenberg and the medievalists Ernst Kantorowicz and Theodor Mommsen.

PUBLICATIONS OF THE GERMAN HISTORICAL INSTITUTE,
WASHINGTON, D.C.

Edited by Hartmut Lehmann,
with the assistance of Kenneth F. Ledford

An Interrupted Past

THE GERMAN HISTORICAL INSTITUTE, WASHINGTON, D.C.

The German Historical Institute is a center for advanced study and research whose purpose is to provide a permanent basis for scholarly cooperation between historians from the Federal Republic of Germany and the United States. The Institute conducts, promotes, and supports research into both American and German political, social, economic, and cultural history, into transatlantic migration, especially in the nineteenth and twentieth centuries, and into the history of international relations, with special emphasis on the roles played by the United States and Germany.

An Interrupted Past

GERMAN-SPEAKING REFUGEE HISTORIANS IN
THE UNITED STATES AFTER 1933

Edited by

HARTMUT LEHMANN

and

JAMES J. SHEEHAN

GERMAN HISTORICAL INSTITUTE

Washington, D. C.

CAMBRIDGE UNIVERSITY PRESS

Cambridge

New York   Port Chester   Melbourne   Sydney

Published by the Press Syndicate of the University of Cambridge
The Pitt Building, Trumpington Street, Cambridge CB2 1RP
40 West 20th Street, New York, NY 10011, USA
10 Stamford Road, Oakleigh, Melbourne 3166, Australia

First published 1991

Printed in the United States of America

Library of Congress Cataloging-in-Publication Data

An interrupted past : German-speaking refugee historians in the United States
after 1933 / edited by Hartmut Lehmann and James J. Sheehan.

p.   cm.

Papers presented at a conference held in Washington, D.C., in 1988.
Includes index.
1. Historians – United States – Congresses.   2. Historians – Germany –
Congresses.   3. Historians – Austria – Congresses.   4. Political
refugees – United States – Congresses.   5. Political refugees –
Germany – Congresses.   6. Political refugees – Austria – Congresses.
7. Historiography – United States – History – 20th century – Congresses.
8. German Americans – Congresses.   I. Lehmann, Hartmut, 1936–.
II. Sheehan, James J.   III. German Historical Institute (Washington, D.C.)
D13.5.U6I58   1991
907'.2043 – dc20   90-26816
                                                                          CIP

British Library Cataloguing in Publication Data

An interrupted past : German-speaking refugee historians in
the United States after 1933.

1. United States. Germany. Historiography
I. Lehmann, Hartmut   II. Sheehan, James J. (James John)
1937–   III. German Historical Institute
907.2022

ISBN 0-521-40326-X hardback

Contents

v

Preface

Ever since the beginning of modern historical writing in the early nineteenth century, the historical profession in Germany has been divided and has had its insiders and outsiders. While historians like Heinrich von Treitschke and Heinrich von Sybel dominated the field by writing German national history with special emphasis on the role of Prussia, others like Onno Klopp and Johannes Janssen, who were interested in the history of Catholicism and in the history of non-Prussian German territories, were much less influential. The assumption that German national history had been the logical outcome both of the Protestant Reformation and of the Prussian military and political endeavors culminated among German historians in the decade before the First World War and during the Weimar republic. Only a minority of historians opposed this view.

After the Nazis seized power in 1933, the historical profession in Germany was divided in yet another way. On the one hand, those historians whom the Nazis considered politically dangerous or alien to the German people were forced to leave their positions in German universities. As a consequence, most of them also left the country. On the other hand, some of the historians who supported Hitler also propagated the National Socialist view of history, while others tried not to get too much involved in politics, although not many managed to steer clear of all manifestations of National Socialist influence.

As far as we know, well over one hundred trained historians – that is, persons with a doctorate in history who had made history the focus of their professional lives – had to leave Germany after 1933. Most of them sought and found refuge in the United States. For reasons that have only partially been researched so far, few of them returned to Germany after 1945.

When I started to study history in Tübingen in 1955, one of my principal academic teachers was Hans Rothfels, who had returned from the University of Chicago only a few years earlier. At the University of Vienna, one of my teachers was Heinrich Benedikt, for whom Great Britain had been the place of refuge from Nazi terror. Some years later, when I was *wissenschaftlicher Assistent* in the history department of the University of Cologne, I had the privilege of meeting and listening to lectures by Dietrich Gerhard, Felix Gilbert, Hajo Holborn, Eric Kollman, Edgar Rosen, and Eugen Rosenstock-Huessy, all of whom came to postwar Germany from the United States. To many students of history of my generation, it was evident that the historians who had been forced into exile by the Nazis represented an important tradition within the German historical profession. They had started to analyze and evaluate critically modern German history in general, and the Nazi regime in particular, even before the Nazi nightmare was over. Moreover, because of their personal experience before, during, and after Hitler, they had lessons to teach that mattered a great deal to all of those who wanted to come to terms with the recent German past. Hajo Holborn, Hans Rosenberg, Fritz Epstein, and many other refugee historians had an impact as teachers of history in postwar Germany because they cared about the future of Germany despite what they had gone through.

The establishment of the German Historical Institute in Washington, D.C., in 1987, offered a unique opportunity to assess the far-ranging impact of the refugee historians' work both in the United States and in Germany. I was also aware of the fact that in many aspects of its work the Institute had the opportunity – indeed the obligation – to build on foundations that had been laid by refugee historians. In my view, a conference on the role and the impact of the refugee historians from Germany to the United States from 1933 to the 1970s, therefore, had a double objective: It was to be a tribute to the scholarly achievements of the historians who had come to these shores under circumstances much less fortunate than ours, and it was to serve us as an orientation for the work that we were about to begin.

When we met in Washington, in December 1988, to discuss the role of the refugee historians in the American and German historical professions, we were able to bring together historians of three generations: some of those whose careers had begun in Weimar Germany and who were themselves witnesses of the story that we tried to look into; some of those who had emigrated to the United States as children, who later decided to study history, and who, interestingly enough, had often made

German history the center of their research; and finally students, and sometimes children, of both of these groups. If the Institute's first conference was an event equally stimulating and moving, this outcome was, in my view, due to this extraordinary combination of dedicated scholars.

I thank James J. Sheehan for the imagination with which he accompanied me in our joint effort to organize and carry through the conference and to publish this volume as well as for his introductions to the volume and its parts and his conclusion. I thank Kenneth Ledford for the expertise with which he edited the manuscripts and for the careful way in which he polished the translations of the German texts; I thank Rudolf Vierhaus and Mack Walker for their help in the publication of this book; and I thank Frank Smith and Cambridge University Press for their advice and their support.

My most sincere thanks go to those historians who had to leave Germany at the beginning of their careers, under difficult and sad circumstances, and who responded when I asked them to come to the Institute's first conference. For some of them the trip to Washington was too strenuous: Hans Baron, for example, and Paul Oskar Kristeller, Gerhart Ladner, Golo Mann, Edgar Rosen, and Martin Weinbaum. Hans Rosenberg was excited when he heard of our plans, but the conference had been scheduled too late for him to be able to attend. I am grateful that others were able to join us: Felix Gilbert, Fred Hahn, Stephen Kuttner, Alfred D. Low, Franz H. Michael, Peter H. Olden, as well as Eleanor Alexander and Marie Kann.

Washington, D.C.   Hartmut Lehmann

Contributors

Professor Kenneth D. Barkin
University of California, Riverside

Ms. Catherine Epstein
German Historical Institute

Professor Fritz Fellner
University of Salzburg

Professor Felix Gilbert
Institute for Advanced Study,
  Princeton

Professor Karen J. Greenberg
Bard College

Professor Michael H. Kater
York University, Ontario

Professor Barry M. Katz
Stanford University

Professor Hartmut Lehmann
German Historical Institute

Professor Robert E. Lerner
Northwestern University

Professor Wolfgang J. Mommsen
University of Düsseldorf

Professor Otto P. Pflanze
Bard College

Dr. Sibylle Quack
German Historical Institute

Dr. Hanna Schissler
German Historical Institute

Professor Carl E. Schorske
Institute for Advanced Study, Princeton

Professor Ernst Schulin
University of Freiburg

Professor Winfried Schulze
University of Bochum

Professor James J. Sheehan
Stanford University

Introduction

JAMES J. SHEEHAN

In the opening pages of his memoirs, Felix Gilbert describes his return to Berlin in the autumn of 1945. Wearing an American army uniform and on orders from the Office of Strategic Services, Gilbert took time out from his official duties to look for the apartment in which he had spent much of his youth. Although he could discover no more than a few colored cobblestones amid the ruins, these were enough to bring back powerful memories of his childhood. In Gilbert's delicate vignette we can find many of the themes that will recur throughout this book: exile and return, America and Europe, loss and recovery. Gilbert calls his memoirs *A European Past,* a title that calls attention both to the forty years the book describes and to the new epoch in his life that began in 1945.

Since the beginnings of our culture, poets have sung about the exile's experience of loss and the struggle to return. Dante, who knew the pains of exile firsthand, wrote of the "salt taste of another man's bread, the steep climb of another man's stairs." But while exile has always represented a special kind of loss, in the twentieth century its consequences have often been particularly serious. Because we live in a world where people's legal identity and status are defined and protected by their states, to be an exile is to suffer the terrible vulnerabilities of statelessness. Exiles now lose not only their homeland and livelihood; they also forfeit their most elementary rights as human beings. Never before has the bread of others been more bitter to the taste.

The exiles with whom this book is concerned were part of that massive flood of nazism's victims whose tragic fate has left a lasting scar on twentieth-century consciousness. In many important ways, the experiences of the refugee historians were like those of millions of others who fled social, economic, and political persecution by the Nazis. All of these refugees had to face the terrible fact that the

1

country to which they felt deep and enduring ties was no longer
theirs. All of them had to reach the painful decision to leave a familiar
world for the uncertain possibilities of a new life. Since we know
the fate of those who stayed, it may be too easy to underestimate
how difficult it was for many to leave – and not only for the men
with which this book is largely concerned but also for their wives
and children, who often had to bear more than their share of the
exile's anguish and anxiety.

Among refugee scholars and intellectuals, historians had some special problems. Since many of them were at the beginning of their
careers, they often lacked the reputations and contacts that would
have given them ready access to an international community of
scholars. On a purely practical level, the historians' sources, unlike
the scientists' equipment, are rarely portable or replaceable. But
deeper than these tangible losses were the bonds of language, culture,
and tradition that linked historians to their nation. In this regard at
least, a conservative like Hans Rothfels was no different from a left
liberal like Hans Rosenberg: For both men, Germany remained the
political center, the main subject of their research, the primary object
of their loyalty or lament.

Considering the obstacles they faced, most of the people whose
lives are described in this book did remarkably well. They and their
families learned a new language, mastered the complex rules of a
new society, made their way in a profession quite different from the
one in which they had been trained. But even those whose passage
into a new career was relatively easy had to overcome formidable
barriers. Almost no one retained the same rank and status that he
had left. And there is no way of assessing those private costs and
psychic burdens that inevitably attend exile. About such things most
of the essays in this book are necessarily silent.

The essays testify, however, to the variety of experience among
the refugees. A few well-established scholars, such as Hans Rothfels,
found good positions rather quickly. After some initial uncertainty,
Hajo Holborn, who had the advantage of ties to the Carnegie Foundation, was hired by Yale, where he spent his long and successful
career. Hans Rosenberg had to make do with a few short-term positions before going to Brooklyn College and, late in his career, an
endowed chair at Berkeley. Many other refugees worked in smaller
schools, where they carried heavy teaching obligations and had few
opportunities for research. And of course those who suffered most

from emigration do not appear in this book: Unable to find an academic job, they simply drop from our view.

That so many refugees did find academic jobs and thus could continue their scholarly work was in part due to a widespread willingness to help, among international organizations, informal networks of scholars, and various colleges and universities. American readers of this book will be grateful to those who came to the refugees' aid in their time of need. But we should be careful not to read this story as simply the triumph of American goodwill over Nazi tyranny. In some ways, the American historical profession that the refugees joined was not so dramatically different from the German profession that they had been forced to leave. Xenophobia, social snobbery, and anti-Semitism were by no means rare among American historians. That these prejudices significantly declined in the late 1930s and 1940s is, at least in part, due to the cosmopolitan influence of the refugee historians and their colleagues in other disciplines. In this, and in many other ways, the émigrés more than repaid whatever debts they may have acquired.

PART I

America first intruded on Germans' imagination during the Revolutionary War. "German newspapers," wrote Johann Heinrich Voss in 1782, "are full of America." To many German intellectuals, the colonists' struggle for freedom was one more sign of the changes taking place throughout late eighteenth-century politics and culture. But few Germans fully understood what was at stake in this distant conflict; they celebrated the colonists' struggle because of what it meant, or seemed to mean, for events closer to home. From this initial encounter until well into the twentieth century, the same process was repeated. Whether they viewed it with admiration or dismay, most German observers projected onto the American scene their own immediate hopes and fears, desires and anxieties. Thus Goethe's famous hymn "Den Vereinigten Staaten" tells us more about the poet's sensibilities than about its ostensible subject, just as Max Weber's famous analysis of Puritanism in *The Protestant Ethic and the Spirit of Capitalism* has more to say about Imperial Germany than eighteenth-century America.

Until the second half of the nineteenth century, Americans paid little attention to German affairs. Unless they were of German background, few citizens of the United States knew or cared much about the complex political or cultural world of Central Europe. With few exceptions, the glorious achievements of German literature and philosophy were not much appreciated in the New World. And who could make sense of the crazy quilt of states in which Germans lived or of the confederation that sought to coordinate their political affairs? Even to the best-informed Americans, these matters seemed far away and of little interest. There were, after all, other, more pressing problems near at hand.

In the century's last decades, some Americans began to find a great deal to interest them in Germany. For the first time it became possible to see certain similarities between the two societies. During the 1860s, both Germans and Americans had fought civil wars in which economically dynamic northern states had imposed their will upon their nation. By the 1890s, both Germany and America were conscious of their economic dynamism and growing international power, and both had begun to challenge Britain's global hegemony. Americans now went to Germany in increasing numbers to study at its great universities, to learn about its advances in science and technology, and to admire its military and bureaucratic institutions. To American academics, Germany seemed especially worthy of emulation. The German professor, generously supported by the state, respected by society, and confident in his own intellectual mission, seemed to represent everything ambitious young American scholars wanted to become. At Göttingen and Berlin, therefore, American students learned the research techniques and professional values on the basis of which they tried to reorganize academic life at home.

In his essay "German and American Historiography in the Nineteenth and Twentieth Centuries" (Chapter 1), Ernst Schulin traces Germany's powerful influence on the emergence of the American historical profession. The work of Ranke, Droysen, and the other great nineteenth-century German historians served Americans as models of how history should be written. At the same time, men such as Herbert Baxter Adams imported into the United States German methods of teaching and research that provided the basis for how young Americans learned to do history and define themselves as historians. Significantly, German influence *on* American history did not produce much American interest *in* German history. American historians turned to Germany in order to discover the intellectual tools and institutional basis with which to create their own national history. As the American historical profession grew stronger and more self-confident, the importance of the German example necessarily waned. Nonetheless, the two scholarly communities continued to be connected by a series of organizational ties and personal relationships. These ties and relationships were disrupted and, in many cases, severed after 1914, as German and American scholars fell victim to the plague of national animosities unleashed by the war.

In Chapter 2, Wolfgang Mommsen draws a somber portrait of the German historical profession after 1918. War, defeat, and revolution had destroyed what many historians regarded as the nation's political and ideological foundation. Bismarck's Germany, whose origins had provided the central theme for national historiography, now seemed all the more precious because of its tragic fate. Only a minority of the older generation made their peace with the new republic, and even these men continued to cherish the lost values of the imperial past. Slowly, and often with great difficulty, a few younger scholars began to define an alternative historical vision. Many of these people were Jews; all of them were committed to the Weimar republic, sharply critical of traditional institutions, and personally uneasy with the prevailing ideological climate within their profession. When the Nazis came to power in 1933, these scholars were forced from academic life. Although their number was small, their departure, as Mommsen writes, produced "a serious distortion of the spectrum of opinions and research traditions in the German historical profession."

Felix Gilbert's memoir of historical study in Berlin (Chapter 3) gives us a moving personal account of the center of historiographic innovation during the republic's last years. As so often happens, Gilbert's personal account does not quite fit with the broader generalizations to be found in many of the other essays in this book. In his experience, the atmosphere in Berlin was highly partisan but relatively tolerant; diverse, but not hopelessly divided. Friendships and personal loyalties could soften – even cut across – political divisions. For Gilbert and his fellow students – many of whose names recur often on the following pages – Berlin was an exciting, stimulating place to be a young historian. His recollections help us to appreciate how much was lost when the Nazis won.

1

German and American Historiography in the Nineteenth and Twentieth Centuries

ERNST SCHULIN

When the International Historical Congress met in Bucharest in 1980, acting president Karl Dietrich Erdmann called that organization the *Ökumene der Historiker*. In 1987, he gave his book on the history of the congress the same title.[1] He could have chosen no more fitting rubric to describe the increasing international unity of historical research in the twentieth century. The express purpose of these international congresses has always been to link the various national historical professions, to connect historians through closer personal acquaintance, through scholarly discourse, and through debate of political–ideological controversies.

Launched safely at The Hague in 1898, the international congresses soon faced heavy weather, which all too often delayed and obstructed safe passage to success. Two world wars, fascism, National Socialism, and Stalinism temporarily brought progress to a total halt. The *Ökumene* to which Erdmann referred has therefore really only existed since the International Congress in Rome in 1955, when historians from both East and West attended for the first time. Let us hope the weather remains fair: Historical ecumenism is, after all, not an inevitable process. More than any other branch of scholarship, the historical scholarships of individual nations remain nationally committed and ideologically bound. Even more than differing methods, directions of growth, and levels of strength, national commitment has led to widely divergent national paths of development, a phenomenon which was already visible in the nineteenth century. The professionalization of historical scholarship was closely associated with its nationalization. Professional historical writing, with its very specific methods and modes of observation, research, and

---

Unless otherwise indicated, all translations are by the author.
1 Karl Dietrich Erdmann, *Die Ökumene der Historiker: Geschichte der Internationalen Historikerkongresse und des Comité International des Sciences Historiques* (Göttingen, 1987).

8

teaching, evolved during the nineteenth century and emerged first in Germany. With a time lag of some twenty or thirty years, it spread from there to Britain, France, America, Russia, and other countries. Because this process was widespread during the nineteenth century, there have been a number of good comprehensive reviews of nine-teenth-century historiography, but there have been no comparable studies on that of the twentieth century.[2]

At the beginning of the twentieth century, historical scholarship in almost all countries found itself engulfed in a crisis of scientific method and concept. German historians debated historical relativ-ism, insisting upon the special position of the humanities – the *Gei-steswissenschaften* – and propagating a new "cultural history," midway between political history and sociology. The new *synthèse historique* in France occupied a similar position. Meanwhile, American historians launched the "New History." Comparable fundamental redefinitions also occurred in Italy, Russia, and Romania. This conceptual crisis was perhaps the most noticeable universal feature of historical schol-arship in the early twentieth century.

World War I not only demolished the high international repute which Germany's historical scholarship had enjoyed, but it also de-stroyed the international links among historians. Since then, histori-cal scholarship in the different countries has developed in parallel with the various actions and reactions in different countries to the political disasters and crises of the century: world wars, the threat of atomic war, the Russian Revolution, the rise of totalitarian systems with their realization of inhuman ideologies, the collapse of the old European state system, the ascendancy of the new superpowers, and the rise of Third World countries. If state interest dominated histori-cal scholarship in some countries, scholarly and public interest was the driving force in others.

National historical scholarships have performed an important function in the affairs of their countries. However, vigor and variety are not the only distinguishing features of scholarship in our century. The pronounced trend toward international communication, toward participation in the *Ökumene der Historiker* which Erdmann described,

2 See my essays "Geschichtswissenschaft in unserem Jahrhundert. Probleme und Umrisse einer Geschichte der Historiker," *Historische Zeitschrift* 245 (1987):1–30, and "Bemerkungen zu einer Geschichte der Historie, vornehmlich im 20. Jahrhundert," *Wissenschaftliche Zeit-schrift der Karl-Marx-Universität Leipzig*, Gesellschaftswissenschaftliche Reihe 37, no. 5 (1988):414–40.

is also quite remarkable. International cooperation has grown by leaps and bounds, especially in the last three decades. The German Historical Institute, and the conference on German-speaking refugee historians in the United States (1933–70), sponsored by the Institute in 1988, are but two examples.

This topic was a most appropriate one for the newly opened German Historical Institute in Washington, because it points to an unusual relationship between two historical professions – a relationship mediated and nurtured through immigrants. Although it could be argued that the United States was, after all, built entirely by immigrants, the massive influx of fully trained scholars who fled Europe under extreme political pressure in the twentieth century lies outside the normal course of migration. America received large numbers of European refugee scholars, displaced by the Russian Revolution, Italian fascism, German National Socialism, the Spanish civil war, and the German annexation of Austria. I need not here, however, approach the larger theme of immigration and its impact upon the intellectual climate of the United States; I will instead confine myself to German-speaking refugee historians. In this introductory essay, I will attempt to explain this encounter – brought about by Germany's political situation in the 1930s – in the context of the links that had developed between the German and American historical professions, beginning in the nineteenth century. This is not very easily done, because the origins, the prior conditions, and the development of the two national traditions differ so greatly.[3] In the beginning, an established, renowned historical profession in Germany exercised its great and formative influence upon a receptive newcomer. The situation has now been reversed. For the last forty years a richly appointed, multifaceted, methodologically advanced scholarly tradition in the United States has reached back to Germany to influence a politically flustered, methodologically stagnant historical profession in a divided nation. The two traditions began as unequal partners – and no more than this is implied in this rough sketch – and, in a different manner, they remain unequal partners in the end. Let me first describe the differences which existed at the beginning, in the nineteenth century.

3 Helpful are Jürgen Herbst, *The German Historical School in American Scholarship: A Study in the Transfer of Culture* (Ithaca, 1965), and the essays for the Centennial Symposium "One Hundred Years of German History in America": Fritz Stern, "German History in America, 1884–1983"; Charles E. McClelland, "German Intellectual History"; Gerald D. Feldman, "German Economic History," all in *Central European History* 19:2 (1986):131–85; Konrad H. Jarausch, "German Social History – American Style," *Journal of Social History* 19 (1985–

Germany set the example for the professionalization of historical scholarship. The shocking changes resulting from the French Revolution and Napoleon's rise to power had brought historical writing in other European countries to a temporary standstill. This was the pause between the Enlightenment and the Romantic Age. At that time, by using the groundwork of scientific and institutional standards created by eighteenth-century academies and universities, German historiography developed its own critical research in all fields of history: ancient history, with Barthold Georg Niebuhr; medieval history, with the edition of the *Monumenta Germaniae historica*; and modern history, with Leopold Ranke. In 1810, history joined philosophy and the natural sciences as a leading field of study at the newly opened University of Berlin. This reform involved a new conception of the Prussian state as well as of the *Bildungsbürgertum* (cultivated middle class). Research, teaching, and historical writing for the educated reading public became integrally linked. At the juncture of reform versus restoration, progress versus tradition, the German middle class looked to history for its identity and orientation. It hoped that historical knowledge would explain the meaning of duration and change. In the process, "historicism" rose to central importance for education and *Bildung* (cultivation). University professors, who were state officials, held key positions in the process, through their access to archives, through their teaching, and through their public influence. Wolfgang Weber has shown us in his book *Priester der Klio* how rapidly, how completely, pupils of the founding fathers of German history – Ranke, Georg Waitz, Gustav Droysen, and Theodor Mommsen[4] – came to occupy all university chairs of history. Because they taught national history rather than *Landesgeschichte* (regional history), they figured prominently in the movement toward national unification and achieved their political ends in 1871. Comfortably assured of state support, the established historians emerged as powerful epigones whose academic standards found great admiration abroad. In their work they justified the growth of the German *Reich* in the European family of nations as both desirable and appro-

6):349–59.

4 Wolfgang Weber, *Priester der Klio: Historisch-sozialwissenschaftliche Studien zur Herkunft und Karriere deutscher Historiker und zur Geschichte der Geschichtswissenschaft 1800–1970* (Frankfurt, 1984). On the importance of German historical scholarship, see also Gustav Schmidt and Jörn Rüsen, eds., *Gelehrtenpolitik und politische Kultur in Deutschland 1830–1930* (Bochum, 1986); Klaus Schwabe, ed., *Deutsche Hochschullehrer als Elite 1815–1945* (Boppard am Rhein, 1988); Gangolf Hübinger, "Geschichte als leitende Orientierungswissenschaft im 19. Jahrhundert," *Berichte zur Wissenschaftsgeschichte* 11 (1988):149–58, and Notker Hammerstein, ed., *Deutsche Geschichtswissenschaft um 1900* (Wiesbaden, 1988).

priate and found little fault with the present state of their nation. They criticized the unfavorable circumstances of their national past or, alternatively, new scholarly trends that insisted upon attributing greater importance to cultural, economic, and social influences than to state interest or the political deeds of great historical figures such as Bismarck.

American historiography began to professionalize much later, only during the later 1870s, and then slowly. Until that time, history in America had been the playground of enthusiasts, of hobby-historians. These authors were often clergymen and lawyers who especially nurtured the cultural heritage of the individual federal states, founding historical societies from which they often received financial backing, with occasional patronage from federal administrations. Famous writers, "gentlemen of wealth and leisure," wrote histories of America or Europe.[5]

History was a much simpler matter for Americans than for Germans. In a broad sense, it was seen as a concern of Europe, with both its centuries-long political rivalries – far away and slightly despicable – and its old and respected cultural tradition. In the narrower sense of national development, history was the progress of the United States beyond the Founding Fathers and the Constitution. The triumph of the Union in the Civil War was but "one more testimony to the providential course America steered."[6] American historiography thus stressed national uniqueness far more clearly than did German historiography and identified itself far more intimately with the advance of civilization.

Because of this view, neither the U.S. government nor the state governments felt any special urgency to promote historical scholarship. Few chairs of history existed at the universities, and interest in the national archives was slack. J. Franklin Jameson complained in 1891, "Except Switzerland, whose case is peculiar, I have found no instance of a civilized European country, not even Bavaria, Württemberg, or Baden, which does not spend more absolutely upon its archives than we do."[7] American historians made such comparisons to the German academic world frequently, because most of them had

5 George H. Calcott, *History in the United States, 1800–1860: Its Practice and Purpose* (Baltimore, 1970), 70.
6 Ernst Breisach, *Historiography, Ancient, Medieval and Modern* (Chicago, 1983), 260.
7 Quoted in Arthur S. Link, "The American Historical Association, 1884–1984," *American Historical Review* 90 (1985): 11. See also Victor Gondos, Jr., *J. Franklin Jameson and the Birth of the National Archives, 1906–1926* (Philadelphia, 1981).

studied in Germany. Among the first to study there was George Bancroft, an admirer of Ranke, followed by Herbert Baxter Adams, who "from 1876 on made systematic use of seminars (in the German style) in the training of historians at Johns Hopkins,"[8] and even the black historian W. E. B. Du Bois, who wrote a thesis on Bismarck, "the man who forged a nation out of a mass of rival peoples," and in 1890 attended Heinrich von Treitschke's lectures in Berlin. Du Bois recalled a scene from those lectures: " 'Mulattoes,' Treitschke thundered 'are inferior.' I almost felt his eyes boring into me, although probably he had not noticed me. 'Sie fuehlen sich niedriger.' 'Their actions show it,' he asserted."[9] On the whole, however, Du Bois felt that he had been well treated in Berlin and concluded that racial animosity was cultural, not hereditary or universal.

Undaunted by lack of official support, American historians resorted to self-help and founded the American Historical Association (AHA) in 1884, whose membership was (and still is) open to amateurs and academics alike. At the time there were no more than fifteen full-time professors of history, but their numbers soon increased. These history professors ensured that history received more attention in the curricula of colleges and universities, as well as secondary schools – which also followed the German model[10] – and after twenty years the historical professionals outnumbered the amateurs.[11]

Dorothy Ross recently pointed out that American historians by no means viewed Ranke, whom the association named an honorary foreign member in 1885, merely as a scholar whose sole aim had been

8 Breisach, *Historiography*, 287. Charles Kendall Adams had introduced this training method at the University of Michigan in 1869; Henry Adams followed him at Harvard in 1870. See Hans Rudolf Guggisberg, *Das europäische Mittelalter im amerikanischen Geschichtsdenken des 19. und des frühen 20. Jahrhunderts* (Basel, 1964), 48; Herbst, *German Historical School*, 34.

9 Quoted in John Baker, *The Superhistorians: Makers of our Past* (New York, 1982), 239.

10 For this purpose the American historian Lucy Salmon made a three-month study in German high schools. See Hartmut Lehmann, "Deutsche Geschichtswissenschaft als Vorbild. Eine Untersuchung der American Historical Association über den Geschichtsunterricht an deutschen Gymnasien in den Jahren 1896–98," in H. Fuhrmann et al., eds., *Aus Reichsgeschichte und nordischer Geschichte* (Stuttgart, 1972), 384–96.

11 The AHA was not the first professional association in America. The American Social Science Association was nearly twenty years older, but the AHA represented a new independence. Historians were no longer content to play second fiddle in a subsection but instead wanted their own professional association. In fact, the AHA remained an association both of historians and of political scientists, at least until 1904, when the American Political Science Association split off. Leading historians in the United States insisted that close links between historians and political scientists were necessary, again following the model of German historical scholarship.

the minute examination of isolated historical facts to demonstrate *wie es eigentlich gewesen* – "how it actually happened." On the contrary, they admired him for his mastery in linking his empirical case studies into a great design of universal historical synthesis.[12] They saw that Ranke and other German historians were firmly committed to state and politics, a commitment which had paid off in political effectiveness. As much as they sought a more scientific methodology, American historians sought more political influence.

Impressed by the experience of the Civil War and the subsequent difficult period of reconstruction and industrialization, American historians (among others, John W. Burgess) sought to use their work to preserve American republican principles in the new mass culture. German and English liberal influences mixed together; the historians' ideal was Teutonic individual independence, especially developed in Anglo-American liberty and self-government. Interestingly, Columbia University appointed a German immigrant, Francis Lieber, to the chair of history and political science. His book was the most influential one in this genre: *On Civil Liberty and Self-Government* (1877). Leading historians in the American Historical Association thought that these trends formed a likely platform from which to persuade the government of history's paramount importance for current politics. Their slogan was the epigram of British historian Edward A. Freeman: "History is past politics and politics present history."[13]

At the same time, no comparable European association of historians existed, except perhaps the Verband Deutscher Historiker. Founded in 1895, it convened the German *Historikertage* (historical conventions), as it has ever since. Britain, France, and Italy followed much later, after 1926, setting up similar national associations only when they became necessary in conjunction with the establishment of the Comité International des Sciences Historiques.[14]

The Verband represents one of the rare parallels of institutional development between American and German historical scholarship at the end of the nineteenth century. Outside of these institutions,

---

12 Dorothy Ross, "On the Misunderstanding of Ranke and the Origins of the Historical Profession in America," in *Syracuse* 9 (1988):31–41.
13 See Ross, "On the Misunderstanding of Ranke," 34; Herbst, *German Historical School*, 113. The words of Freeman were inscribed by Herbert Baxter Adams on the walls of his seminar room at Johns Hopkins.
14 Peter Schumann, "Die deutschen Historikertage von 1893 bis 1937. Die Geschichte einer fachhistorischen Institution im Spiegel der Presse," Ph.D. diss., Marburg/Lahn; Erdman, *Die Ökumene der Historiker*, 148.

however, the two national historical professions extended the first official feelers toward each other, creating a German–American professorial exchange. (Bernhard vom Brocke has treated this exchange at some length.)[15] The initiative came from the American side, from John W. Burgess and Nicolas M. Butler. Both had studied in Germany and wished to promote the knowledge of American history in Germany. Immigrant German historians, especially medievalist Kuno Francke of Harvard (formerly of Strassburg) and American constitutional historian Hermann von Holst (formerly of Freiburg) were eager to draw German colleagues to America, if only as visiting professors.

Francke thought that American academic life, "though intellectually far less stringent and invigorating, was yet far healthier physically and morally, more natural, with greater promise for the future" than the German one and considered that it would be "gainful in an eminently important way" if the exchange "were to lead to some reflections on the need for reform of many a public institution in the dear fatherland."[16] Another forceful advocate of the professorial exchange program was Friedrich Althoff of the Prussian Ministry of Culture, who had plans for the worldwide spread of German *Kulturpolitik*. Once he had gained the approval of the Kaiser, who took the matter up with President Theodore Roosevelt, Althoff dispelled the misgivings of Berlin historians that the proposed academic parity with American universities might be beneath their own dignity. The scheme was launched by an exchange of visits arranged in 1905, first between Berlin and Harvard, later between Berlin and Columbia and Chicago. Among the German visiting professors were Hermann Oncken, Erich Marcks, and Eduard Meyer; on the American side were John William Burgess and William S. Sloane. The outbreak of war in 1914 severed this connection. American historian Albert B. Hart canceled his appointment for the winter term 1914–15, and Leipzig cultural historian Karl Lamprecht had to do likewise – the more regrettably so since he had waged a long battle against the Berlin faculty, which had opposed his nomination for the exchange.

In 1914, a decade of important and stimulating direct links be-

15 Bernhard vom Brocke, "Der deutsch–amerikanische Professorenaustausch. Preussische Wissenschaftspolitik, internationale Wissenschaftsbeziehungen und die Anfänge einer deutschen auswärtigen Kulturpolitik vor dem Ersten Weltkrieg," *Zeitschrift für Kulturaustausch* 31 (1981):128–82.
16 Quoted in ibid., 141.

tween many branches of American and German scholarship, came to an end. In the field of history, one cannot simply conclude that a highly successful and growing cooperation thereby ended. One must also emphasize that during this decade new and old historical views merged, on both sides. Not only did German influence on American historical scholarship change in this process, but it declined.

The ebbing of German influence had been recognized from the beginning of German *Kulturpolitik*. One of the chief aims of that policy was to reverse the decline in the number of American students attending German universities, which had set in during the 1890s. For years Americans had made up the largest single contingent of foreign students, closely followed by Russians. Improved opportunities in Britain and France reduced the number of American students in Germany. Moreover, American universities began to offer significantly more courses in history. The "New History" clearly played a significant part. As early as 1891, Frederick Jackson Turner used his paper "The Significance of History" to speak out against those historians to whom history was principally or solely political history. He commented, "There is another and an increasing class of historians to whom history is the study of the economic growth of the people, who aim to show that property, the distribution of wealth, the social conditions of the people, are the underlying and determining factors to be studied."[17] In opposition to the Germanist thesis of Lieber and others, Turner stressed the uniqueness of America and its democracy. His frontier thesis is therefore widely known as "America's declaration of historiographical independence from Europe." Liberty and democracy, Turner argued, had not grown in the forests of Germany but rather in those of America.[18]

Edward Eggleston was the first to use the term "New History" at the annual meeting of the American Historical Association in 1900. His concept of New History was a kind of cultural history. James Harvey Robinson also employed the phrase, with wider effect. The New History arose in connection with the Progressive move-

17 This essay of Turner's is reprinted in Fritz Stern, ed., *The Varieties of History: From Voltaire to the Present* (London, 1970), 197–208, 199.
18 Breisach, *Historiography*, 314. See also Carl Becker's remarks on his teacher Turner in a letter to Beard, February 1939, quoted in Michael Kammen, ed., *"What Is the God of History?": Selected Letters of Carl L. Becker, 1900–1945* (Ithaca, 1987), 268. "In short, the explanation of American institutions was to be found, not in the German forest, but in the American wilderness." On the retardant German influence and its subsequent reversal, see also the informative interview by David M. Potter, "John A. Garraty," in John A. Garraty, ed., *Interpreting American History: Conversations with Historians* (New York, 1970), 320.

ment and with the social pragmatism of John Dewey, who taught at Columbia University, where Robinson and later Charles Beard were active. There is obviously no need to treat the New History at great length; its significance for our context is that it marked an emancipation from both the older American and the then-dominant German historical theory, although not from German influence altogether.

Turner borrowed many of his ideas from Arnold Heeren and Wilhelm Roscher; Robinson, who wrote his dissertation under von Holst at Freiburg in 1890, was influenced by Gustav von Schmoller. After 1900, Robinson remained in contact with Karl Lamprecht, who was a controversial and prominent advocate of new-historical conceptions in Germany.[19] Of course, these connections did not restore the former paramount influence of German historiography upon American historical scholarship. New-historical concepts developed in parallel and then merged on the international level.

The international connections of historians became very clearly apparent at the International Congress of Arts and Sciences, which convened upon the occasion of the World Exhibition of 1904 in St. Louis. Nearly one hundred European scholars attended, forty from Germany alone (presumably because one of the organizers of the Congress was Hugo Münsterberg, philosopher and psychologist, formerly of Freiburg, later of Harvard). Adolf von Harnack, Ernst Troeltsch, and Max Weber were present. The New History and its international community of proponents dominated in the Historical Section, postulating – as Woodrow Wilson formulated, in his opening address – "the early morning hours of a new age in the writing of history." Turner, Robinson, and William S. Sloane presented papers, as did Karl Lamprecht and British historian John B. Bury.[20]

In Germany, meanwhile, traditional history remained strong and even gained in power prior to World War I. Traditional historians dominated the lists of nominees for the American exchange program, and traditional topics prevailed at the German *Historikertage*. The Berlin history faculty even sought to prevent an international congress from convening there, because they feared it might lead to "unfruitful discussions on methods" and to "willful suppression of the truly crucial problems of power shifts and national struggles that alone

19 Luise Schorn-Schütte, *Karl Lamprecht, Kulturgeschichtsschreibung zwischen Wissenschaft und Politik* (Göttingen, 1984), 291.
20 Woodrow Wilson, "The Variety and Unity of History," in Howard J. Rogers, ed., *Congress*

ought to preoccupy our scholarship."[21] Such inflexible attitudes de-
tracted from Germany's influence on the international historical
scene.

One can only speculate about how American contacts with Karl
Lamprecht and his Leipzig Institut für Kultur- und Universalge-
schichte would have fared without the war. Besides the methodological affinity of his work to the New History, Lamprecht was greatly
influenced by the international peace movement, to which Butler
hoped to link the professional exchange program. Lamprecht's
achievements received widespread international acknowledgment,
especially in America. The first American review of his *Deutsche
Geschichte* appeared in the *American Historical Review* of 1898 under
the title "Features of the New History," written by Earle Dow (and
reputedly the first use of the term). W. E. Dodd wrote on Lamprecht
in 1903, Carl Becker in 1913. (Dodd, who was later U.S. ambassador
to Germany from 1933 to 1938, had studied under Lamprecht at
Leipzig but had written his dissertation under Marcks.) As time
passed, however, Lamprecht's evolutionist theories and scientific
concepts looked less convincing to American historians. In 1917,
after Lamprecht's death, Dodd wrote to Carl Becker, "I used to
think history as a science was possible, led to that idea by Lamprecht;
but I have long since got over that."[22]

World War I and ideological enmity effectively silenced the German–American dialogue. The work of Eduard Meyer can serve as
one example. His studies in religious history had benefited substantially from his residence in America, which had facilitated research
into a richly documented modern fundamentalist sect, the Mormons,
from whom he hoped to deduce the origins of Christianity and Is-
lam. After the war, however, Meyer began to express a hatred of
America in his work, tore up his American and British honorary
degrees, and effectively stalled the revival of scholarly and student
exchanges.[23] This may be an extreme example, but because of
Meyer's high standing in the profession it was very telling.

  of Arts and Science, Universal Exposition, St. Louis, 1904, 8 vols. (Boston, 1906), 2:3
21 Quoted in Erdmann, *Die Ökumene der Historiker*, 66.
22 Quoted in Schorn-Schütte, *Karl Lamprecht*, 303.
23 Eduard Meyer, *Ursprung und Geschichte der Mormonen, Mit Exkursen über die Anfänge des
  Islams und des Christentums* (Halle, 1912). *Nordamerika und Deutschland* (Berlin, 1915). *Der
  amerikanische Kongress und der Weltkrieg* (Berlin, 1917). *Die Vereinigten Staaten von Amerika.
  Geschichte, Kultur, Verfassung und Politik* (Frankfurt am Main, 1920). See the portrayal of
  Meyer by Karl Christ, *Von Gibbon zu Rostovtzeff* (Darmstadt, 1972).

The lost war and Versailles imposed new strictures upon German historical scholarship and led to a new retreat to a nationalist position. German historians in the 1920s saw their chief task as the justification of the country's historical path since Bismarck, the rejection of Germany's war guilt – in short, the defense of Germany's "special path," the *Sonderweg*. They did not like American and British international predominance, but they preferred it to French or Russian rule. They saw no need to accept, even less to honor, the political foundations of the Versailles settlement, such as democracy and the League of Nations. The majority of German historians disapproved of the new Weimar republic, and they were disappointed by America's withdrawal from European politics. The exclusion of German historians from the first postwar International Historical Congress at Brussels in 1923 mortified them, for they had long played a leading role in such assemblies. German historians turned inward. Even Friedrich Meinecke, a distinguished historian and untiring critic of domestic reactionaries, showed little interest in international cooperation.[24] Despite America's ascent to world-power status, German historians displayed little interest in American history or in works by American historians. As far as I can discover, German historians translated no American historical works into German and published no books on American history themselves.[25] Such lack of interest in American history is remarkable when we compare it to the marked interest of Dutch historian Johan Huizinga. In 1919, Huizinga wrote to Turner, "It has been a great surprise to me to see how much we Europeans could learn from American history, not only as to the subject itself, but also with regard to historical interpretation in general."[26] He published two booklets on America, one before and one after his travels there. His experience in America kindled his rising critical concern. He believed that he detected an anticultural, antihistorical trend in America and feared that this trend might encroach

24 See Bernd Faulenbach, *Ideologie des deutschen Weges. Die deutsche Geschichte in der Historiographie zwischen Kaiserreich und Nationalsozialismus* (Munich, 1980). On Meinecke's reserve, see Erdmann, *Die Ökumene der Historiker*, 150.
25 Exceptions were Friedrich Schönemann, who pursued the modern course of study known as *Kulturkunde*, and Alfred Vagts, whose Ph.D. thesis was entitled "Mexiko, Europa und Amerika" (1928) and who had been an exchange student at Yale. Friedrich Schönemann, *Die Vereinigten Staaten von Amerika*, 2 vols (Stuttgart, 1932). (Only the first volume was historical; the second treated contemporary political democracy, culture, and religion.) Alfred Vagts, *Deutschland und die Vereinigten Staaten in der Weltpolitik*, 2 vols. (New York, 1935).
26 Quoted in Michael Kammen, *Selvages and Biases: The Fabric of History in American Culture* (Ithaca, 1987), 163. Huizinga's two booklets on America were translated into English

upon Europe. He preceived a shift in historiography from narrative to structural history. It may well be that German historians harbored similar intellectual criticisms, but I know of no comparable German exposition on the faults of the American historical craft.

American historians' attitude toward Germany was, perhaps, more ambigious. The uncritical nationalism of most of the German professors from whom they had once learned so much about historical objectivity deeply disappointed them. The mood of anti-German hostility evident in America after 1914 was a great personal tragedy for German-born historians like Francke. The prevailing attitude of American historians toward German scholarship can be extracted from the presidential addresses to the annual meetings of the American Historical Association. In 1916, shortly before America's entry into the war, medievalist George Lincoln Burr presented a comprehensive review of current German historical theory. He judged German theorists such as Wilhelm Dilthey, Eduard Spranger, and Georg Simmel to be more important – even more stimulating – than Frenchmen such as Henri Berr. In 1919, after the war, William R. Thayer denounced the entrenched, anticivilizationist, older German historians Heinrich von Sybel and Treitschke, whose Darwinist notions had dehumanized a subject – history – "which should be the most human of all."[27]

Late in 1922, eminent medievalist Charles H. Haskins addressed the annual meeting of the American Historical Association. Other than James Henry Breasted, Haskins was probably the only contemporary American historian with any perceptible influence on German scholarship (if we disregard the much earlier Alfred Thayer Mahan, with his public and academic influence). Haskins had acted as specialist on French historical borders for the Paris Peace Conference. Now he called for the training of more American specialists in the history of Europe. He did not mention Germany in particular but spoke of Europe at large. Americans, he said, relied too exclusively upon European historians for their European history. Too many Americans, unfortunately, believed the United States to have been "providentially cut off from Europe by Columbus, or the Revolution, or

under the title *America: A Dutch Historian's Vision, from Afar and Near,* translated with an introduction by Herbert H. Rowen (New York, 1972).

27 George Lincoln Burr, "The Freedom of History," *American Historical Review* 22 (1916–17):253–71. William R. Thayer, "Fallacies in History," *American Historical Review* 25 (1919):179–90, 179. See also Herman Ausubel, *Historians and Their Craft: A Study of the Presidential Addresses of the American Historical Association, 1884–1945* (New York, 1965).

the rejection of the Treaty of Versailles." But Europe and America were "in the same boat, along with the still older Orient, all common material for history. The historian's world is one."[28]

Finally, in 1926 Dana Carlton Munro pointed out to the American Historical Association that World War I had led to the revival of political history. It had helped to restore military and diplomatic history to something of their once-favored position.[29] Indeed, America's entry into World War I did stimulate interest in the study of European political history. President Wilson sought to recast traditional foreign policy and found much support. But there were also opponents – the isolationists and the foreign-policy realists – who believed that Wilson's democratic ideology was out of touch with reality and who insisted on the primacy of America's political and economic interests. All of these factors contributed to the turn toward political history. The question of the causes of the war sparked a long battle over the Treaty of Versailles between revisionists and antirevisionists. Fritz Stern points out that this controversy – principally in the form of the scholarly dispute between Sidney B. Fay and Bernadotte Schmitt – established the equal standing of American historical scholarship with that of Europe. I would argue that in this particular field American scholarship was even superior, since among Europeans each nation continued to adhere to their own biased, nationalist interpretations.[30]

In this regard, it was possible for Americans to approximate the German viewpoint (for example, Sidney Fay and Harry E. Barnes). Moreover, it was through the efforts of American historians – notably Waldo G. Leland – that German historians gained readmission to the international historical community. For example, the visiting professors' exchange reemerged between 1931–5, if only as a one-way arrangement (the Roosevelt fellowship at Berlin). The exchange ended only with the implementation of Hitler's Jewish policies.[31]

Little else can usefully be added to the story of relations between American and German scholarship from 1914 to 1933. On the

28 Charles H. Haskins, "European History and American Scholarship," *American Historical Review* 28 (1923): 215–27, 226.
29 Dana C. Munro, "War and History," *American Historical Review* 32 (1926–7):219–31.
30 Fritz Stern, "German History in America," 152.
31 Erdmann, *Die Ökumene der Historiker*, 137. Vom Brocke, "Der deutsch–amerikanische Professorenaustausch," 161. On the attempts at Göttingen to set up a German–American exchange, cf. Hermann Wellenreuther, "Mutmassungen über ein Defizit: Göttingens Geschichtswissenschaft und die angelsächsische Welt," in Hartmut Boockmann and Hermann Wellenreuther, eds., *Geschichtswissenschaft in Göttingen* (Göttingen, 1987), 261–6, 280.

whole, American interest in European and German history was notably stronger than German interest in American history. Americans
quite naturally gave priority of interest to Britain and France, yet
Guy Stanton Ford taught Prussian history, and a number of books
appeared on Germany's very recent history: on the German revolution of 1918–19 (Ralph H. Lutz, 1922); on German colonies (Mary
E. Townsend, 1921 and 1930); on the Pan-German League (Mildred
S. Wertheimer, 1924); and on recent German political developments
generally (John F. Coar, 1924; Rupert Emerson, 1928; James W.
Angell, 1932).[32] This production was certainly more than could be
found in Germany about recent developments in America.

American historians were preoccupied with their own country's
history. Despite the renewed interest in European civilization and
political history, historians applied the tools of the New History to
the field of American history with new vigor. This was the era of
Charles Beard's greatest impact. In cooperation with Turner, Robinson, Vernon L. Parrington, and Carl Becker, he promoted economic,
social, and cultural history that was critical both of the present condi-
tion of the United States and of conventional American views of its
past. Beard inveighed against the idealized view of the origin of
the nation, the popular assertion of America's national and social
consensus, ruling industrial capitalism, and modern foreign politics.
He raised his criticism both before and after the onset of the Depression. In the face of Stalinism, fascism, and National Socialism in
Europe, his critique became increasingly developed, attaining the
character of a coherent historical theory. He believed scientific history, especially the study of economic systems, to be of enduring
importance, but he thought that scientific objective knowledge of
the past was out of the question, "a noble dream." Equally dreamlike
was the likelihood that conclusive evidence of the progress of humankind could ever be found, as many of his fellow "new histori-

32 Guy Stanton Ford, *Stein and the Era of Reform in Prussia, 1807–1815* (Stanford, Calif., 1922);
Ralph H. Lutz, *German Revolution 1918–1919* (Stanford, Calif., 1922); Mary E. Townsend,
Origins of Modern German Colonialism, 1871–1885 (New York, 1921); idem, *Rise and Fall of
Germany's Colonial Empire, 1884–1918* (New York, 1930); Mildred S. Wertheimer, *Pan-
German League, 1890–1914* (New York, 1924); John F. Coar, *The Old and the New Germany*
(New York, 1924); Rupert Emerson, *State and Sovereignty in Modern Germany* (New Haven,
1928); James W. Angell, *The Recovery of Germany* (New Haven, 1932). See also Leonard
Krieger, "European History in America," in John Higham, Leonard Krieger, and Felix
Gilbert, eds., *History* (Englewood Cliffs, N.J., 1965), 273. Even after 1933, important
studies on German history appeared in the United States: for example, Eugene Anderson,
Nationalism and the Cultural Crisis in Germany, 1806–1815 (New York, 1939). Cf. Stern,
"German History in America," 153.

ans" asserted. Beard nevertheless thought that the historian ought to strive to convert that dream into reality: "Written history is an act of faith," he maintained.[33]

Beard's theory, formulated between 1933 and 1935, was of triple relevance to Germany: It challenged Ranke's alleged objectivity, which had figured prominently in the scholarly concepts of most American historians and which Beard himself called "historicism"; it challenged Oswald Spengler's biologist concepts and the related racial theories of National Socialism; and it evoked (together with Benedetto Croce) both older and contemporary German theorists whose criticism had revealed the relativism of Ranke's historicism. With some justice, Beard's diverse reflections on Germany were never interpreted as proof of his familiarity with German historiography and its theoretical foundation (although he had studied in Germany). His conclusions are best interpreted as a sign of American and German historiography going separate ways after 1914.

Beard had been introduced to German theorists (quickly, and late) by Alfred Vagts, a young historian and vehement critic of German mainstream history who had been an exchange student in the United States. Vagts returned to America and worked in Washington, D.C., from 1927 to 1930 on his *Habilitation* thesis, which explored German–American relations during the two decades prior to World War I, and he there married Beard's daughter Miriam. In 1932 the young couple emigrated to London, later returning to the United States. Vagts acquainted Beard with the writings of Kurt Riezler, Karl Mannheim, Karl Heussi, Theodor Lessing, and others. Together they published in 1937 the essay "Currents of Thought in Historiography," which was highly critical of Meinecke and his book on historicism.[34] Meinecke, renowned internationally as Germany's leading historian, was an outspoken critic of the National Socialist regime and therefore had been forced to resign from the editorship of *Historische Zeitschrift* in 1935. A year later, in 1936, he became a celebrated guest at Harvard. Although Beard had also included in his attack

33 Charles A. Beard, "Written History as an Act of Faith," *American Historical Review* 39 (1933–4): 219–31; "That Noble Dream," *American Historical Review* 41 (1935):219–31.
34 Charles A. Beard and Alfred Vagts, "Currents of Thought in Historiography," *American Historical Review* 42 (1936–7):460–83. See Hans-Ulrich Wehler's introduction to the collection of essays he edited, *Alfred Vagts, Bilanzen und Balancen. Aufsätze zur internationalen Finanz und internationalen Politik* (Frankfurt, 1979). On the theoretical discussion, see also Fritz Stern, "Objektivität und Subjektivität–Ein Prinzipienstreit in der amerikanischen Geschichtsschreibung," in *Festschrift Ludwig Bergstraesser*, ed. A. Herrmann (Düsseldorf, 1954); 167–82. See also Herbst, *German Historical School*, 219.

other of his colleagues who continued to cover the old ground of historicism, his work created a feeling of ambivalence about Meinecke among American historians. However, this subject goes beyond our present concern.[35] Beard's attitude is of significance because it was a visible sign of the complex relationship between American and German historiography after 1933, blending scholarly traditions of interchange, perceptions of Hitler's Germany, and the feelings of historians who were refugees from Germany.

The essays in this volume focus entirely on the refugee historians. They thus treat the difficult conditions faced by all immigrant scholars: the economic depression in the United States, which impeded the career prospects of even native scholars and kept American xenophobia alive; and widespread anti-Semitism, which made it hard for the refugees, many of whom were Jewish, to obtain university posts, especially in the humanities. The great initiatives which helped overcome some of these difficulties are well known, but the names of the groups concerned should be repeated with gratitude: the Emergency Committee in Aid of Displaced Foreign Scholars; the School of Humanistic Studies, founded by Abraham Flexner, founder and first director of the Institute for Advanced Studies in Princeton, in answer to the anticultural policy of the Nazis; and the "University in Exile," created by Alvin Johnson, founder of the New School for Social Research. Through these and other means, and because of the abhorrent developments inside Nazi Germany, American anti-Semitism gradually receded, to the benefit of both immigrant and native Jewish scholars.[36]

The importance of the refugee historians for American historical scholarship will also be taken up in detail in the following essays, so I shall only draw general outlines. Even that is no easy task, since the specialists have not yet rendered a clear picture of American historical writing during the 1930s and 1940s.

Largely because of the dynamic power of the New History, American historiography was fully developed before the new arrival of

35 Friedrich Meinecke, *Werke*, ed. Hans Herzfeld, Carl Hinrichs, and Walter Hofer, 7 vols. (Stuttgart, 1957–68): vol. 6, *Ausgewählte Briefwechsel*, pp. 166–73. Hans Herzfeld, "Friedrich-Meinecke-Renaissance im Ausland?" in Mitarbeiter des Max-Planck-Instituts für Geschichte, eds., *Festschrift für Hermann Heimpel* (Göttingen, 1971), 1:42–62. Michael Erbe, "Zur Meinecke-Rezeption im Ausland," in Erbe, ed., *Friedrich Meinecke Heute* (Berlin, 1981), 147–65.
36 See Laura Fermi, *Illustrious Immigrants: The Intellectual Migration from Europe, 1930–41* (Chicago, 1968), 29, 73. Lewis A. Coser, *Refugee Scholars in America: Their Impact and Their Experiences* (New Haven, 1984), 271–94.

foreign influences. American domestic historical research remained fully free from foreign influence. The arriving refugees, however, did not enter a field comfortably united in a belief in assured progress. On the contrary, conflicting theoretical countercurrents led to periodic crises, which is predictable in a period of scholarly flux. Beard's discussion of fundamentals, particularly his stance in favor of relativism and against evolutionism (to which Harry F. Barnes continued determinedly to adhere)[37] weakened the New History. Moreover, it impaired the links between history and the social sciences which had been established and promoted with the help of foundations during the 1920s. Such links nevertheless persisted and even solidified during the 1940s, particularly among economic historians. By the end of World War II, cooperation among disciplines had advanced farther than in any European country and was much admired abroad as a true American specialty. Conservatively inclined historians took a critical view of this trend to social science methodology and denounced it roundly as Marxist, quite as they had earlier done with Beard himself. In 1935 Beard had opposed the artificial isolation of historical observation and had pleaded for a broader outlook: "This means a widening of the range of search beyond politics to include interests hitherto neglected – economic, racial, sexual, and cultural in the most general sense of the term. Certainly by this broadening process the scholar will come nearer to the actuality of history as it has been."[38] His advice seems to have been heeded: Pluralism has since been the hallmark of American historiography. Conventional political history is practiced parallel to economic and social history, intellectual history and history of civilization.

Ever since Robinson, intellectual history in America had been wedded to social history in the common pursuit of the interplay of ideals and interests. With the foundation of the *Journal of the History of Ideas*, intellectual history established an independent existence. Arthur O. Lovejoy, editor of the journal, insisted upon maintaining a fair balance between the intrinsic interests of intellectual history and its interdisciplinary function as a debating platform for all cultural sciences. The terms "culture" and "cultural history" came into general use. As Jacques Barzun remarked, "A revulsion of feeling against

---

37 See Ernst Breisach, "Harry Elmer Barnes' Geschichte der Geschichtsschreibung und die Krise der Progressive History," *Wissenschaftliche Zeitschrift der Karl-Marx-Universität Leipzig*, Gesellschaftswissenschaftliche Reihe 37, no. 5 (1988):439–44.
38 Beard, "That Noble Dream," reprinted in Stern, *Varieties of History*, 314–28, 328.

the practical and business life took place in the United States in the Thirties, which quite transcended the resentment against an economic system that had broken down."[39] Sensing that Western culture was in danger, historians explored and analyzed cultural creativity, cultural crises, and cultural currents. At the same time, history of civilization, encompassing both America and Europe, encountered competition from the study of extra-European civilizations. Foundations served as the patrons of cultural anthropology and social psychology, particularly through the device of area-studies programs, which gained support during and after the war.

History of ideas and cultural history are fields of study in which the refugees were visibly effective, although it cannot be said that they created them. In general, the influence of German social scientists on America seems to have been greater than that of German historians. The number of immigrant economists and social scientists was disproportionately high, and their concentration at the New School for Social Research conferred great influence. In their capacity as theorists, many of the immigrants influenced American historians. The level of theoretical discourse rose visibly because of the influence of the refugees (as we saw in the cases of Beard and Vagts). John Higham singles out as important Ernst Cassirer (important later for Lovejoy's "History of Ideas"); Karl Löwith; Carl Hempel; and Hajo Holborn.[40] At the same time, *Geistesgeschichte* was imported into the United States. In his lecture "Modern German Historiography," given in Chicago in 1933, Eckart Kehr referred to the history of ideas as the most successful school under Meinecke's leadership, a specialty confined to Germany, and argued that its emergence was understandable only because of the social circumstances of the German bourgeoisie. Kehr blamed it for Germany's loss of influence on American historical scholarship.

Kehr, whom Fritz Stern called "the accidental forerunner of the Great Migration," died in May 1933 in Washington, D.C. Had he lived to see the influence of the immigrant Meinecke-trained scholars in the United States, he would have had to revise his opinion about any loss of influence and about the German *Sonderweg*.[41] The immi-

---

39 Jacques Barzun, "Cultural History: A Synthesis," in Stern, *Varieties of History*, 387–402, 389.
40 Higham et al., *History*, 142.
41 Eckart Kehr, "Neuere deutsche Geschichtsschreibung," in idem, *Der Primat der Innenpolitik* (Frankfurt, 1976), 254–67, 260. See also my essay "German *Geistesgeschichte*, American 'Intellectual History,' and French *Histoire des mentalités* since 1900: A Comparison," *History*

grant political scientists and sociologists pursued intellectual interpretations of German totalitarian conditions, basing their theories
upon the history of ideas. Even philosopher Herbert Marcuse favored history of ideas as a counterweight to positivism.[42] Indeed, a
great many immigrant historians were former pupils of Meinecke,
with marked interest in the analysis of ideas: Hajo Holborn, Hans
Baron, Felix Gilbert, and Gerhard Masur. Non–Meinecke-trained
scholars, such as philosopher-historian Paul Oskar Kristeller and medievalists Theodore E. Mommsen and Ernst Kantorowicz, stimulated
research into the Middle Ages and the Renaissance. Research also
focused upon the nineteenth- and twentieth-century European ideologies that had had such an intense and lasting influence on the alarm-
ing conditions of the 1930s. This research was of direct and important contemporary relevance, and it led to an intimate cooperation
between American scholarly and political life. The Research and
Analysis Branch of the Office for Strategic Services (OSS) was the
center of this cooperation, where, under the direction of William
Langer, American specialists on European history joined forces with
refugees during World War II.

European history – particularly German history – in fields ranging
from the Middle Ages to the present was thus mediated by refugees
in the United States with more vigor and discernment after the 1930s
than earlier, when European history had been taught either as political history or as a great spiritual, civilizing process. Political, intellectual, and social developments in Europe were presented as a mutually
controlling interplay of interests, in the same way as American New
History had done with America's domestic history. German (and
later also Austrian) historians brought not only their excellent specialized knowledge to America but also, through their personal experiences, firm critical attitudes toward German historical development. They were thus much more open to American political
principles and prevalent economic and sociohistorical views in their
new homeland than they had been in Germany. Their greatest effi-
cacy, however, lay in what they imported with them: the history of
ideas and the concept of the interplay of ideas, state, and society.

Scholarly contact between refugees and American historians after
1933 was enforced by political circumstances. Fritz Stern describes

---

of European Ideas 1 (1981):195–214. Stern, "German History in America," 155.
42 Joachim Radkau, *Die deutsche Emigration in den USA* (Düsseldorf, 1971), 57.

the situation with the following words: "When . . . Germany turned into a monstrous tyranny, we became the guardians of German history; from 1933 to 1945, German history was being written here and in England or not at all."[43] The effects of this contact, however, became clear only during and especially after World War II. Accordingly, a glance at the postwar situation is necessary.

Immediately after World War II, Germany was in a pitiable state. Devastated and divided, it had lost all former power through the disastrous war that it had brought upon itself. Historical scholarship's fine old internationally renowned traditions were a thing of the past. The profession was at great pains to come to terms with its own recent history, which should have given sufficient cause for self-critical reflection. Historians in the German Democratic Republic, moreover, were forced to adopt a strictly prescriptive historical reorientation. Historians in the Federal Republic, despite relatively more freedom, still had to find some sort of agreement with the notions of the Western powers. They displayed no more interest in American history and historiography than they had after the First World War. Only some shorter pieces by Fritz Wagner, Otto Vossler, and Fritz Fischer come to mind.[44] American wartime propaganda and Cold War propaganda were more a hindrance than an incentive in this respect, for Germans did not wish to appear as a satellite of the new superpower. The emigrant historians did not greatly help either. They had not been much concerned with American history during their immigrant days, least of all Hans Rothfels, the emigrant historian who returned to Germany to settle permanently and subsequently became one of the most influential historians there. Gerhard Masur used his Colombian residence to write a biography of Simón Bolívar, but there is hardly a single parallel case in the United States. In 1961, Felix Gilbert published an intellectual history of the beginnings of the partly idealistic, partly realistic

43 Stern, "German History in America," 132. On evaluating the influence of refugees, see also Gerald Stourzh, "Die deutschsprachige Emigration in den Vereinigten Staaten, 1933–1963," *Jahrbuch für Amerikastudien* 10 (1965):59–77. Georg G. Iggers, "Die deutschen Historiker in der Emigration," in Bernd Faulenbach, ed., *Geschichtswissenschaft in Deutschland* (Munich, 1974), 97–111. Gordon A. Craig, *Deutsche Geschichte aus amerikanischer Sicht* (Munich, 1981). Peter Th. Walther, "Emigrierte deutsche Historiker in den USA," *Berichte zur Wissenschaftsgeschichte* 7 (1984):41–52. Reference can be made also to Felix Gilbert, *A European Past: Memoirs, 1905–1945* (New York, 1988).

44 Fritz Wagner, *USA. Geburt und Aufstieg der neuen Welt. Geschichte in Zeitdokumenten 1607–1865* (Munich, 1947). Otto Vossler, *Geist und Geschichte. Von der Reformation bis zur Gegenwart. Gesammelte Aufsätze* (Munich, 1965).

American foreign policy of the eighteenth century. Archeologist Karl Lehmann described Thomas Jefferson as a lover of ancient civilizations. As a fruit of his work in the OSS, Hajo Holborn presented his observations on the enormous, novel importance of the American military government in a 1947 study on its organization and policies. But these publications were intended for American readers and were not translated into German. For German readers, Dietrich Gerhard enlarged the scope of his comparative study to include comparisons of the Old and the New World. In 1954, Golo Mann wrote an introduction to American thought and practice entitled *Vom Geist Amerikas*. Political scientist Ernst Fraenkel analyzed the American system of government; Hannah Arendt compared the American Revolution with the French. It remained for a younger generation of West German historians – especially Erich Angermann and Hans-Ulrich Wehler – to kindle research interest in American history.[45]

At first, ties between the professions relied principally upon personal contact. American and immigrant historians welcomed the opportunity to see how West German historians would approach and judge the very recent past. Until his early death in 1967, Klaus Epstein was an outstanding mediator, as were Gordon A. Craig and Hans Rosenberg by virtue of their visiting professorships and publications.[46] For many postwar decades, Americans and Britons were the greatest influence upon German historians and upon their reevaluations of Germany's history in the nineteenth and twentieth centu-

45 Gerhard Masur, *Simon Bolivar und die Befreiung Südamerikas* (Constance, 1949). Felix Gilbert, *To the Farewell Address: Ideas of Early American Foreign Policy* (Princeton, 1961). The production of this latter book pertains to influences upon Germany because the book originated as a series of lectures given in Cologne in 1959–60 on early American foreign politics. Karl Lehmann, *Thomas Jefferson, American Humanist* (Chicago, 1947). Hajo Holborn, *American Military Government: Its Organization and Policies* (Washington, 1947). Dietrich Gerhard, *Alte und neue Welt in vergleichender Geschichtsbetrachtung* (Göttingen, 1962). Golo Mann, *Vom Geist Amerikas. Eine Einführung in amerikanisches Denken und Handeln im zwanzigsten Jahrhundert*, 3rd, ed. (1954; Stuttgart, 1961). Ernst Fraenkel, *Das amerikanische Regierungssystem* (Cologne, 1960). Hannah Arendt, *Über die Revolution* (Munich, 1966). Erich Angermann, *Die Vereinigten Staaten von Amerika* (Munich, 1966). Hans-Ulrich Wehler, *Der Aufstieg des amerikanischen Imperialismus 1865–1900* (Göttingen, 1974). In addition, while in American exile Karl Obermann, later a historian in the German Democratic Republic, wrote a biography of German socialist Joseph Weydemeyer, who emigrated to America in 1852: Karl Obermann, *Joseph Weydemeyer: Pioneer of American Socialism* (New York, 1947); idem, *Joseph Weydemeyer, ein Lebensbild 1818–1866* (Berlin, 1968).

46 Klaus Epstein, *Geschichte und Geschichtswissenschaft im 20. Jahrhundert* (Frankfurt, 1972), a German translation of his reviews of new German publications on contemporary history. Gordon A. Craig, especially through his book *The Politics of the Prussian Army, 1640–1945* (Oxford, 1955; German translation, 1960). Hans Rosenberg, especially through his book *Grosse Depression und Bismarckzeit. Wirtschaftsablauf, Gesellschaft und Politik in Mitteleuropa* (Berlin, 1967).

ries. No comparable influence derived from France. It is striking how important the refugees became for mediating the new social history of ideas and the new socioeconomic interpretations in the Federal Republic. They contributed vitally toward innovation in German historical scholarship, which proceeded much more slowly than many wished but was finally accomplished in the 1960s and 1970s.

After World War II, American historical scholarship had become the world's leader, the most vigorous and multifaceted. Europeans saw the full impact of its achievements first at the 1955 International Historical Congress in Rome (until then the United States had mostly played the part of financier in this organization). In terms of moral and scholarly authority, German historical scholarship contrasted very unfavorably with its American counterpart. As Michael Kammen blandly put it, "Unlike the Germans, we did not have two scary skeletons in the closet that made historical knowledge an absolute requisite for self-understanding and national identity."[47] Certainly, on any past or present view, Germany emerged as the scene of strife and separation, while the American historians pointed to unity and to the "consensus" in their great nation. This view of American history stood against the conflict research of the old, now outdated, New Historians. It also resulted from comparisons with the history of the rival European nation-states. The fact that this neoconservative orthodoxy soon became the target of attacks and subsequently dissolved into a renewed plurality does not relate directly to the topic at hand.[48] It is important because it provided the basis for further research into different European, and especially German, conditions. The refugee historians participated actively in this research and were most effective, because they were now the leaders of methodological schools of thought. More precisely, as Volker Berghahn pointed out, the refugees' children by then were already performing that task. With critical yet discerning interpretations of Germany's ideological and social development, they attempted to dispel the horrible vision of Germany and its history that had formed in the American mind since the time of Hitler and to which A. J. P. Taylor's and William L. Shirer's books had contributed greatly.[49]

---

47 Michael Kammen, *Selvages and Biases*, 19.
48 See also, among others, Bernard Sternsher, *Consensus, Conflict, and American Historians* (Bloomington, 1975). Daniel Joseph Singal, "Beyond Consensus: Richard Hofstadter and American Historiography," *American Historical Review* 89 (1984):976–1003.
49 Volker Berghahn, "Deutschlandbilder 1945–1965. Anglo-amerikanische Historiker und moderne deutsche Geschichte," in Ernst Schulin, ed., *Deutsche Geschichtswissenschaft nach*

Active in this effort were, above all, George Mosse, Fritz Stern, Klaus Epstein, Peter Gay, and Georg G. Iggers, as well as American historians of the same cohort: Gordon Craig, Leonard Krieger, and Carl Schorske. Similar attitudes were adopted somewhat later in Britain.

To summarize: Anglo-American critical interest in German history influenced and assisted in the modernization of West German historical writing. Meanwhile, during the last two or three decades, connections intensified to such a degree that, with all their changing concepts and fashions, international scholarly developments can be said to have been fairly similar. This is encouraging testimony to international cooperation in our time. It is by no means an inevitable process and is on that account vulnerable to countercurrents. The very vulnerability of the process of cooperation causes one to hope that fair winds will prevail and that the contribution made by the refugees, an outcome of their forced emigration, will continue to be greatly beneficial.

dem Zweiten Weltkrieg (1945–1965) (Munich, 1989), 239–71. Heinz Wolf, *Deutsch-jüdische Emigrationshistoriker in den USA und der Nationalsozialismus* (Bern, 1988).

2

German Historiography during the Weimar Republic and the Émigré Historians

WOLFGANG J. MOMMSEN

The history of German historiography during the Weimar period is closely correlated with the question of why the courageous attempt to establish a democratic order in Germany after the breakdown of the imperial regime in 1918 failed, a failure which resulted in the rise to power of National Socialism. In general, German historiography during this period must be seen as a major factor strengthening the trend in public opinion to look back to, and to judge, contemporary events against what seemed the happy days of Bismarck and Wilhelm II. There was a strong tendency to denounce the Weimar system as alien to the German historical tradition and imposed by the victorious Western powers against the wishes of the majority of Germans. Max Lenz, the holder of Ranke's chair at the University of Berlin, the most prestigious chair of history in Germany, declared it the task of the historical profession to mobilize the "moral energies" of former, greater generations of Germans against what he called "the pygmies of the day" in order to pave the way for a brighter future for the German nation-state. With good justification Bernd Faulenbach summarized the trends of German historiography in the interwar period under the heading *Ideologie des deutschen Weges*.[1]

Although German historiography of the 1920s remained firmly entrenched in the tradition of an idealistic historicism linked up with the idea of the powerful nation-state as a sort of teleological goal of German history, there existed in actual fact a great variety of historiographic positions, often at loggerheads with one another. The deep political cleavages in German public opinion – the bitter struggle between the Right and the Left, while those with positions

I should like to express my gratitude to Catherine Epstein, who assisted me by supplying me with bibliographies of all the émigrés.

Unless otherwise indicated, all translations are by Kenneth F. Ledford.

1 Bernd Faulenbach, *Ideologie des deutschen Weges. Die deutsche Geschichte in der Historiographie zwischen Kaiserreich und Nationalsozialismus* (Munich, 1980).

in the middle found it hard to hold their own – which marked the history of Weimar politics from the start, were reflected in the historians' battles, though perhaps not always with the same degree of radicalism. The intellectual climate was obviously not one in which serene historiography, aloof from political struggle, could flourish; rather, the opposite was the case. Teaching positions at the universities, and in the relatively few well-endowed research institutions in history, continued to be controlled by the old guard of historians, who made it difficult if not impossible for newcomers, especially those from the Left, who refused to play by the traditional rules of the game, to gain access to teaching or research positions. Even so, German historiography of the Weimar period was in many ways very productive and witnessed a great deal of pioneering work which was later taken up, after 1945. The consequences of the rise of National Socialism to power for German historiography have so far not been fully analyzed; research is still in an initial stage, in spite of a few most valuable studies, such as those by Karl-Ferdinand Werner, Klaus Schreiner, and Helmut Heiber.[2] Even though it must be said that the National Socialists neither succeeded in a complete *Gleichschaltung* of German historiography nor in their attempt to establish a new school of National Socialist historiography, the impact of National Socialism upon the historical profession was profound. The historical craft lost many of its most prominent members and was progressively demoralized, under the impact of National Socialist propaganda and manipulation.

With but a few notable exceptions, German historiography proved theoretically and mentally altogether unprepared to mount an effective intellectual defense against National Socialist ideology; the historicist belief that history is a meaningful process containing its justification in its inner self made the historians ready to compromise with and adapt to the new regime, even before this was directly demanded by the authorities. The fact that a considerable number of historians, mostly of the middle generation, had to leave Germany, usually but not always because the anti-Semitic policies of the National Socialist regime left them no alternative, contributed to the

2 Karl-Ferdinand Werner, *Das nationalsozialistische Geschichtsbild und die Geschichtswissenschaft* (Stuttgart, 1967); Klaus Schreiner, "Führer, Rasse, Reich. Wissenschaft von der Geschichte nach der NS-Machtergreifung," in Peter Lundgreen, ed., *Wissenschaft im Dritten Reich* (Frankfurt, 1985), 163–252; Helmut Heiber, *Walter Frank und sein Reichsinstitut für Geschichte des neuen Deutschland* (Stuttgart, 1966).

moral crisis of historiography vis-à-vis National Socialism. The enforced emigration of many of the best historians, including quite a few young historians who only later entered the historical profession, amounted to a significant brain drain. After 1933, German historiography was, to put it in Johan Huizinga's words, *gefesselte Wissenschaft*, no longer allowed to speak freely and, more importantly, progressively cut off from the free exchange of views with historians of other countries. On the other hand, most German historians found it not too difficult to adjust to these conditions; with some notable exceptions, business went on as usual, albeit with considerable lip service if not substantive adaptation to the new regime.

In this chapter we are concerned with those historians who were forced to emigrate from Germany to other countries, mostly, though not always directly, to the United States. The willingness of the Americans to give both a home and the opportunity for further research to these historians must be considered one of the momentous humanitarian and scholarly achievements of our time. Here we are, however, exclusively concerned with the role which these historians played within the German historical profession before they left Germany. It is the intention of this essay to assess their contribution to the development of German historiography in the 1920s and to place them within the different ideological camps separating the various schools of academic historiography in Weimar Germany. In doing so I concentrate, with but few exceptions, on those historians who worked in the fields of modern and contemporary history. I will leave aside those who worked in special fields of various kinds, because it is impossible for me, as a generalist, to assess their status and methodological positions within their disciplines with any degree of certainty. I suppose, however, that had they been included, the general pattern which emerges from this analysis would not be much altered. Finally, this will allow me to discuss the issue of what it has meant for the development of German professional historiography to have lost an important group of historians during the prime of their productivity. It is no doubt somewhat risky to raise questions of this sort, since the answers are based on counterfactual assumptions. But it would seem worthwhile, all the same. I should like to advance the hypothesis that though the group of historians which emigrated in the 1930s was, numerically, comparatively small, it was sufficiently large to effect a serious distortion of the spectrum of opinions and research traditions present in the German historical profession. It goes without saying that resistance to political manipulation of the past in the interest of the National Socialist regime was further weakened by the disappearance of these scholars from the German scene, particularly since, for the most part, they had been staunch supporters of the democratic system of Weimar. More importantly, the distortion of the spectrum of historical positions had a significant influence on the development of German historical scholarship in the 1950s and 1960s, since, with but few exceptions, the émigré historians did not return to Germany after 1945, for reasons we need not go into here. There is, of course, another side to this story. The émigré historians, by establishing influential schools of German and Central European historiography in their new countries, significantly contributed to closing the gap between the German and the Anglo-Saxon intellectual traditions which had long cast a shadow over the development of historical thought.

The German historical scene in the 1920s was overshadowed by the experiences of the defeat of Imperial Germany and the failure of the German revolution of 1918–19. Most historians, like the German intelligentsia in general, experienced these events as a severe shock which initially resulted in mental disorientation and confusion. They had grown up under the comparatively comfortable conditions of Wilhelmine Germany and now saw their optimistic world view, underpinned by their historicist inclinations, severely shaken, if not altogether shattered. This is particularly true of the large group of historians who had grown accustomed to the idea that the emergence of the German nation-state and Germany's gradual rise to world-power status had been preordained, as it were, by world history itself. Even historians who held comparatively moderate political views, like Friedrich Meinecke, who had come to believe that constitutional reform could no longer be delayed, considered the revolution of 1918–19 a national catastrophe, "because the revolution incalculably increased our misfortune, rendered us utterly defenseless against the external enemy, and introduced unimaginable dangers in internal affairs."[3] Political passions were high, and they affected the historical profession perhaps even more strongly than the public in general. In some ways the wave of nationalist thinking which had swept through the German historical profession during the First World War now reached a new peak, and those who preached moderation were initially, at least, only a small group.

After 1918 the great majority of political historians considered it

---

3 *Nach der Revolution* (Munich, 1919), 59–60

their prime duty to remind the German public of the great deeds of the past and, in particular, to keep alive the memory of the Bismarckian empire. They presented this memory in stark contrast to the dreary present, which they depicted as a period of temporary decline which would of necessity be followed by a revival of Germany's national greatness, provided that the people remained faithful to the great ideals embodied in Germany's national history. Erich Marcks, Max Lenz, Dietrich Schäfer, Eduard Meyer, and, among the younger generation, Hermann Oncken and Karl Alexander von Müller, to name just a few of the most prominent historians of the day, preached in public speeches the "idea of national rebirth."[4] Likewise, they called for a new great statesman, comparable to Prince Bismarck, who, in his own stride, would lead Germany into another period of national grandeur.[5]

The preoccupation of many German historians during the interwar period with Bismarck and his work, and the publication of a splendid leather-bound edition of Bismarck's works, both belong in this context. However, many historians soon came to believe that it was their duty to lend their services to the nation in fighting against the so-called *Kriegsschuldlüge*. In doing so they could count upon much clandestine government support. However, many professional historians expressed their disagreement with the rather crude methods of the semiofficial Zentralstelle für Erforschung der Kriegsursachen.[6] This situation explains why, in the 1920s, an unusual degree of research energy, even compared with the prewar period, was channeled into fairly traditional diplomatic historiography. In this context the neo-Rankean principle of "primacy of foreign policy" was not only revived but given a new dignity. The political objectives of the numerous studies devoted to the origins of the First World War, the European state system, and international politics were often quite

---

4 For the phrase *nationale Wiedergeburt* see, *inter alia*, Hermann Oncken, *Nation und Geschichte. Reden und Aufsätze 1919–1935* (Berlin, 1935), 12–13.

5 See, for instance, Karl Alexander von Müller, *Deutsche Geschichte und deutscher Charakter. Aufsätze und Vorträge* (Stuttgart, 1926), 236, referring to Bismarck's fall from power: "His empire, in the form in which it was constructed, has today fallen, but his spirit is not yet dead. . . . Our race has atoned for the ingratitude toward greatness, for the contempt for the truly God-given leader which lies in his fall. In this state of impotence, we succumb to mediocrity and cry like a hart for water in our need for one who is supposed to lead us. That his spirit has not yet died leaves us the hope that he will one day arise anew in our people, that the hour will come in which the lightning of a genius will again flash from the gloomy clouds of our confusion and consume the mountain of our shame."

6 See Ulrich Heinemann, *Die Verdrängte Niederlage. Politische Öffentlichkeit und Kriegsschuldfrage in der Weimarer Republik* (Göttingen, 1983), 105–9.

openly declared; Hermann Oncken, for one, published his essays about the Rhine policies of France under the heading "Im Kampf um die Westfront."[7] His voluminous study *Die Rheinpolitik Napoleons III.* must also be seen in the context of Weimar revisionism against the Treaty of Versailles.[8]

The preoccupation with international relations was seen by many, including Hans Rothfels, as justified not only on political but also on moral grounds. Rothfels argued that German historians had to fight against the falsification of German history which the Allied powers and Allied public opinion had brought forth in the context of the controversy about Article 231 of the Treaty of Versailles. The conflict with the Western powers about the causes of World War I, and in a wider sense about the interpretation of German history, was not only one of territory, reparations, economic influence, and the restoration of Germany's national independence; it was also about rival *Geschichtsbilder.* Gerhard Ritter's influential book *Machtstaat und Utopie,* for instance, was an elaborate justification of the German path of development which had always placed state authority and military needs higher than liberal principles, whereas the English people, enjoying the relative security of their insular status, allegedly could afford parliamentary institutions at a relatively early stage of their national development.[9]

Indeed, the fundamental issue concerned the idea of Germany's special path of development, which had long informed the writings of German historians. At issue was whether this path was still essentially correct or whether, in view of the fact that it had led the German nation into the abyss, a thorough revision of the German *Geschichtsbild* was necessary. As early as 1919, in a famous series of essays, *Deutschland und Westeuropa,* Ernst Troeltsch pleaded for a symbiosis of the German and the West European intellectual traditions, which were, after all, as he pointed out, offspring of a common European heritage. Whereas the Germans, under the spell of Lutheran religiosity, had cultivated, above all, respect for authority and deference to state power, the Anglo-Saxon tradition, influenced by Calvinism and Puritan religiosity, had emphasized the principles of individualism, personal freedom, and rational social conduct. But

---

7 See Hermann Oncken, *Nation und Geschichte* (Berlin, 1935), 135–247.
8 *Die Rheinpolitik Kaiser Napoleons III. von 1863–1870 und der Ursprung des Krieges von 1870/71* (Berlin, 1926).
9 *Machtstaat und Utopie* (Leipzig, 1940).

Troeltsch's arguments had, for the time being at any rate, little effect, although they left a deep imprint upon the minds of at least some of his students.

In actuality, Ernst Troeltsch, though from the start one of the very few scholars who actively supported the new democratic order, was not a genuine democrat. Rather, he belonged to a large group which came to be called *Vernunftrepublikaner* – that is, those who accepted the new political conditions in Weimar without enthusiasm but as a matter of fact and who decided to work on this new basis, since there seemed to be no reasonable alternative.[10] Friedrich Meinecke, perhaps the most prominent historian of this group, even managed to find a conventional historicist justification for this course of action: "The ideal task of combining good democracy with good aristocracy, which we set for ourselves, has already been imperiously set for us by historical development itself – and we simply cannot lose faith in the sense and reason of historical development."[11] He argued that the fortunes of the nation were not inseparably connected with the old *Herrschaftsstaat*, and for this reason he gave qualified support to the Weimar system. However, in his own historiographic work he retreated into a sublime intellectual history which focused upon the antinomian nature of freedom and state power, as well as on the unbridgeable distance between the principle of individuality (the dominant feature of modern historicism) and the various types of rationalist world views.

After 1918 there were but few historians who demanded a decisive break with the authoritarian traditions of German historiography and a fundamental reorientation of German historiography. Among them were some historians of an older generation who were eventually forced to emigrate, historians who already during the Wilhelmine period had held progressive or even democratic views – as Veit Valentin and Arthur Rosenberg for example. Walter Goetz was spokesman for this group of progressive historians; he pleaded for a renewal of German historiography. Historians should stop praising prewar conditions and blaming those who had, allegedly, arbitrarily destroyed them; instead, they ought to tell the public how Germany

10 Cf. Wolfgang J. Mommsen, "Deutschland und Westeuropa. Krise und Neuorientierung der Deutschen im Übergang vom Kaiserreich zur Weimarer Republik," in *Troeltsch-Studien*, vol. 4, ed. Horst Renz and Friedrich Wilhelm Graf (Gütersloh, 1987), 118–20.
11 *Nach der Revolution*, 65.

had gone wrong in the past, thus providing the nation with what it needed most in its depressed state: *Klarheit über sich selber.*[12]

This daring plea for a reorientation of German historiography immediately provoked violent opposition. Perhaps foremost among those who objected to Goetz's position was Georg von Below. Already in 1920 Below had sharply attacked Goetz and other progressive historians for their alleged cooperation with what he called the new *parteiamtliche Geschichtsschreibung.* In his opinion, there was no need for change; on the contrary, political necessities required remaining faithful to the well-established tenets of German historiography as it had developed since Ranke, Sybel, and Treitschke: "We would want to alter the formal means of our historical method just as little as the objective knowledge which our scholarship has attained. . . . It is our standpoint to remain staunch, to hope, to believe and to struggle, to apply unconcerned the old historical methods."[13] Below rigorously defended the traditional historicist method, not least because he associated it with the principles of German folkdom and "German freedom," which contrasted sharply with West European individualism and the egalitarian principles of the Enlightenment. Adalbert Wahl, whose *Deutsche Geschichte 1870–1914*[14] must be considered a highly influential account of the history of Imperial Germany, was even more outspoken; this book was written from a traditional conservative vantage point which placed all the blame on the rise of democracy. Wahl identified the prime cause of the 1918 defeat and everything that followed from it as the pernicious influence of "the Ideas of 1789" on Germany. With the revolution of 1789 the French people, with disastrous consequences, had dissociated themselves in a most frivolous manner from their own history. Unfortunately, the Germans had partly followed them on this pernicious path, and they must by all means avoid moving any farther in this direction. Instead they should stick to their own national heritage, best represented by the historical example of the *Freiheitskriege* against the French.[15]

To be fair, dogmatic conservatives of the old breed, like Adalbert

12 "Die deutsche Geschichtsschreibung der Gegenwart," in Walter Goetz, *Historiker in unserer Zeit. Gesammelte Aufsätze* (Cologne, 1957), 416, 418.
13 *Die parteiamtliche neue Geschichtsschreibung. Ein Beitrag zur Frage der historischen Objektivität* (Langensalza, 1920), 63–4.
14 4 vols. (Stuttgart, 1926–36).
15 "Die Ideen von 1789 in ihren Wirkungen auf Deutschland," *Zeitwende* 1 (1925): 115, 126.

Wahl, were gradually losing ground even in Weimar Germany. Their place was increasingly being taken by nationalists who adopted *völkische* arguments and combined them with a *grossdeutsch* position. These nationalists did not even hesitate to criticize Bismarck's foreign policy as too timid and ineffective. In the late 1920s the traditional national-conservative historians who considered Bismarck *das Mass aller Dinge* were increasingly on the defensive. In 1928 Gerhard Ritter found it necessary to give an eloquent defense of Bismarck's *kleindeutsch* policy in a public lecture at Freiburg; his remarks were directed against the new variety of pan-German historians.[16]

Otto Hintze followed a rather independent line. Before the war Hintze had been among the staunchest supporters of the German semiauthoritarian system of government, and he had sincerely assumed this to be the natural result of historical conditions which had determined Imperial Germany's rise to European and world-power status. During the war he had been a champion of the so-called ideas of 1914, largely on the ground that Imperial Germany's exposed position in the center of Europe did not permit any other course of action.

The spirit and character of a nation depend not alone upon its internal social structure, but in even greater degree upon the political necessities that spring from its geographical position and its relation to other states and Powers . . . Germany in particular is subject to so relentless a pressure on her borders that, before all things, she is forced, through the imperative law of self-preservation, so to strengthen herself in a military sense as to be able, in case of necessity, to maintain herself in the face of a world of enemies. . . . The degree of political freedom permissible [and here he relied upon a quotation from Seeley] in the forms of government must evidently be inversely proportional to the political and military pressure exerted against the boundaries of the state.[17]

Hintze had been personally shattered by the collapse of Imperial Germany and the Hohenzollern dynasty in 1918. However, initially he refused to change his views radically: "We have no reason now to imitate the political ideologies of our oppressors, intoxicated by victory."[18] Yet by 1925 he freely admitted that "the adoration of the state," typical of the Germans in the past, had been an aberration

---

16 *Bismarcks Reichsgründung und die Aufgaben der Zukunft. Ein Wort an Bismarcks grossdeutsche Kritiker* (Freiburg, 1928).
17 Quoted in W. M. Simon, "Power and Responsibility: Otto Hintze's Place in German Historiography," in Leonard Krieger and Fritz Stern, eds., *The Responsibility of Power: Historical Essays in Honor of Hajo Holborn* (London, 1968), 207.
18 Ibid., 211

from the right path and ought to be supplanted by a sober, even *misstrauische* attitude toward the state.[19] Hintze conceded that the system of imperialist world-power politics which had determined German policies before 1914 had led to the catastrophe, but he suggested that Germans need not bow before the Western powers, since the hypertrophy of power politics had been a universal phenomenon in modern European and indeed world history. He was also now prepared to admit that part of the reason for Imperial Germany's defeat had been its failure to introduce democratic reforms in order to strengthen the internal cohesion of the body politic. He developed a new type of comparative constitutional history on a universal-historical plane, which maintained that state power was the core of the historical process and yet systematically took into account the interior structures conditioning the policies of states and nations. In doing so he adapted Max Weber's ideal-type reconstruction of occidental history for his own purposes, although on a more pragmatic methodological level.

This survey of German historiography in the 1920s and early 1930s, demonstrating a great variety of methodological positions which were usually closely intertwined with political positions, is certainly anything but complete. It leaves much to be desired, yet a more detailed presentation would take up far too much time. However, it suffices as a framework within which the particular historiographic positions of the future refugee historians may be assessed with some accuracy. To be precise, the age group under discussion here includes all those historians who won academic positions or influence in Weimar Germany, while those who received their academic training or parts of it abroad are not a subject of this study. Needless to say, the German-trained historians were not a homogeneous group, even though the great majority had a Jewish religious background or belonged to the Jewish cultural community in Germany. However, they did have one essential thing in common: They all came from the German *Bildungsbürgertum*. Otherwise, they were of different intellectual, philosophical, and political persuasions.

The first group of future refugee historians which deserves mention here played a largely marginal role in the period under discussion. They consisted of outsiders, either because they entered into an academic career late in life, as did, for instance, Gustav Mayer

19 *Soziologie und Geschichte*, 242.

(1871–1948), the well-known biographer of Ferdinand Lassalle and Friedrich Engels, or because they were not accepted by the academic community, largely for political reasons, like Veit Valentin, the author of a masterful history of the German revolution of 1848–9. Gustav Mayer came from a well-established Jewish family and initially studied economics with Gustav Schmoller in Berlin and Georg Adler in Basel. After Mayer finished his dissertation in Basel, "Ferdinand Lassalle as an economist," he maintained a special interest in the development of the early working-class movement. Yet, although he had great sympathy with the socialist movement, or, more precisely, with its more moderate intellectual representatives, he never became a socialist himself. He was and remained a progressive liberal who believed that a more just and democratic society could only be attained if the working classes cooperated with the progressive sections of the bourgeois classes. For a long time Mayer did not seriously consider an academic career, and indeed, his chances of joining the German historical profession as an outsider who had not undergone a proper professional training were slim; in addition, his Jewish background and radical political views were not conducive to a successful academic career under Wilhelmine conditions.

Starting in 1906, Mayer published extensively on the early working-class movement in Germany. He wrote a biography of Johann Baptist von Schweitzer, Lassalle's rather unfortunate successor in the leadership of the Allgemeiner Deutscher Arbeiter Verband (ADAV) and then did studies on the radical democratic-party movement in the 1860s which ended up in no-man's-land after Bismarck's triumph in 1866. During the 1860s the democratic and working-class movements had still worked together for a united democratic German republic, although such a republic had no chance of realization even in a distant future. In a nutshell, Mayer wrote the history of the losers, and in particular of those groups that had stood for political ideals which had fallen into disrepute, and even oblivion, in Wilhelmine Germany. Since national-liberal and neo-Rankean interpretations of nineteenth-century German history commanded general recognition and universal acclaim, both within the exclusive academic establishment and among the general public, Mayer's topics were considered marginal at best. Under these conditions his numerous publications received little more than scant recognition, and then only among a small group of official historians. It was only during the First World War that Mayer, who by this time had published an impressive oeuvre, entertained the possibility of entering the academic profession, albeit influenced by the assumption that the Social Democrats were no longer considered outcasts but had become genuine partners of the bourgeois parties and the government in the common war effort. However, in the heated nationalist atmosphere in Berlin in the fall of 1917 his *Habilitation* at the University of Berlin failed, although supported by Friedrich Meinecke and Gustav Schmoller; nationalistic diehards, under the leadership of Georg von Below and Dietrich Schäfer, torpedoed his faculty colloquium.

It was only after the First World War that Mayer was given the opportunity to teach at the University of Berlin. At the behest of the Prussian government, but against the wishes of the faculty, he was given an *Extraordinat* for his book *Die Geschichte der Demokratie, des Sozialismus und der politischen Parteien*. In practical terms he remained an outsider, inasmuch as his position did not carry any of the traditional rights and privileges associated with a full professorship at the University of Berlin. His chance to train gifted students and pave the way for their entry into an academic career were minimized. His research achievements were, given the rather awkward conditions under which he worked, most impressive. His edition of Lassalle's papers, as well as his biography of Engels, laid essential foundations for the study of German labor history. In this context, his sensational discovery of the correspondence between Lassalle and Bismarck in 1863 deserves special mention. For more than fifty years these letters had been carefully hidden from the public in the Prussian Ministry of State, since they were likely to tarnish Bismarck's image: Bismarck had repeatedly denied in Parliament that he had ever had any contacts with Lassalle at all. Mayer, on the other hand, saw in the intimate contacts between Bismarck and Lassalle, however premature Lassalle's hopes may have been to achieve a historic breakthrough for the democratic working-class movement by an alliance with the Prussian minister-president, a sign that cooperation between the German state and the working class was possible after all. Likewise, Mayer's studies on early German party history command the respect even of present-day researchers in this field, as Hans-Ulrich Wehler pointed out in his afterword to a new edition of Mayer's studies on radicalism, socialism, and bourgeois democracy.[20]

20 See the afterword by Wehler to Gustav Mayer, *Radikalismus, Sozialismus und Bürgerliche Demokratie* (Frankfurt, 1969), 188–9.

Veit Valentin's story is very different, although he failed to establish himself within the German academic community for many of the same reasons. His career was brought to a halt by his violent clashes with the nationalist majority of the philosophical faculty at the university in Freiburg, caused by public criticism of his extreme annexationist views and of private remarks that he had made concerning the dubious role of Alfred von Tirpitz, who had become the hero of Germany's extreme Right.[21]

Valentin had been one of the most brilliant students of Erich Marcks at Heidelberg University, and his early academic career had been splendid, not least thanks to his former teacher's protection. He had been deeply influenced by Erick Marcks's aestheticist variety of neo-Rankean historiography, which sought to bring across the deeply rooted emotions, beliefs, and values motivating the men who, in Erich Marcks's words, "make history," or who symbolize the cultural values of important social groups or, perhaps, of the nation itself. In his methodological position, Valentin deviated but little from the conventional notions of historicism, which emphasized empathy and individuality. His power of plain narrative description was considerable, and like Erich Marcks he tended to summarize his findings in descriptive entities which may be described as collective individualities. In this respect his methodological views did not deviate markedly from those of the established historians in control of the German historical profession. However, with his liberal Frankfurt background he gradually emancipated himself from the cultural aestheticism of the Heidelberg milieu. Instead he was fascinated by the liberal and democratic undercurrents which he discovered in the political and intellectual mentality of this old free city of the Holy Roman Empire and the German Confederation, in which the anti-Prussian emotions of 1848–9, and even of the early period of the foundation of Imperial Germany, had never completely died down. His first major study, published in 1919 – *Die erste deutsche Nationalversammlung*, a precursor of what was to become a definitive study of the German revolution of 1848–9 – although written before the revolution of 1918–19, gave expression to these anti-Prussian feelings, substantiated by a painstaking analysis of the Frankfurt Paulskirche proceedings. "The greatest obstacle to the victory of the

---

21 See, *inter alia*, the official documentation by the University of Freiburg edited by Felix Rachfahl, *Der Fall Valentin. Die amtlichen Urkunden. Im Auftrag der Philosophischen Fakultät der Universität Freiburg* (Munich, 1920). Even Rachfahl conceded that this affair had been one of the darkest chapters in the history of the German universities.

Paulskirche was Prussia – the state, the tradition, the political style, even more than individuals."[22] But, more importantly, Valentin significantly shifted the interpretation of this crucial period of German history; to him the ideal of liberty, rather than that of national unity, was all-important. In this he deviated from the view of a whole generation of national-liberal historians, men such as Droysen, Sybel, Treitschke, and their heirs – for example, Hermann Oncken and Friedrich Meinecke. "The struggle for freedom was less visible than the struggle for unity – but it was, from the historical perspective, the deeper and more powerful struggle."[23] This shift in emphasis meant also that Valentin was driven to pay much more attention to those groups in German society that had been the staunchest supporters of the idea of liberty, even if this implied a revolutionary upheaval of the established order. Accordingly, Valentin began to analyze the role of the lower classes, including artisans and laborers, in the revolution of 1848–9.

During the First World War, Valentin became a partisan of constitutional reform, and he also strove against the far-reaching war aims supported by almost all segments of German society. During a stay at the Gouvernement-General in occupied Brussels, he had seen enough outrageous expansionist schemes to be convinced that such propaganda must not be allowed to continue. Valentin was, however, by no means a radical; thanks to his considerable literary gifts he was able to address not only the profession but the public at large. As a result, he was hired by the German Foreign Office to write a popular history of German foreign policy since 1890, in which he was to fend off the Western radical critique which blamed German chauvinist policies for the war. Valentin tendered a sober account of German policies, which was, though critical in many respects, on the whole still rather timid and even apologetic about German policies in the decade before 1914. Even so, the book, when it eventually was published with the consent of the authorities in 1919, still occasioned violent protests by the Right.

In the introduction, Valentin defined himself as a member of the generation which had been deprived by the war of all of its hopes and prospects.[24] Even so, he argued that the best he could do for the German people in this situation was to approach the past in a critical

22 *Die erste deutsche Nationalversamlung. Eine geschichtliche Studie über die Frankfurter Paulskriche* (Munich, 1919), 156–7.
23 Ibid., 157.
24 Ibid., ix.

spirit, rather than with the constant self-praise which had led Germans to their present misfortune. He now declared himself explicitly in favor of the historian's political function. He assigned to historical scholarship an "ursprüngliches historiographisches Amt der Gesinnungsbildung für Gegenwart und Zukunft" while dissociating himself from "Rankes geruhsamer Nazarenerblässe" which had supported the existing order, or, to be more precise, the traditional forces in state and society.[25] His own message was that the Germans should have taken the spirit of 1848, and not of 1871, let alone that of 1914, as their political guideline. He also expressed some regret that the German revolution of 1918–19 had been halted in its early stages, rather than being carried through to the point at which a safe foundation for a new democratic order had been laid. He criticized the compromise nature of the Weimar constitution as still containing too many authoritarian elements and defended the idea of the League of Nations.[26] All this was outrageous in the eyes of the public. At the same time, he could not expect recognition for this work from the historical profession; on the contrary, he now was depicted as a *Tendenzhistoriker* who had compromised himself as a serious scholar by associating himself unreservedly with the new democratic order.

It is no wonder that Valentin was denied an adequate academic position which might have allowed him to bring his views across to the younger generation during the Weimar period. He was merely given a professorship at the Handelshochschule Berlin, which was little more than a sinecure, and later the respectable, academically influential position as archivist, and eventually director, of the Reichsarchiv in Potsdam. His great study of the German revolution of 1848–9, published in 1930–1, failed to make an impact upon German historical scholarship. Only two years later, with the rise of National Socialism to power, this sort of democratic historiography was no longer considered tolerable. Valentin was immediately dismissed from his job as archivist on the grounds that his activities in various democratic and pacifist organizations had compromised him as a civil servant. His fate as a determined democratic liberal, who in spite of respectable research achievements was never considered acceptable by official academic historiography, was in many ways

---

25 Cf. Hans Schleier, *Die bürgerliche deutsche Geschichtsschreibung der Weimarer Republik* (Cologne, 1957), 75.

26 See, *inter alia*, Veit Valentin, *Von Bismarck zur Weimarer Republik. Sieben Beiträge zur deutschen Politik*, ed. Hans Ulrich Wehler (Cologne, 1979).

representative of the trends prevailing in the German historical profession in the 1920s and 1930s.

A rather different, but in many ways comparable, case was that of Arthur Rosenberg (1889–1943). Rosenberg was by training an ancient historian and student of Eduard Meyer and had established himself as a renowned historian with studies on the social history of the early Roman republic. It was only when he became a member of the Parliamentary Committee of Inquiry into the Origins of the Defeat of Imperial Germany that he became interested in contemporary history. His sympathy with the extreme Left and his membership in the German Communist party were unique at the time; even so, he was allowed to retain his *ausserordentliche* professorship at the University of Berlin until 1933, although no longer for ancient history but for the new and still-undefined discipline of sociology. Arthur Rosenberg's two books, *Die Entstehung der Weimarer Republik* (published in 1928) and later his *Geschichte der Weimarer Republik* (written in exile in Liverpool and published late in 1935), must be considered, along with Johannes Ziekursch's *Geschichte des deutschen Kaiserreiches 1871–1914*, the first narrative account of German history from 1871 to 1930 written from a genuinely democratic viewpoint. Even though he had explicitly stated, in the preface to *Die Entstehung der Weimarer Republik*, that he was writing without regard to party opinion or party prestige,[27] he argued that it was a significant failure of the Social Democrats, in December 1918 and early 1919, that they did not push the revolutionary movement any farther – that is, that they did not cooperate with the Workers' and Soldiers' Councils in order to establish a stable and enduring foundation for a new democratic order. By doing full justice to the positions of the parties of the Left, however, and without being dogmatic about the issues of revolution and socialization, Arthur Rosenberg helped to restore balance to the writing of contemporary German history, which had always been heavily tilted toward the bourgeois classes. Though surpassed by modern research in detail, these books still make fascinating reading today. Indeed, contemporary scholarship has accepted Rosenberg's findings to a surprising degree. Today his views are no longer seen as particularly radical, let alone Communist. At the time when Rosenberg published his *Entstehung der Weimarer Republik*, he

---

27 Arthur Rosenberg, *Entstehung und Geschichte der Weimarer Republik*, ed. Kurt Kersten (Frankfurt, 1955), 15–16.

earned the contempt of his Berlin colleagues, however. Quite apart from their disagreement with his democratic views, they were antagonized by Rosenberg's daring to write about the origins of Weimar in a sort of positive vein. He presented the history of Imperial Germany not in bright contrast to the misery of Weimar politics but as the rather depressing but inevitable prehistory of the revolution and the democratic republic of Weimar.[28]

Perhaps the most outstanding figure among the historians of the interwar period who later had to leave Germany was Hans Rothfels.[29] Born in 1891, he had still witnessed the happy days of the last decade before 1914 in Freiburg, where he found an intellectual home in Friedrich Meinecke's seminar. Rothfels came from a liberal Jewish background, but, after years of intellectual incertitude and inner crisis, he eventually converted to the Protestant faith. At the same time, he came to a conservative position identified with an enlightened Prussianism which did not admire the Prussian aristocracy but rather maintained an ideal of the state as both a conservative and progressive force in history and society. Rothfels found in Friedrich Meinecke a historian who offered not only intellectual inspiration but also orientation in a disoriented world. Meinecke's theory that the political traditions of both German idealism and of Prussia belonged together, and, indeed, appeared to have reached a harmonious balance in Wilhelmine politics, must have given Rothfels confirmation that he was on the right path. When the war broke out, Rothfels at once decided to volunteer for the military. He had not the slightest doubt that it was his duty to serve his fatherland with all his energy in its hour of war. The experience of the First World War, from which he emerged severely handicapped, was certainly fundamental to Rothfels' intellectual orientation in the years to come. His dissertation, "Politics and War in Carl von Clausewitz's Thought," was influenced by Meinecke, who had shown great interest in topics and thinkers of the early nineteenth century, the period of the formation of German nationhood.

But in Clausewitz's writings Rothfels found his own opinions confirmed. For example, Rothfels believed that there was an intimate

---

28 For instance, Hermann Oncken, "Wandlungen des Geschichtsbildes in revolutionären Epochen," *Historische Zeitschrift* 189 (1959): 124–38, 136.
29 See Hans Mommsen, "Geschichtsschreibung und Realität: Zum Gedenken an Hans Rothfels," in Wolfgang Benz and Hermann Graml, eds., *Aspekte deutscher Aussenpolitik im 20. Jahrhundert* (Stuttgart, 1976), 9–27.

interrelationship between "greater-Prussian patriotism and the German national idea," and that domestic affairs were of secondary importance compared with the Prussian state's position in the midst of rival powers in the middle of Europe; not surprisingly, Rothfels considered Ranke and Clausewitz to be very similar kinds of thinkers. The state, as an entity predating the nation, was to become Rothfels' primary concern in the years to come.

Like many other historians of his generation who were strongly affected by Imperial Germany's defeat and collapse in 1918, Rothfels considered it his duty to join in the intellectual struggle against the Treaty of Versailles and its historical premises. But unlike others, Rothfels believed that the refutation of the German responsibility for the First World War was not, as such, enough. He asked the question of whether "the truly historical guilt, the responsibility of the nation, does not begin exactly where the innocence in the sense of Versailles is corroborated."[30] Therefore, in his view, the mere reverberation of past glories would not do. Instead, he searched for the long-term causes of the collapse of Imperial Germany, and he found them primarily in the fact that the state-oriented policy pursued by Bismarck had been allowed to be subordinated to the forces of a populist nationalism, particularly during Wilhelm II's reign. Rothfels' early work was concerned above all with a thorough reconstruction of the true principles of Bismarck's foreign policy, which, in contrast to the foreign policy of his successors, had never left out of consideration the essential requirements of the state. His book *Bismarcks englische Bündnispolitik* was intended to do justice to a particularly sensitive aspect of Bismarck's foreign policy, namely Germany's relationship to Great Britain, which by then had come under fire from many quarters. Likewise, he examined the reasons for Bismarck's dismissal from power in 1890, which he, like many other conservative historians, considered a decisive turning point in modern German history.[31] But he did not stop here. He carefully scrutinized the history of Imperial Germany and attempted to identify the ideological forces which had led to its downfall, in spite of Bismarck's masterful policies. In his view, Bismarck had pursued two objectives above all: international peace and the defense of the social

---

30 Quoted in Heinemann, *Die verdrängte Niederlage*, 108.
31 See Hans Rothfels, "Zur Bismarck-Krise von 1890," *Historische Zeitschrift* 123 (1921):267–96, 287: "Der Epochencharakter des Jahres 1890"; "nicht so sehr für den Inhalt, als für die Form der deutschen Politik," this year had meant a decisive caesura.

order against the destructive forces about to undermine state and society alike. Rothfels found that the real nature of Bismarck's state-oriented policies had been obscured by the national-liberal interpretations of his fellow historians; not Bismarck's alleged alliance with German nationalism but, on the contrary, his staunch defense of the idea of the state against the nationalist and democratic forces of his age had been his greatest achievement.[32] The dilemma of German politics began in 1890 with the deviation from Bismarck's conservative path. Rothfels' collection of texts from Bismarck's works, *Otto von Bismarck. Deutscher Staat* published in 1925, proved enormously influential; it set the stage for a new image of Bismarck which focused upon his intellectual roots in the Prussian tradition rather than upon his role as founder of the German *Reich*. Bismarck's notion of the state, with its obligation to the people in their entirety, was, in Rothfels' opinion, the key to his political success. While this book was full of admiration for the personality of Bismarck, it was at the same time a harsh critique of current conventional interpretations of Bismarck. Rothfels did not hesitate to invoke Bismarck himself against the fashionable interpretations of Bismarck as "iron chancellor": "The figure of Bismarck . . . is the main prosecution witness against the illusory self-reliance of the epigones, against all false images of grand times, against every German tendency toward satisfied comfort."[33]

The strength of Bismarck was, according to Rothfels, that he did not allow himself to be carried away by the predominant tendencies of the age. Instead, he remained devoted to traditional values such as a deep-seated Protestant faith, an unswerving loyalty to his king, a feeling of responsibility for the well-being of the people at large, and, above all, a sense of reality in political affairs which was free from doctrinaire opinions of any sort. This idealized image of Bismarck as a true heir to traditional Prussian virtues – as a European rather than a German statesman, who succeeded in preserving the peace in Europe for more than a generation with his masterful diplomacy, free from all ideological premises – proved extremely influential even in the early period of the Federal Republic. In later years, Rothfels attempted to supplement this interpretation of Bismarck by

---

32 Rothfels first presented these views about Bismarck in his inaugural lecture at the University of Berlin in October 1923: "Bismarcks Staatsauffassung. Eine akademische Antrittsvorlesung," in *Archiv für Politik und Geschichte* 2 (1924): 119–34.
33 *Prinzipienfragen der Bismarckschen Sozialpolitik* (Königsberg, 1929), 5.

turning attention to Bismarck's social policies as a prime example of the benefits which could be derived from social policies that, allegedly free from all party considerations, were pursued exclusively in the state's interest. To some degree at least, Rothfels maintained, Bismarck had succeeded in integrating the hitherto destructive force of the socialist working class into the political system of Imperial Germany.

The gist of Rothfels' argument was that the path of German history had ended in disaster precisely because it had violated the first principle of Bismarck's policy, namely the "primacy of the state over the nation."[34] After Rothfels moved to Königsberg in 1926, where he held a chair in modern history at the university, he turned his attention especially to the problems of East-Central Europe. He attempted to defend the time-honored predominance of the German nationality in the regions of Eastern Europe, and therefore he ruled out the applicability of the principle of national self-determination, which seemed to be the only viable democratic solution to preserve peace and stability in Europe. Rothfels persuasively argued that the Western ideas of national self-determination and the democratic nation-state were altogether unsuitable for the social and ethnic conditions of East-Central Europe, with its plurality of different national and cultural groups living together in a most complicated social mix. He believed that in these regions a stable and mutually satisfactory social order could be found only by returning to the Bismarckian principle of putting the state first and the nation second. In his view, the traditional German rule in parts of Eastern Europe had been governed neither by narrow nationalism nor by selfishness but conditioned by the necessities of the international order.

In all this, it concerned European ideas of order, the ethos of power, which sets boundaries for itself, which contains nothing of a missionary or agitating spirit but rather at the same time becomes a guarantee of the society of states as a matter of the Germans' own interest; it is a matter of a conservative principle of objectivity and authority, directed against subjective arbitrariness and liberal crusading instincts, against the explosive forces, in the final analysis against the explosive combination of democracy and nationalism.[35]

To put it in a nutshell, Rothfels tried to formulate a transnational

34 *Otto von Bismarck. Deutscher Staat* (Munich, 1925), xxxi.
35 "Bismarck und die Nationalitätenfragen des Ostens," *Historische Zeitschrift* 147 (1933): 89–105, 90.

alternative to the idea of the liberal nation-state which governed Western political thought.

All the same, Rothfels was anything but an ordinary conservative historian; with men like Adalbert Wahl he had in fact nothing at all in common. In some respects his views were close to those of the so-called *Tat-Kreis*, and he may be described as a moderate adherent to what is conventionally called the Conservative Revolution. In his championship of the idea of the state as a stabilizing and controlling force in society, whose supreme task consists in keeping the destructive forces of ideological mass movements at bay, he may well be seen as a disciple of Thomas Hobbes and Machiavelli, rather than a conventional conservative. It is obvious that for these reasons Rothfels was a strong opponent of National Socialism from the start. All the same, he felt deeply hurt when the National Socialists dismissed him from his chair and forced him to leave his students behind with the trivial argument that Jews must not be allowed to teach German history. For him, perhaps more than many others, the rise of National Socialism was a personal catastrophe, because it seemed to repudiate much of what he had believed. The National Socialists eventually destroyed the premises for a future understanding between the German and the Slav peoples for which Rothfels had worked so hard. Even under these degrading conditions, Rothfels refused to leave Germany. He remained deeply devoted to Germany's future political well-being until the very last moment.

Quite a different position was taken by those future refugee historians who belonged to an age group born just before or shortly after the turn of the century; they were, in terms of life experience, just a few, although decisive, years younger than the generation just described. This younger group was fortunate enough not to serve in the bloody battles of the First World War; it did not belong to the so-called *Frontkämpfergeneration*. The members of this group differed but little in age, and in hindsight it would appear that the group was rather homogeneous. We think above all of Dietrich Gerhard, born in 1896; Hans Baron, born in 1900; Gerhard Masur, born in 1901; Hajo Holborn, born in 1902; Eckart Kehr, also born in 1902; Hans Rosenberg, born in 1904; and Felix Gilbert, born in 1905. They all began their university studies in Berlin under the aegis of Ernst Troeltsch, Max Lenz, Friedrich Meinecke, and in part also Hans Rothfels, who was *Privatdozent* at the University of Berlin from 1923 to 1926. Unlike their elders, they did not encounter major difficulty in their early academic careers, even though they by and large supported the democratic system of the Weimar republic and had little in common with the more orthodox varieties of the *deutsche Sonderweg* paradigm predominant in the German historical profession during these decades. It is perhaps no coincidence that all of them eventually became students of Meinecke. His intellectual brilliance, his universalist approach to historical problems, but also his tolerant attitude toward alternative methodological approaches attracted them; in addition, his moderate political position by and large conformed to their own views.

The dominant generational experience of this group was the collapse of the prewar bourgeois social order, which had been – or at least had seemed to be – a solid basis for an enlightened, liberal, sophisticated intellectual culture, found in particular among the educated Protestant and Jewish elites. These elites, however, had been closely intertwined with the business elites and hence were wealthy enough to afford a comparatively leisured existence. War, revolution, and inflation were, as Felix Gilbert described in his recently published memoirs, traumatic experiences for this generation. Apparently for them history came to be seen as a mode of thought which could provide a new sense of identity and continuity in a time of social upheaval and political crisis;[36] such was, at any rate, the message of Friedrich Meinecke's lectures. The notion of the continuity of the historical process – that is to say an almost irrational trust in the meaningfulness of history – recurs again and again in Meinecke's historical writings. For that matter, it is no surprise that a considerable number of young talents came together in Meinecke's seminars, not least of all those young Jewish students who felt a deep sense of insecurity now that the traditional German political culture was in upheaval and the social fabric was threatened from both the extreme Left and Right.

In upbringing and intellectual preferences, as well as in their political views, the future refugee historians who met in Meinecke's seminars differed a great deal. Given this fact, it is remarkable that most of them started out with topics bordering on Meinecke's own research interests – in particular, a focus on the political and historical thought of outstanding personalities of the earlier nineteenth century. Felix

36 See Felix Gilbert, *A European Past: Memoirs, 1905–1945* (New York, 1988), and the review by Carl E. Schorske in *New York Review of Books*, November 10, 1988.

Gilbert's dissertation was "Johann Gustav Droysen und die deutsche Frage" and Hans Rosenberg's was "Die Jugendgeschichte Rudolf Hayms"; Dietrich Gerhard's early historical essays, published in *Historische Zeitschrift*, dealt with Ranke, Leo, and Niebuhr. Only later did Gerhard turn to international history. Hans Baron was originally under Ernst Troeltsch's spell; his early masterly study *Calvins Staatsanschauung* closely followed a line of interpretation which Troeltsch had outlined in his unforgettable masterpiece *Die Bedeutung des Protestantismus für die moderne Welt*. But even though Baron soon became a specialist in Renaissance studies, he in many ways remained faithful to Meinecke's methodology, combining a biographical and history-of-ideas approach; Baron's essay "Das Erwachen des historischen Denkens im Humanismus des Quattrocento," published in 1932 in a special issue of *Historische Zeitschrift* dedicated to Meinecke, pays direct homage to his teacher.[37]

The individual perhaps closest to Meinecke's own approach to history, which emphasized individuality as the key to historical understanding but also recognized the importance of historical theory, was Gerhard Masur. Masur wrote a book on Ranke's notion of world history and followed it up with a monograph on Friedrich Julius Stahl. In later years Masur became an expert in the field of theory of historiography and universal history, a field largely neglected by German historiography because of its strong bias against anything which had to do with theory and philosophy of history. Masur's paper on the occasion of the Sixth International Congress of Historians in Oslo in 1928, "Geschehen und Geschichte," must be seen as an important contribution to the discussion about the epistemological status of historical knowledge, a debate which was at the time largely conducted among German philosophers. Masur's paper paid homage to the then-fashionable trend of historical thought in that *das verstehende Ich* was considered the very core of historical cognition.[38] In the typical late-historicist manner, Masur emphasized that historical empathy is not a photographic copy of past reality but "ein aktiv schöpferisches Verhalten, ein Bestimmen und Formen, eine Produktivität des schöpferischen Geistes."[39] But

---

37 *Historische Zeitschrift* 147 (1933): 5–20. In n. 1 Baron directly refers to the fact that his study was written "unter Geschichtspunkten, die mir zuerst durch Friedrich Meinecke nahegetreten sind."

38 Gerhard Masur, "Geschehen und Geschichte," *Archiv für Kulturgeschichte* 19 (1929): 183–209, 201.

39 Ibid., 199.

at the same time Masur strongly objected to mere irrationalist approaches to the past, as, for instance, represented by Theodor Lessing's *Geschichtsschreibung als Sinngebung des Sinnlosen*. In many ways Masur was perhaps Meinecke's closest follower, not least for the great power of his linguistic presentation of both historical and theoretical subjects.

Only Hajo Holborn from the start turned to issues of German foreign policy, in the tradition of a Rankean conception of international history. His first study, written before he had finished his dissertation, was devoted to Count Radowitz's diplomatic mission to St. Petersburg during the "war-in-sight" crisis of 1875, when a war with France seemed imminent.[40] After 1919, the generally accepted interpretation of Radowitz's mission – as an attempt to sort out Russian irritation about a German diplomatic initiative in Constantinople concerning Serbia, which the Russians thought violated the special relationship between the two monarchies – had been challenged by French scholarship. Allegedly Bismarck had tried to buy the neutrality of Russia in the imminent Franco-German war by offering far-reaching concessions to Russia in the Oriental question. In the fashion of the day, which seemed to require defending Bismarck's image as the preserver of peace, Holborn dutifully refuted these charges on the basis of a careful analysis of the official files and the private correspondence of Radowitz, which was made available to him by the Radowitz family. The war-in-sight crisis of 1875 had not, according to Holborn, been a preliminary stage of the First World War, and there was no substantiation of the claim that Radowitz's mission had been merely part of a strategy of preventive war against France. In typical Rankean fashion, Holborn concluded that the crisis in Russo-German relations in 1875 had been caused by personal animosities, not fundamental disagreements; indeed, eventually "die dauernden und immanenten politischen Gewalten" (that is to say, the objective interest of both czarist Russia and Imperial Germany in the preservation of the European established order) "behaupteten ihre Rechte" against mere transitory personal factors.[41] This line of reasoning still adhered to the conventional pattern of diplomatic history fashionable in the neo-Rankean tradition. This is the case also with Holborn's study on Germany's relations with the

---

40 *Bismarcks europäische Politik zu Beginn der siebziger Jahre und die Mission Radowitz* (Berlin, 1925).
41 Ibid., 90.

Ottoman Empire during Bismarck's rule, written soon afterward; however, this study amounted to an implicit critique of the intensive German engagement in the Middle East during the Wilhelmine period. This involvement, in his view, had grossly violated the basic principle of Bismarck's Oriental policies, which prohibited any major financial engagement of German capital in the Ottoman Empire.[42] It is also noteworthy that Holborn dissociated himself from Onckens' rather nationalistic interpretation of Napoleon III's Rhine politics, which, in Oncken's opinion, had overstepped the boundaries of a *realistische Staatengeschichte*. Holborn did so with Rankean arguments and a finesse in the analysis of individual patterns of motivation which reminds us of Meinecke's method.[43]

In a study of Ulrich von Hutten, Holborn then moved closer to the historiographic presentation typical of the Meinecke school.[44] A further point needs to be made. Hajo Holborn, like most of his colleagues, soon went beyond the traditional geographical restrictions of German diplomatic history. His dissertation on Imperial Germany's policies vis-à-vis the Ottoman Empire tackled a theme which had been largely neglected by the Bismarck orthodoxy. Bismarck's message that "the Orient was not worth the bones of a single Pomeranian grenadier" was brought home to a German public grown accustomed to the idea that indirect control over the vast regions of the Ottoman Empire was a legitimate objective of German "world politics." In doing so, the book represented an indirect critique of the excesses of Wilhelmine imperialist policies.

All the same, it must be admitted that Holborn's early writings remained within the Rankean paradigm of the relative autonomy of foreign politics, a paradigm which had never been questioned by Meinecke and which young Rothfels had also underlined. However, Holborn struck a new note in his endeavor to get beyond a more nationalist approach to the problems of German foreign policy. On the contrary, a holder of the Carnegie Chair for Foreign Affairs and History at the Deutsche Hochschule für Politik in Berlin, he did his best to write about international relations in a conciliatory manner, attempting to present the point of view of all of the major nations

---

42 Hajo Holborn, *Deutschland und die Türkei 1878–1890* (Berlin, 1925).
43 Hajo Holborn, "Onckens Werk über die Rheinpolitik Napoleons III.," *Historische Zeitschrift* 139 (1929): 303–13, esp. 308, regarding Onckens' moral condemnation of Napoleon's policies, and 312–13.
44 *Ulrich von Hutten* (Berlin, 1929).

involved, not just the German one. A good example is his essay "Kriegsschuld und Reparationen auf der Pariser Friedenskonferenz von 1919."[45] Here he drew attention to recent French research upon the origins of paragraph 231 of the Versailles peace treaty which emphasized the juridical, in contrast to the moral, meaning of this paragraph. He followed this up with a detailed analysis of the history of Woodrow Wilson's Fourteen Points, in order to corroborate the German point of view that the claims for reparation had no basis in the original peace proposal made by the president of the United States. But on the other hand, he demonstrated for the first time that the infamous war-guilt declaration of paragraph 231 did not originate with the Commission des Responsabilités des Auteurs de la Guerre, contrary to widely held views in Germany at the time. This analysis was – and indeed it was meant to be – a first step toward a nonpartisan scholarly analysis of this issue that had been so divisive in the interwar period, not least in the interest of helping to create a more peaceful world.

In some ways a more rational approach to international politics, less prone to nationalist fervor, but also free of idealized notions of the state, had been prepared by Meinecke himself. Meinecke's book *Die Idee der Staatsraison in der neueren Geschichte* argued that there is an unbridgeable dichotomy between reason of state and the principles of morality and had thus supported the contention that power politics are not reducible to ideals, however important the latter may be in guiding statesmen's actions in their conduct of foreign affairs. The ongoing influence of the Rankean tradition was also apparent in the early work of Dietrich Gerhard, who studied the great empires of the seventeenth and eighteenth centuries, notably those of Great Britain, Russia, and France, and the great shifts in the international arena caused by the imperial rivalries of the late eighteenth century.

Hajo Holborn's work, but even more so that of Dietrich Gerhard, represented a way of writing international history reminiscent of the historiography of the neo-Rankeans, although Holborn and Gerhard approached their subject matter with a rather critical intent. In addition, their historiography was entirely free of the aggressive nationalism and the enthusiasm for *Weltpolitik* which had motivated the older generation of historians. They also did not share the strong anti-French bias found in Oncken's studies of Napoleon III's Rhine

---

45 Leipzig, 1932.

policies. Dietrich Gerhard's inaugural lecture as *Privatdozent* in Berlin
was devoted to the history of the British Empire.[46] It accentuated
the role of the mercantile spirit and of striving for power as two
closely interrelated factors which had determined the rise of the British Empire. Peaceful policies were, in his view, only a late arrival on
the stage of imperial history, after the commercial predominance of
Britain had already been well established. However, he emphasized
that the motive for British imperialism was not territorial gain but
commercial gain. In some ways this study foreshadows modern notions of the interpretation of empire, such as the idea of a perennial
shift between methods of informal, primarily commercial, penetra-
tion and those of formal colonialism, or of the role of "men on the
spot" (notably the governors general in India), who often forced the
hand of the government in London. He also pointed to substantial
changes in the nature of British imperial rule that came about with
the rise of modern industrial capitalism, changes that, as time went
on, progressively pushed the older type of commercial capitalism
more and more into the background. He argued that Germans ought
to understand British expansion not just in terms of national rivalry
but also as part of a universal process of the expansion of Europe
over the whole globe, in which Germany was involved (however
indirectly) in a substantial way, if only because of the repercussions
of the rise of British imperial power on the international economy.
Gerhard ended on a pessimistic note, observing that the history of
European expansion could no longer be written in optimistic terms,
as had been common in Ranke's days. By now the dark aspects of
the expansion of the European spirit to the other continents could no
longer be overlooked. These thoughtful observations, now almost
entirely fallen into oblivion, were based upon a substantial mono-
graphic study of Anglo–Russian relations in the later eighteenth century.[47] Contrary to Gerhard's own initial expectations, this turned
out to be less a study of international policy than an analysis of the
closely intertwined nature of international diplomacy, commercial
relations, and international trade, under the auspices of the formation
of two new empires, whether of a continental nature, like the czarist
one, or maritime, like the British Empire. According to Gerhard, it
was during the Napoleonic Wars that a new international system

---

46 "Hauptprobleme einer Geschichte des britischen Empire," *Historische Zeitschrift* 149
   (1934):57–74. (The lecture was actually given in 1932.)
47 Dietrich Gerhard, *England und der Aufstieg Russlands* (Munich, 1932).

came into being which, for the first time in modern history, encompassed vast regions of the non-European world as well. This was Rankean history of a new sort which considered the economic and commercial dimensions of international politics as factors of equal importance.

Even Hans Rosenberg initially wrote international history in a Rankean mode. He sought to keep clear of moralist or partisan views and to describe the forces at work in foreign relations in terms of objective power interests. In his first book, *Die Jugendgeschichte Rudolf Hayms*, Rosenberg counted himself among those historians who arrive at their judgments "not by deduction from a moral code or party ideal, but rather, as corresponds to the eternal nature of politics, from the insight into the struggle of interests and the objective necessities which emerge from this struggle."[48] But, in much the same way as Dietrich Gerhard, he soon was driven beyond the confines of the Rankean paradigm. Only a few years later, however, Rosenberg came to define these "interests" no longer exclusively in terms of power, prestige, and status within systems of states. Instead, he now increasingly emphasized the economic and sociopolitical factors determining foreign policy, be it the interest of dominant aristocratic elites in holding their own against the rising lower classes or the economic advantage of the commercial classes which profited from imperialist policies.

Although these historians developed rather different directions in their later work, all of them were strongly influenced by Meinecke's idealist approach to political history, which focused on the actions of great statesmen and the ideas of great thinkers of the age in an attempt to trace ideas and emotions as the real, dynamic elements of the historical process. Although none of them ever directly attempted to copy Meinecke's form of intellectual history, which tended to focus upon the peaks of the historical process rather than upon events as a whole, they inherited his great sensitivity and likewise his sense of moral responsibility as a historian. One is inclined to praise Meinecke's remarkable liberality both in methodological and political respects. He not only tolerated the fact that many of his students were to follow paths rather different from his own but actively encouraged them to do so.

The group of historians under discussion here formed the core, or

---

48 *Die Jugendgeschichte Rudolf Hayms*, 200.

at least a sizable section, of what may be called the Meinecke school (even though in technical terms there was no such thing). Their historical work, as it progressively developed, was devoted essentially to three main themes:

a. Political history, with particular emphasis upon the ideas that determine the motives and the intellectual orientation of those human beings who either directly exercise political power or who, perhaps even more importantly, provide intellectual guidelines for creative statesmanship;
b. Problems of historiography and universal history, intrinsically connected with a sort of sublime history of ideas of which Meinecke himself was a supreme master, as is witnessed in particular in the work of Felix Gilbert and, even more so, that of Gerhard Masur;
c. A variety of history of international relations that no longer focused narrowly upon issues related to the war-guilt campaign; instead it encompassed empire building and power politics beyond the confines of Europe, including the commercial and economic dimensions of power politics.

Some of Meinecke's students, however, proved increasingly dissatisfied with the serene, partly Rankean, partly idealist approach to foreign politics practiced by Ranke and some of his disciples. Hans Rosenberg published in 1934 a pioneering study of the economic crisis of 1857, which demonstrated the interrelationship between economic cycles, with their ramifications on the social and psychological level, and the political events of these years. It was principally Eckart Kehr who, thanks to a passionate political engagement, overcame the traditionalist paradigm of political history and developed a systematic socioeconomic approach to political history. For this new departure he derived a good deal of inspiration from Max Weber's political and sociological writings, which had little in common with the favorable explanatory models of the historians in the neo-Rankean tradition. Eckart Kehr launched a frontal attack against the theory of the "primacy of foreign politics," which, as we have seen, had been made a platform of defense of traditionalist historiography against criticism from the left. The unfortunate academic career of Eckart Kehr has been fully documented by Hans-Ulrich Wehler in his introduction to the posthumous publication of Eckart Kehr's historical essays, which in the 1960s provoked a heated controversy between social historians and adherents of *Politikgeschichte* – a controversy that ought already to have been conducted in the 1930s.[49] Eckart Kehr's dissertation, *Schlachtflottenbau und Parteipolitik 1894–1901,*[50] defended by Meinecke against the criticism of many of his colleagues in the Berlin faculty, played havoc with the naval enthusiasm of the German intelligentsia. Kehr relentlessly exposed the political and economic interests which had motivated Tirpitz's naval policies in the late 1890s, including the role of heavy industry. (It is perhaps worthwhile remembering that Valentin's troubles with the historical profession were precipitated by some derogatory remarks of his about Tirpitz, made public at the time, by Paul Cossmann, editor of *Süddeutsche Monatshefte*.) Kehr went on to subject many of the favorite themes of the "*Sonderweg*" paradigm to a thoroughgoing scrutiny – for instance, the Prussian bureaucracy of the Reform Era and the anglophobia of the German ruling classes. He radically questioned the traditional interpretation of German foreign policy in the last decades before the First World War and argued that it was dominated throughout by domestic considerations, namely the exploitation of foreign affairs for the purpose of defending the privileged position of the ruling elites against the rising tide of democracy.

It is no wonder that Kehr was considered by the majority of his German colleagues to be the *enfant terrible* of the German historical profession.[51] Indeed, all his numerous essays, written at a prolific pace within a very few years, directly challenged the validity of the "*Sonderweg*" paradigm still dominant among Weimar historians. While Kehr's views were considered anathema by most of his colleagues, with the exception of Meinecke and Paul Fridolin Kehr, then head of the Reichsarchiv (for among the younger generation only Hans Herzfeld and Wilhelm E. Mommsen defended Kehr's views), Kehr was soon recognized abroad as a remarkable historian. Despite political objections to Kehr by the members of the German selection committee, he was granted a Rockefeller scholarship in 1931. However, only four months after his arrival in the United States Kehr died, at the premature age of thirty-one, in Washington,

49 Cf. Eckart Kehr, *Der Primat der Innenpolitik. Gesammelte Aufsätze zur preussisch-deutschen Sozialgeschichte im 19. und 20. Jahrhundert*, ed. Hans-Ulrich Wehler (Berlin, 1965), 1–30.
50 *Schlachtflottenbau und Parteipolitik 1894 bis 1901. Versuch eines Querschnitts durch die innenpolitischen, sozialen und ideologischen Voraussetzungen des deutschen Imperialismus*, Eberings Historische Studien, no. 197 (Berlin, 1930).
51 For instance, Hermann Oncken to Walter L. Dorn, cf. Hans-Ulrich Wehler, "Einleitung," in Kehr, *Primat der Innenpolitik*, 1–29, 15.

D.C., four months after Hitler's rise to power. Only thanks to the endeavors of Hans-Ulrich Wehler were Kehr's writings given general attention after the Second World War. Even now, in the postwar era, his writings have met a stormy reception, creating a controversy which to this day has not fully subsided.

Two other junior scholars who attempted to develop a socioeconomic interpretation of the study of power politics and imperialism in the nineteenth and early twentieth centuries in a similar vein fared little better: Alfred Vagts (born in 1892) and George W. Hallgarten (born in 1901). Already during his student years Vagts had established close contacts with the American historical profession. This explains in part why he, even though a member of the *Frontkämpfergeneration*, never came under the spell of the dominant paradigms of German historiography during the Weimar period. From the start, Vagts devoted his attention to the interplay of power politics and international high finance; he was among the first to expose the important role of foreign investment and financial links in the international system.[52] However, he was prevented from qualifying as a lecturer at Hamburg by political events; after extended archival research in Great Britain and the United States he eventually abandoned his plan of returning to Germany. His monumental study *Deutschland und die Vereinigten Staaten in der Weltpolitik* is, in fact, a tightly argued study of German imperialist policies during the Bülow era. Based upon extensive archival research, it was published in New York in 1935, thanks to the assistance of Charles Beard.[53] Its immediate impact upon research was practically nil; in the Federal Republic it is almost forgotten.

George F. Hallgarten's magnum opus *Imperialismus vor 1914* had a similar fate. Hallgarten was a student of Oncken's. His dissertation was on a comparatively conventional, though thematically progressive, topic: the sympathy of the German national movement in the 1840s for the Polish liberation movement.[54] Only occasionally do we find passages that anticipate the critical approach to the political traditions of the German bourgeoisie, as, for instance, when he pointed to the strict limitations of the national ideology heralded "by

---

52 See his essay "Internationale Finanz und internationale Politik" in Alfred Vagts, *Bilanzen und Balancen. Aufsätze zur internationalen Finanz und internationalen Politik*, ed. Hans-Ulrich Wehler (Frankfurt, 1979), 13–35.
53 *Deutschland und die Vereinigten Staaten in der Weltpolitik*, 2 vols. (New York, 1935).
54 See George W. Hallgarten, *Studien über die deutsche Polenfreundschaft in der Periode der Märzrevolution* (Munich, 1928).

the liberals . . . and their intellectual leaders; they had applauded the idea of nationality only insofar as it was in line with their own interests."[55] He ended his book with a grand vision, which in hindsight must be considered remarkable. The rise of new, huge state formations outside the boundaries of Europe, such as the United States, pointed to the necessity of overcoming the perennial nationality conflicts, with their destructive consequences for all national groups alike, and to strive for the unification of Europe.

But Hallgarten supported these observations through his argument that, for the time being, old and new forms of imperialism still had the upper hand in international politics, and this induced him to take up a new topic, namely the history of European imperialism. In his studies of modern imperialism, Hallgarten sought to develop a new explanatory model of imperialist politics that would take into account the intricate connection between economic and political forces, rather than concentrating on the actions of governments and statesmen alone. Unlike Vagts, however, Hallgarten focused upon the informal networks of personal relationships between representatives of high finance and the agents of imperialist policies; such networks rarely provided indisputable proof of causal links between the economic and political forces which spearheaded the process of imperialist expansion. At the time, this was a momentous achievement, despite its just-mentioned methodological shortcomings. But again, even though Hallgarten succeeded, at considerable personal expense, in having an abbreviated version of his work published in 1935, the immediate impact of his work upon historical scholarship was rather limited. By the 1950s, when at last a full version of his study was published, Hallgarten's *Imperialismus vor 1914* was no longer methodologically up-to-date. However, with the emigration of Vagts and Hallgarten and others to the United States, German historical scholarship within this particular field came to an almost complete halt. Even today it has not yet fully recovered from this break in a previously well-established tradition of research.

Much the same may well be said of international relations. With the emigration of Hajo Holborn and Dietrich Gerhard, two experts in international history were no longer around to provide a counterweight to the mainstream of history of international relations in Germany, which had succumbed to temptations of an altogether

55 Ibid, 10.

nationalist sort. It goes without saying that the emigration of Hans Baron, who in many ways must be considered a legitimate heir of Ernst Troeltsch, and of Felix Gilbert, deprived Germany of scholars who soon were to establish a worldwide reputation in the study of Renaissance history. It may be said anyway that Renaissance studies in Germany, both in history and in art history, came to a virtual halt after 1933. The Meinecke school had shown a considerable interest in historiography and its philosophical aspects; after 1933 this field of inquiry also became barren. Meinecke's famous *Die Entstehung des Historismus*, published in 1936, was in many ways an isolated monument of the former, greater days of German historiography.

The picture given here of the role of that age group of future refugee historians who established themselves as reputable scholars during the Weimar period could be far more differentiated and colorful. Some of the most original scholars who cannot be easily assigned to any school or metholodological tradition have not been mentioned. For example, Siegmund Neumann, who in hindsight qualifies as one of the most important political scientists of the interwar period, developed a theory of pluralism which is still an essential element of modern political thought. His pioneering work on German party history provided the point of departure for the modern analysis of party movements developed in West Germany from the 1950s onward. The great medievalist Ernst Kantorowicz, whose *Friedrich II.* was one of the most successful historiographic works produced during the interwar period, also ought to be mentioned.[56] Special attention is deserved by Eugen Rosenstock-Huessy, who was perhaps the most original figure of all, and who does not fit into any of the conventional categories of German historiography in the 1920s because his work represented a cross section of historical, sociological, and literary approaches to the past. He spoke to his audiences in Stefan George's emotional language but boldly crossed the borderlines between political, social, and intellectual history and pleaded with them to accept the order of Weimar as a firmly new departure, fully in line with the traditions of German history.[57] Many more famous names cross our minds when we move beyond the boundaries of the historical profession itself, names of scholars who were

---

56 See Friedrich Baethgen, "Ernst Kantorowicz, 3.5.1895–9.9.1963," in *Deutsches Archiv* 21 (1965):1–17.
57 See, *inter alia*, E. Rosenstock, *Politische Reden. Vierklang aus Volk, Gesellschaft, Staat und Kirche* (Berlin 1929), 32–3.

forced to leave Germany in the 1930s and who found a new intellectual home in the United States, scholars such as Carl Joachim Friedrich or Hans Plessner.

The loss in intellectual potential which the German academic community suffered as a consequence of National Socialist policies is certainly immeasurable. In historiography, the consequences may have been, in the short run at least, perhaps less dramatic than in other disciplines such as the sciences or art history; all the same, they were momentous. In some special fields, like Renaissance studies or international history, German historiography has never fully recovered from the loss of a significant number of highly creative and original scholars. In other fields the consequences cannot be assessed with quite the same certainty. In political terms, the enforced emigration of the historians under review here also had important consequences which became visible only after 1945. The dismissal of many historians from their positions after 1933, and their eventual emigration, further undermined the already weak defenses of the German historical profession against the onslaught of the National Socialist ideology; the moderate Left was fatally weakened, and the few historians who sympathized with Social Democracy were almost annihilated. Likewise, to some degree the moderate neoconservatives lost considerable ground to those who stood for a combination of conservative views and an integralist nationalism not always free of *völkische* and Pan-German elements. It may be said that because of these developments the range of methodological and political positions found in the German historical profession, when it slowly began to reestablish itself after 1945, was substantially tilted to the right, and that it took another generation to restore the balance.

The battles about the reorientation of German historiography which occurred in the 1960s and early 1970s were bitter; in some ways, they were controversies which took place only belatedly. For the younger generation which spearheaded this battle, the inspiration from the older generation of refugee historians was of vital importance, and in hindsight Hans-Ulrich Wehler deserves our gratitude, because he arranged for the publication of the largely forgotten works of many refugee historians deprived of normal academic careers due to National Socialism. These historians include Gustav Mayer, Veit Valentin, Alfred Vagts, Eckart Kehr, and Hans Rosenberg. Even though none of the refugee historians under review here ever accepted a permanent academic position in the Federal Republic,

with the notable exception of Hans Rothfels, their contribution to
the recovery of German historiography after the years of darkness
and indoctrination, as well as near total isolation from the international academic community, was remarkable.[58] But this is a subject
which lies beyond the task of this essay. There is only one thing left
for me to say, namely to express my deep gratitude to the English,
and, in particular, to the American academic community for readily
opening their universities and research institutions to German scholars who were forced to leave Germany under disgraceful conditions
which still weigh heavily upon our conscience as a nation.

---

58 See on this point also the recently published study by Heinz Wolf, *Deutsch-jüdische Emigrationshistoriker in den USA und der Nationalsozialismus* (Bern, 1988).

3

The Historical Seminar of the University of Berlin in the Twenties

FELIX GILBERT

In this chapter I propose as my subject the Berlin historical seminar in the twenties. I might have chosen to discuss Friedrich Meinecke's seminar, of which several German refugee historians were members in the twenties and in the early thirties: Hans Baron, Dietrich Gerhard, Hajo Holborn, Gerhard Masur, Hans Rosenberg. Yet it seems to me preferable to speak in general about the experience of studying history in Berlin; such a discussion will also help to establish the nature and the importance of the influence which Meinecke exerted on those who were to become historians. The Berlin historical seminar in the twenties is a rather wide subject, and this will explain – and I hope excuse – why this chapter takes the form of a personal reminiscence rather than scholarly analysis.

Before studying in Berlin, I had studied in Heidelberg and Munich. I never wavered, however, in my decision to complete my studies in Berlin. There was one very decisive reason why studying history in Berlin, and particularly modern history, was very attractive. Of course, at that time modern history was not global history; it meant European history, with emphasis on German history, and when you studied modern history at the University of Berlin you had a wide choice of whom you wanted as your teacher, and you could slowly and gradually decide on the era and on the field in which you wanted to concentrate. There were three full professors teaching modern history in Berlin: Erich Marcks, Friedrich Meinecke, and Fritz Hartung. Moreover, a number of younger lecturers (*Privatdozenten*) were teaching there and increased the variety of offerings in history. I heard in Berlin the first lecture course given by Hans Rothfels just after his *Habilitation*, and I learned about the history of socialism from Gustav Mayer, whom, after 1918, the Prussian Ministry of Education had made a professor in Berlin; Mayer and I became good friends, however, only some years later, when we were both exiles in London. In Berlin there was also much life in medieval history, which, even when you were studying modern history, you were obliged to take as your minor field: The *Monumenta Germaniae historica*, a center for medieval studies, was then housed at the Staatsbibliothek, next to the university, and a number of older and younger medievalists worked on the *Monumenta*. Through a back door, you could get directly from the reading room of the Staatsbibliothek to the *Monumenta*, and in this way, through my friend Theodor E. Mommsen, who was then an assistant at the *Monumenta*, I met two medievalists whom I later encountered frequently in the United States: Gerhart Ladner and Ernst Kantorowicz. From time to time I strolled with them around the great fountain in the large courtyard of the Staatsbibliothek.

The twenties in Berlin were postwar years; that meant years of reexamination and revision of traditional notions. The defeat in the First World War had shaken the ruling assumptions of German historical scholarship: that the Bismarckian national state was the result of a long development which would continue and which would raise Germany to a world power, and that diplomacy and foreign policy would be decisive in bringing about the successful outcome of this process. It is now frequently overlooked that Meinecke's *Weltbürgertum*, with its concentration on the intellectual developments which prepared the genesis of German national unification, represented a challenge to the dominating historical school, with its emphasis on power politics; Meinecke's book was a new departure – or at least the beginning of a new departure – in historiography. Also, although Ernst Troeltsch had died at the beginning of the twenties, his emphasis on the variety of possible attitudes to the past – his historical relativism – exerted a powerful influence upon students of history throughout the entire twenties. Moreover, reconsideration of the traditional historical approaches was further encouraged by changes which the revolution and the socialist Prussian government had brought about in the philosophical faculty. In the history and economics departments, various socialists had been appointed to professorships, and Karl Marx had become an important influence on the study of the past.

There were two figures, certainly entirely different from each other, who were widely admired because they impersonated something of this striving for a new approach: Eckart Kehr and Ernst Kantorowicz. Eckart Kehr, assistant to the director of the historical seminar in Berlin, and as such known to everyone in the seminar, aimed at the heart of the traditional approach by rejecting the primacy of foreign policy; Ernst Kantorowicz was forgiven even by democrats for being a member of the elitist Stefan George circle because of his opposition to the institutionalization of medieval history and its exclusive concentration on the publishing of documents.

Discussion and dispute about the direction which historical scholarship should take were intensified by the combination of various generations or age groups then studying history in Berlin. A mixing of age groups always takes place at German universities, but because the war had delayed the studies of many or had halted their advance into academic careers, the postwar situation brought together people who had grown up under very different political circumstances, and naturally their opinions differed. There was a fundamental difference between those who had been in the war and us, the postwar generation; this contrast became very evident on the occasion of a celebration in Meinecke's honor. Whereas we – the younger generation – did not like the speech in which Siegfried Kaehler placed Meinecke in the context of traditional scholarship, Kaehler and Rothfels gave us of the postwar generation clearly to understand that they found a play that we produced on this occasion, which made fun of the popular myths of Prussian history, inappropriate and somewhat tasteless. I am afraid this objection was not unjustified; I can say that, because Kehr and I had written the play. Yet, there was also a middle generation of Meinecke students: Gerhard, Masur, Ulrich Noack, and Holborn, lecturing or doing research in Berlin, and they represented a bridge, some of them leaning more to the war generation, others to the postwar generation. I remember Kehr saying to me about Holborn, "Holborn – Oh, he is one of us!"

Of course, these differences among age groups were frequently tied to political differences. Life at that time, and particularly life at the University of Berlin, was very much politicized. These political differences and contrasts erupted on various occasions, and I remember one of these incidents well. Emil Lederer had been appointed to a professorship by the Prussian government, against the wishes of the professors of economics; when Lederer arrived in Berlin, there were violent demonstrations in front of the hall in which he lectured, and it was quite a struggle to make one's way into his course. However, the simultaneous presence on the faculty of several professors of modern history made it possible for the students to gravitate toward the professor with whose views they felt most comfortable. Once, when Erich Marcks gave a party to his students, he said, "We can talk here freely; we are all on the right side." I was told this by a student of Marcks's, my friend Heinz Holldack; Holldack was politically very much to the left, and I wish to emphasize that despite this fact he was and remained a great favorite of Marcks's. Thus, the division into a political Right, in the school of Marcks, and into a political Left, in the school of Meinecke, was not very strict. Theodor Eschenburg, probably the history student most actively involved in politics, worked under Hartung, and Eschenburg had no difficulty in having students of both the Marcks and the Meinecke schools in the political club which he founded and which, with the exclusion of Nazis and Communists, comprised all political shadings.

I have talked about differences and conflicts, yet there was also a kind of common spirit – a common pride about studying in the Berlin historical seminar. Its members were conscious that this was an old institution, of importance for the development of German historical scholarship; the presence of the past, of history, was almost visible in the Berlin historical seminar. In justification of this statement, let me briefly recall the surroundings in which the students of the Berlin historical seminar worked.

Four days a week, at nine in the morning, we assembled in the so-called *Kommode*, the former royal library, built in the eighteenth century, where Meinecke gave his survey course which extended over six semesters. Then, usually in some lively discussion, we crossed Unter den Linden, and, through an entrance gate flanked on right and left by the statues of William and Alexander von Humboldt, entered the palace of Prince Henry, Frederick the Great's brother, which had become the university. We went upstairs, for the historical seminar occupied the left wing of the second floor of the palace. We passed by the professor's offices and the seminar rooms, on our way to the large library rooms with their long tables, at which we sat working a good part of the day. If you had not yet entered on more specialized studies, the books in this library contained all you needed. Clearly, they had been brought together about the middle of the last century, and, somewhat to my continuous annoyance, the name "Machiavelli" was still written in the catalog with a double *c*. When we looked up from our books and out of the window, we were at the same height as Rauch's statue of Frederick the Great; the king, riding steadily forward, seemed to admonish us to get ahead.

PART II

Soon after the Nazis took power in 1933, the creative world described in Felix Gilbert's memoir collapsed. Those who had supported German democracy faced a choice between silence and repression, while Jews, of whatever their political persuasion, had to endure an ever-increasing constriction of their legal rights and social status. Michael Kater describes, in Chapter 4, how this process of political persecution and professional isolation affected left-wing and Jewish historians. But in order to understand the fate of these historians, it is also important to bear in mind that for most of the German historical profession nazism did not represent a sharp break with the past. The overwhelming majority of the members of the profession stayed at their posts, met their classes, did their research, and carried on with their lives. The Nazis evidently believed that these scholars represented no threat to their regime – and they were, of course, quite right. With very few exceptions, German historians remained silent as colleagues and students were driven from their midst. Some of them surely disapproved of what was happening, but they kept their disapproval to themselves. The Austrian story, as Fritz Fellner tells it in Chapter 7, has a somewhat different shape and chronology, but the conclusion is the same: Here too, the ranks of the profession closed again, after its dissenting members had either left or been expelled.

Deprived of their livelihoods and abandoned by their colleagues, democratic and Jewish historians were forced to throw themselves on the mercy of others. As Karen Greenberg's essay demonstrates (Chapter 5), efforts to find suitable employment for these refugees involved a cooperative effort by international agencies and a variety of American colleges and universities. In the midst of an economic depression and within a profession still narrowly focused on Ameri-

71

can history, it was a daunting task to discover teaching jobs for foreign scholars, many of whom were still in the early stages of their careers. Considering these difficulties, a remarkable number of refugees were able to continue to work as historians – even if only a few found positions commensurate with their talents and achievements.

It is understandable that when a group of historians tells the story of the refugee scholars, they tend to concentrate on academic careers and professional accomplishments. But, as Sibylle Quack sharply argues in Chapter 6, this emphasis leaves out some of the essential human dimensions of emigration. By examining the role of women, Quack recovers something of what emigration meant for people's everyday lives. Her account leads us to a better appreciation of the suffering and sacrifice that even the most successful refugee families had to endure. Catherine Epstein continues this line of analysis, in Chapter 8, with what she calls a *Schicksalsgeschichte* of the refugees. Her picture of some ninety German-speaking historians indicates a diversity of origins and experience that is easy to overlook when we concentrate on a few prominent and successful scholars.

In the last two essays in this part of the volume, our attention is once again directed toward the best-known refugees – that small but significant group of historians who worked for the Office of Strategic Services during the Second World War. As Barry Katz's history (Chapter 9) and Carl Schorske's memoir (Chapter 10) make clear, the OSS united American and German scholars in an enterprise that required them to learn from and teach each other. In the highly unusual setting of the OSS, we can see for the first time some of the larger questions that will dominate the concluding essays in the volume: How much were the refugee historians changed by their American experience? What were the extent and the limits of their influence? Finally, How did historians differ from other refugee scholars?

4

Refugee Historians in America: Preemigration Germany to 1939

MICHAEL H. KATER

Two types of university historians were forced from their teaching and research positions, and into exile, by the National Socialist regime: first, non-Jews of a left-liberal or Marxist persuasion, and second, Jews. A third, mixed, type was derivative: Leftist Jews were at risk both for their racial background and for their ideology. This combination was historically grounded. Characteristically, left-wing politics had accompanied the emancipation of Jews in Germany since the Enlightenment and had in fact marked the noticeably greater access of Jewish candidates to university posts in the comparatively tolerant climate of the Weimar republic.[1]

The emigration of leftist and Jewish academics was preceded by official legislation, but in certain cases it received a significant boost from semiprivately organized, and sometimes altogether spontaneous, harrassment.[2] Proscriptive legislation against Jews and Marxists proceeded in three major steps. First came the Law for the Restoration of the German Civil Service, which, on April 7, 1933, deprived both politically unreliable and non-"Aryan" university personnel of their civil-service status, canceling their tenure privileges and dismissing them, with few, albeit notable, exceptions. By December 1934, junior faculty who fell into these categories were barred from *Habilitation*, the university lecturer certification demanded of all Ger-

For financing the research for this essay, I am much indebted to the Social Sciences and Humanities Research Council of Canada. I also have to thank Mr. Lewis Bateman, Professor Giles Constable, Ms. Catherine Epstein, Professor Georg G. Iggers, Dr. Peter Walther, and W. W. Norton, New York, for their valuable assistance.

Unless otherwise indicated, all translations are by the author.

1 Reinhard Rürup, *Emanzipation und Antisemitismus. Studien zur "Judenfrage" der bürgerlichen Gesellschaft* (Göttingen, 1975); Bernd Faulenbach in *Frankfurter Allgemeine Zeitung*, January 4, 1989.
2 For the latter as a constituent factor in the shaping of Nazi society, see Michael H. Kater, "Everyday Anti-Semitism in Prewar Nazi Germany: The Popular Bases," *Yad Vashem Studies* 16 (1984): 129–59.

man professors. And in September of 1935, as part of the "Nuremberg Blood Laws," the Reich Citizenship Ordinance was promulgated, robbing Jews of the rights and privileges of ordinary citizens and thus reducing them to "guests," legally at the mercy of the authorities.[3] These (negative) measures to eliminate the influence of leftists and Jews, on the one side, were complemented by (positive) enactments designed to Nazify the entire university structure, on the other, with the "Aryan" rector at the helm as *Führer*.[4] "Aryan" historians who fell victim to the incriminating clauses on political grounds were few: They included the full professors Walter Goetz in Leipzig, Franz Schnabel in Karlsruhe, and Bernhard Schmeidler in Erlangen.[5]

The typology of unofficial or quasi-legal harassment is harder to describe, because by its very nature it is not as well documented. By analogy to the government enactments, racial and political aliens were intimidated so as to discourage them from holding out at the workplace or even in their homes, while potential collaborators were pressured, co-opted, and appropriately rewarded.

The intimidation of scholars was usually planned and executed by members of the National Socialist Student League (NSDStB) or brown-shirted student Storm Troopers (SA), often with the active support of entrenched Nazi academics.[6] It was as capricious as it was unpredictable. Thus, before his dismissal as associate professor of

---

3 Gerd Rühle. *Das Dritte Reich. Dokumentarische Darstellung des Aufbaues der Nation*, 2nd ed., 6 vols. (Berlin, 1934–9), 1:112–13; Wolfgang Kunkel, "Der Professor im Dritten Reich," in Helmut Kuhn et al., *Die deutsche Universität im Dritten Reich. Acht Beiträge* (Munich, 1966), 115–16; Karl Dietrich Bracher, in Bracher, Wolfgang Sauer, and Gerhard Schulz, *Die nationalsozialistische Machtergreifung. Studien zur Errichtung des totalitären Herrschaftssystems in Deutschland 1933–34*, 2nd ed. (Cologne, 1962), 322; Arno Weckbecker, "Gleichschaltung der Universität? Nationalsozialistische Verfolgung Heidelberger Hochschullehrer aus rassischen und politischen Gründen," in Karin Buselmeier et al., eds., *Auch eine Geschichte der Universität Heidelberg* (Mannheim, 1985), 274–5.

4 Hellmut Seier, "Der Rektor als Führer. Zur Hochschulpolitik des Reichserziehungsministeriums 1934–1945," *Vierteljahrshefte für Zeitgeschichte* 12 (1964): 105–46. The Nazi coordination of university administrations was not uniform; it occurred swiftly in some places (Tübingen) and more hesitatingly in others (Heidelberg). See Uwe Dietrich Adam, *Hochschule und Nationalsozialismus. Die Universität Tübingen im Dritten Reich* (Tübingen, 1977), 46–84; Birgit Vezina, *"Die Gleichschaltung" der Universität. Heidelberg im Zuge der nationalsozialistischen Machtergreifung* (Heidelberg, 1982), 75–77.

5 Helmut Heiber, *Walter Frank und sein Reichsinstitut für Geschichte des neuen Deutschlands* (Stuttgart, 1966), 181; Hans Schleier, *Die bürgerliche deutsche Geschichtsschreibung der Weimarer Republik* (Berlin [East], 1975), 107; Manfred Franze, *Die Erlanger Studentenschaft 1918–1945* (Würzburg, 1972), 343–4.

6 On the general principle of this, see Michael Stephen Steinberg, *Sabers and Brown Shirts: The German Students' Path to National Socialism, 1918–1935* (Chicago, 1977), 135–9; Weckbecker, "Gleichschaltung," 278.

internal medicine at the University of Berlin, Bernhard Zondek, who was Jewish, was forced to witness the beating of his Jewish assistants by the SA in March of 1933.[7] At Rostock, two medical colleagues of Zondek's, pediatrician Gustav Posner and stomatologist Hans Moral, also Jewish, were set upon by organized Nazi students until, still in the summer of 1933, they committed suicide.[8] Moreover, Nazi students insulted Frankfurt philosopher Kurt Riezler in the lecture hall until he was forced into retiremeat.[9] Among historians, Professor Richard Laqueur had been molested at Tübingen by right-radical students, as early as the spring of 1932, for having publicly supported Hindenburg's reelection as president. Three years later, in Halle, Laqueur too would be sacked; this specialist in ancient history emigrated to the United States in 1939.[10] Since 1932, at Cologne, the half-Jewish history lecturer Hans Rosenberg had had to endure the opposition engendered by right-wing senior colleagues surrounding Martin Spahn, and in Frankfurt the boycott of medievalist Ernst Kantorowicz began.[11] Few historians suffered as severely as Jewish archivist Ernst Posner, who, although as a World War I veteran he had not been affected by the law of April 1933, was dismissed from the Prussian State Archives in 1935, and later was thrown into Sachsenhausen concentration camp for six weeks in the aftermath of the November 1938 pogroms.[12]

Skeptical non-Jewish historians (as well as teachers in other university disciplines) might be kept in check with constant pressure to

7 Hermann Zondek, *Auf festem Fusse. Erinnerungen eines jüdischen Klinikers* (Stuttgart, 1973), 163–5.
8 Forschungsgruppe Universitätsgeschichte, ed, *Geschichte der Universität Rostock 1419–1969. Festschrift zur Fünfhundertfünfzig-Jahr-Feier der Universität*, 2 vols. ([Rostock], [1969]), 1:263–4.
9 *Wer Ist's?*, 10th ed., ed. Herrmann A. L. Degener (Berlin, 1935), 1306; Hans Maier, "Nationalsozialistische Hochschulpolitik," in Kuhn et al., *Universität*, 79; "Dreams of a Better Life: Interview with Toni Oelsner," *New German Critique* 20 (1980):31–56, 42.
10 Adam, *Hochschule*, 23; "Richard Laquer," in Herbert A. Strauss and Werner Röder, eds., *International Biographical Dictionary of Central European Émigrés, 1933–1945* (Munich, 1983).
11 See Heinrich August Winkler, "Ein Erneuerer der Geschichtswissenschaft: Hans Rosenberg 1904–1988," *Historische Zeitschrift* 248 (1989):534; Gerald D. Feldman's remarks in *Bulletin of the German Historical Institute*, 4 (Spring 1989):13; and Hans-Ulrich Wehler, *Historische Sozialwissenschaft und Geschichtsschreibung. Studien zu Aufgaben und Traditionen deutscher Geschichtswissenschaft* (Göttingen, 1980), 267. Spahn's vita is in *Wer Ist's?*, 1518–19. For Kantorowicz, see Friedrich Baethgen, "Ernst Kantorowicz," *Deutsches Archiv für Erforschung des Mittelalters* 21 (1965):6–7.
12 Posner eventually joined the history department of American University in Washington, D.C. Paul Lewinsohn, "Introduction: The Two Careers of Ernst Posner," in Ken Munden, ed., *Archives and the Public Interest: Selected Essays by Ernst Posner* (Washington, D.C., 1967), 9; "Ernst Posner," in Strauss and Röder, *Dictionary*.

conform to the new Nazi role model, by all kinds of intimidation and threats. Such "personal terrorism" has been described in a letter from the very early days of the regime, when the great majority of Germans were inclined to give Adolf Hitler all the credit for trying to turn things around: "The uniformed bandits come into your apartment and ask what newspapers you subscribe to; they go into the cafés and collect money and everyone gives because he is afraid," wrote a friend of young Berlin historian Felix Gilbert one day after the Reichstag fire.[13] Failure to comply would result in professional handicap before actual expulsion, banishment, or incarceration. The setbacks that a young, defiant medievalist, Gerd Tellenbach, endured at the beginning of his career in Heidelberg, Würzburg, and Giessen – being passed over for a chair and then going without deserved promotion for years – explain why less steadfast colleagues joined the Nazi party or affiliated organizations such as the SA early, without, perhaps, believing in the Nazi dogma.[14] Tellenbach's published memoirs are not alone in qualifying the apologetic assertion made by Karl Ferdinand Werner, in the late 1960s, that in essence the historical profession denied itself to the Nazis.[15] In fact, knowledge about the protective function of any sort of affiliation with the regime was so common that even a Jewish historian tried to avail himself of it, because he happened to be married to a Nazi "Aryan": Professor Hans Herzfeld of Halle, after having visibly supported the "National Socialist revolution" in 1933, one year later, as a card-carrying member of the nationalistic Stahlhelm, moved over to the SA in the hope of retaining his chair – all to no avail, for he was ejected in 1936.[16]

Today one encounters difficulty in researching the circumstances and the extent of the displacement of German historians who suffered under Hitler. One reason for this is the relative dearth of first-

13 Heinz Holldack to Eckart Peterich, Dresden, February 28, 1933, in Felix Gilbert, *A European Past: Memoirs, 1905–1945* (New York, 1988), 130.
14 For Tellenbach, see Vezina, *Heidelberg*, 136; Gerd Tellenbach, *Aus erinnerter Zeitgeschichte* (Freiburg, 1981), 34–7, 42–5. The counterexample of another historian, Nazi-party member Heinrich Dannenbauer, rewarded with a Tübingen chair as early as 1933, is in Adam, *Hochschule*, 122.
15 Karl Ferdinand Werner, *Das NS-Geschichtsbild und die deutsche Geschichtswissenschaft* (Stuttgart, 1964), esp. 41–69. A much more critical position than Werner's is in Georg G. Iggers, *Deutsche Geschichtswissenschaft. Eine Kritik der traditionellen Geschichtsauffassung von Herder bis zur Gegenwart* (Munich, 1971), 319–26.
16 Schleier, *Geschichtsschreibung*, 108.

hand information about such cases. Secondary sources more often than not tell only half the story, as the recorded data on Heidelberg historian Prof. Eugen Täubler show: Beyond the basic fact that this fifty-nine-year-old Judaica scholar arrived in Cincinnati to teach at Hebrew Union College in 1941, we know little more about him.[17] With very few exceptions, memoirs, including those of scholars who eventually arrived in America, keep strangely silent about any incident of harassment suffered before an escape was managed, and identifying the specific events that crystallizes a refugee's decision to leave Germany often is next to impossible. Private papers of the persons involved are hardly available for consultation, and this author's personal letters of inquiry brought no fruit.[18]

Moreover, upon closer examination we find that relatively few historians were affected. Thus in a list of nearly 200 scholars suspended from their duties by the civil-service law of April 1933, published in the *Manchester Guardian*, only one historian is named, the aforementioned Walter Goetz of Leipzig. A "List of Banned Authors" of uncertain date, comprising "only a small part of those whose works are banned today in Nazi Germany and in occupied France," contains the name of not a single persecuted historian among 189 luminaries, some of them of a bygone age – and not even German – but including Paul Tillich, Ernst Bloch, and Albert Einstein.[19]

Indeed, research has revealed that among the total dismissals of scholars from universities and archives on political and racist grounds, historians were underrepresented. If it is now fairly certain that close to one-third of all teaching personnel, junior and senior, were terminated between 1931–2 and 1938, with a disproportionately large share in the medical and legal faculties, historians may be assumed to have been near the 10-percent mark.[20] Furthermore, there

17 See Dagmar Drüll, *Heidelberger Gelehrtenlexikon 1803–1932* (Berlin, 1986), 266; *List of Displaced German Scholars* (London, 1936), 44; Weckbecker, "Gleichschaltung," 287; "Eugen Täubler," in Strauss and Röder, *Dictionary; Israelitisches Wochenblatt* (Basel), July 25, 1975.
18 My written request in summer 1988 to Professor Hanna Holborn-Grey of the University of Chicago for information about her late father, Professor Hajo Holborn of Yale University, remained without answer. A letter to Professor Hans Baron was answered by Mrs. Edith Baron (Urbana, Ill., September 19, 1988), informing me that her husband had just suffered a stroke and was unable to reply. On Baron, see "Hans Baron," in Strauss and Röder, *Dictionary*.
19 *Manchester Guardian Weekly* (May 19, 1933), 399; "List of Banned Authors," n.d., Writers' War Board, Manuscript Division, Library of Congress, Washington, D.C.
20 See Christian von Ferber, *Die Entwicklung des Lehrkörpers der deutschen Universitäten und Hochschulen 1864–1954* (Göttingen, 1956), 144, 196; Herbert A. Strauss, "Wissenschaftler

is evidence that in smaller universities such as Erlangen or Königsberg comparatively fewer persons were molested for racist or political reasons and scholars were dismissed at a lower rate.[21] The latter observation pertains to history as much as to medicine or law. It identifies a phenomenon that was peculiar to provincial universities of limited size: These lacked the cosmopolitanism of larger centers that often inspired tolerance; it was here that Nazi controls were most effectively applied.[22]

All these considerations, however, cannot be read to mean that history was an especially apolitical science and consequently that the persona of the historian was less politically charged, and hence less oppressed, than, for instance, that of the teacher of medicine. On the contrary: The symptom of underrepresentation in persecution in these years points to history as a highly politicized discipline long before 1933, so much so, in fact, that by the time the Nazis took over they found comparatively few left-liberals, Marxists, and Jews to remove, notwithstanding the freedom of opportunity of the Weimar-republican scene.[23] The charge of one Nazi historian, for instance, that "a not inconsiderable percentage of Jewish scholars"

in der Emigration," in Jörg Tröger, ed., *Hochschule und Wissenschaft im Dritten Reich* (Frankfurt am Main, 1984), 54–5; Maier, "Hochschulpolitik," 82–3. *List of Displaced German Scholars*, 41–44, subsumes sixty scholars under "History," of whom approximately half were full-time academic historians in our sense of the word. Reinhard Kühnl's figure of 15% for historians is somewhat exaggerated: "Reichsdeutsche Geschichtswissenschaft," in Tröger, ed., *Hochschule*, 102.

21 See Franze, *Studentenschaft*, 343–7; Bracher, in Bracher, Sauer, and Schulz, *Machtergreifung*, 321. In a letter to Ms. Catherine Epstein, Dr. Edith Lenel writes, "Since I finished the work for my doctorate in 1934 [for Professor Hans Rothfels, in Königsberg], harassment by the Nazis had not yet occurred" (Newton, Pa., May 17, 1988. I thank Ms. Epstein for making a copy of this letter available to me).

22 See Michael H. Kater, "Die nationalsozialistische Machtergreifung an den deutschen Hochschulen: Zum politischen Verhalten akademischer Lehrer bis 1939," in Hans Jochen Vogel et al., eds., *Die Freiheit des Anderen. Festschrift für Martin Hirsch* (Baden-Baden, 1981), 70–4; Aharon F. Kleinberger, "Gab es eine nationalsozialistische Hochschulpolitik?," in Manfred Heinemann, ed., *Erziehung und Schulung im Dritten Reich*, 2 vols. (Stuttgart, 1980), 2:27–9.

23 See, for instance, Strauss, "Wissenschaftler," 59–60. This conjures up the question of why in 1933, in academic medicine – a field which in the biopolitical order of the Nazis was equally ideologically charged – there were, absolutely and relatively speaking, more Jewish faculty subject to dismissal than in history (Michael H. Kater, *Doctors under Hitler* [Chapel Hill, 1989], 139–43). The complex answer lies in the peculiar socialization of Jewish physicians, which underwent forceful development from the Second Empire on and spilled over into the academic establishment. See Claudia Huerkamp, *Der Aufstieg der Ärzte im 19. Jahrhundert. Vom gelehrten Stand zum professionellen Experten. Das Beispiel Preussens* (Göttingen, 1985); Michael H. Kater, "Professionalization and Socialization of Physicians in Wilhelmine and Weimar Germany," *Journal of Contemporary History* 20 (1985):678–701.

was involved in the production of the leading professional journal *Historische Zeitschrift* beyond 1933 was as patently specious as it was malicious.[24]

In the Weimar republic, the best of the German historians worshiped the idea of state supremacy, ideally personified by Hohenzollern monarchs.[25] A few of these historians – Friedrich Meinecke, Otto Hintze, and Gerhard Ritter – accepted post-1918 democracy and its attendant parliamentarism with more·or less reluctance; the only historian of stature who was openly exposed on the moderate political Left was Walter Goetz.[26] The nationalist historians' emphasis on Prussian glory, the primacy of foreign policy, and the need for external and continental (that is Eastern European) colonization was usually tied up in a formula condemning the Peace of Versailles and clamoring for its revision.[27] This precluded – even at that time – a deeper preoccupation with internal historical circumstances or domestic policy, as well as any interest in the novel thematic and methodological historiography required by social history. To express interest in social history, for that matter, was commonly equated with being a socialist.[28] Scholars like Gustav Mayer or Eckart Kehr, who showed a marked predilection not only for social history but for the history of social democracy, were by definition suspect.[29]

The national-conservative disposition of leading historians such as Dietrich Schäfer, Erich Marcks, and Georg von Below, who need not, but could very well have been, members of a reactionary party like the German National People's Party (DNVP),[30] rendered the acceptance and complete integration into the profession of Jewish historians extremely difficult, if never entirely impossible. The reasons for this were the ingrained anti-Semitic prejudices even among

24 Wilhelm Grau, *Die Judenfrage als Aufgabe der neuen Geschichtsforschung* (Hamburg, 1935), 13–14. Heiber qualifies this issue in *Frank*, 180, 697.
25 For the general principle of this, see Iggers, *Geschichtswissenschaft*, 295–310; Bernd Faulenbach, "Die Historiker und die 'Massengesellschaft' der Weimarer Republik," in Klaus Schwabe, ed., *Deutsche Hochschullehrer als Elite 1815–1945*. Büdinger Forschungen zur Sozialgeschichte 1983 (Boppard, 1988), 225–46. For a pronouncedly Marxist perspective, see Kühnl, "Geschichtswissenschaft," 94–102.
26 Iggers, *Geschichtswissenschaft*, 298–304; Ernst Schulin, "Gerhard Ritters Briefe und die erste Biographie über Ihn," *Historische Zeitschrift*, 241 (1985):362–6; Lewis A. Coser, *Refugee Scholars in America: Their Impact and Their Experiences* (New Haven, 1984), 279.
27 See the literature mentioned in n. 25, this chapter.
28 Iggers, *Geschichtswissenschaft*, 305–7.
29 Wehler, *Sozialwissenschaft*, 243; idem, "Gustav Mayer," in idem, ed., *Deutsche Historiker*, (Göttingen, 1971), 2:122–5; Joachim Radkau and Imanuel Geiss, eds., *Imperialismus im 20. Jahrhundert: Gedenkschrift für George W. F. Hallgarten* (Munich, 1976), 266.
30 Faulenbach, "Historiker," 242–3.

liberal-bourgeois historians of Hermann Oncken's ilk, as well as the traditional association of Jewish emancipation and professional careerism with social, or worse, socialistic progress. Jews, after all, were widely believed to have been the principal movers behind the birth and evolution of the distrusted egalitarian republic of Weimar. Oncken is on record for having made at least one anti-Semitic remark, against his colleagues Hans Rothfels during the denouncement of the republic, and the rational republican Friedrich Meinecke was believed, as late as 1988, by one of his outstanding pupils to have favored the *Habilitation* "only of those Jews who had converted to Christianity."[31]

This tight network of nationalist historians left few niches into which leftists or Jews could move, much less lodge themselves, before or after 1933. Insofar as those established historians had been concerned with the continuity of what they regarded as hallowed traditions beyond 1918, they attached equal weight to maintaining the same value system beyond 1933, with a singular but nevertheless important modification: The idea of monarchy now was discarded in favor of the notion of strong-man leadership, or *Führertum*, in this fashion to go with the times. The addition of the *Führer* dimension to their historical constructs, which the American historian Oscar Hammen judged in 1941 to have long been prefigured,[32] appears to have constituted the sole concession to "modernity" which traditionalists of Marcks's type were prepared to make; some of his colleagues, of course – Albert Brackmann, Adalbert Wahl, and Karl Alexander von Müller – turned into veritable handmaidens of the dictatorship.[33] But even about Oncken, who at Berlin became a victim of the intrigues of Nazi historian Walter Frank, American ambassador William E. Dodd, himself a history professor from Chicago, observed in 1935, "I do not think that Oncken is in any way radically opposed to the present regime, now that it has swung so completely over to the conservative side."[34]

31 Heiber, *Frank*, 191–2; quotation from Gilbert, *European Past*, 75.
32 Oscar J. Hammen, "German Historians and the Advent of the National Socialist State," *Journal of Modern History* 13 (1941):173–5. Also see Bernd Faulenbach, "Deutsche Geschichtswissenschaft zwischen Kaiserreich und NS-Diktatur," in Faulenbach, ed., *Geschichtswissenschaft in Deutschland. Traditionelle Positionen und gegenwürtige Aufgaben* (Munich, 1974), 82.
33 On all three historians, see Heiber, *Frank;* specifically on Brackmann's involvement in National Socialist *Ostforschung*, see the innovative study by Michael Burleigh, *Germany Turns Eastwards. A Study of Ostforschung in the Third Reich* (Cambridge, U.K., 1988).
34 Entry for March 11, 1935, in *Ambassador Dodd's Diary, 1933–1938*, ed. William E. Dodd, Jr., and Martha Dodd (New York, 1941), 220. Also see Heiber, *Frank*, 172–230.

Of the three refugee-historian groups identified at the beginning
of this chapter – non-Jewish leftists, bourgeois Jews, and Jewish
leftists – the first two groups were the smallest. Ideal-typically
speaking, against the background of reigning traditionalist historiography, it was unlikely for an "Aryan" historian to be politically left
of center, and for his Jewish colleague not to be so. The group of
left-liberal democrats, none of them a radical Marxist or a card-
carrying Communist party member, was led by Veit Valentin, Eckart
Kehr, and Hajo Holborn. (It would have been possible to deal with
still other historians, for instance Alfred Vagts or Theodor E.
Mommsen, but documentation on them is not as plentiful, and for
all their worth they do not appear as important as the other
three.)[35]

Veit Valentin was born in 1885 into a patrician Frankfurt family.
At the age of twenty-three he obtained his doctorate with a dissertation about prerevolutionary (1848–9) Frankfurt. His *Habilitation* occurred when he was only twenty-five. This pupil of the conservative
Erich Marcks then became a lecturer at the University of Freiburg.
After the outbreak of World War I, he was called to Berlin to research German foreign policy before 1914, a study commissioned
by the Imperial War Ministry.

Valentin's opposition to the conventional nationalist historiography of the day developed over differences he entertained with right-
wing Freiburg historian Georg von Below on Pan-German expan-
sionism and annexationist war aims. Soon the young scholar, who
may have lacked personal tact and diplomatic finesse, was dragged
into court and into disputes with the Freiburg university administration, with the result that in 1916 he was compelled to resign his
Freiburg teaching position.

In the Weimar era, Valentin remained ostracized from the German
historical establishment; this naturally forced him to move farther
toward the left-of-center camp. A convinced pacifist, he joined the
German Democratic Party (DDP) and collaborated with the League
for Human Rights. Besides prolific publishing, much of it publicistic
rather than scholarly, he taught at the Berlin Commercial College
and at that mainstay of democracy, the Deutsche Hochschule für
Politik. His chief livelihood, however, was a regular position with
the Reichsarchiv. As a scholar, Valentin made his mark with a fully

35 See Wehler, *Sozialwissenschaft*, 286–91; Gilbert, *European Past*, 102–11, 127–9; "Theodor
Ernst Momagen" and "Alfred Vagts" Strauss and Röder, *Dictionary*.

detailed history of the 1848–9 revolution (printed in 1930–1), which rejected the reactionary outlook championed even then by Heinrich Ritter von Srbik, and implicitly expressed a firm commitment to the Weimar democracy. In the words of Hans-Ulrich Wehler, it was therefore "no miracle" that Valentin was dismissed, on the basis of the April 7 law, from his archival position in June 1933; he immediately fled to London. Not until September 1939 did Valentin arrive in the United States, but to the end of his life he was never able to find a permanent academic post. He died in 1947, while working at the Library of Congress as a Rockefeller Foundation fellow.[36] Valentin truly became the victim of the post-1918 traditionalists, whose victory was fully realized only after Hitler came to power.

As a leftist historian, Eckart Kehr was much more extreme than Valentin. Born into a well-connected family of Prussian academics, Kehr published his revised Berlin dissertation, on the connection between naval construction and party politics at the turn of the nineteenth century, in 1930. The thoroughly researched tome was a consummate criticism, not only methodologically – that is of the conventional way of composing history according to foreign-policy criteria – but also thematically, of the ruthless warmongering policy of Wilhelmian mandarins, including historians. Characteristically, the book was hailed by democratic reviewers but rejected by the traditionalist chairholders in the faculties. While Yale historian Charles A. Beard lauded the work, Hans Rothfels of Königsberg University refused to endorse Kehr's *Habilitation*. Rothfels' decision later was applauded by the equally patriotic historians Gerhard Ritter and Hermann Oncken.[37] Kehr, meanwhile, had solidly established the reputation that would precede him from now on, that of a "red" radical – not least because he had seen fit to publish a number of political articles in the Social Democratic organ *Die Gesellschaft*.[38]

In 1931 the young scholar, already suspect in the eyes of his elders, competed for the Stein Prize with the work that Rothfels had rejected: an economic and financial analysis of Prussia in the Napoleonic era. The arbiters of the historical commission at the Reichsarchiv, Ritter included, conceded to Kehr good workmanship and superlative control of the subject matter but once again rejected his

36 This sketch according to Wehler, *Sozialwissenschaft*, 292–97 (quotation 297); Schleier, *Geschichtsschreibung*, 361–96.
37 Wehler, *Sozialwissenschaft*, 233–6; Schleier, *Geschichtsschreibung*, 482–97.
38 Schleier, *Geschichtsschreibung*, 487–98; Gilbert, *European Past*, 83.

unorthodox criticism of Baron vom Stein's bureaucracy, penned, not least, to excoriate certain shortcomings in late Wilhelmian administration. Kehr lost the contest to a mediocre competitor. In a letter to George Wolfgang Hallgarten on December 8, 1931, Kehr complained that the German full professors were bent on destroying his "entire university future."[39]

It was then that Kehr decided to avail himself of opportunities for further historical study in the United States.[40] With difficulty (over the protests of Hermann Oncken), he received the necessary backing from German senior academics, so that a Rockefeller grant would sustain him in America for several months; he was assured of the aid of his like-minded friend Alfred Vagts, latterly in the United States as the son-in-law of Professor Beard.[41] The committed socialist arrived on the East Coast in January 1933. He met with Bernadotte Schmitt at Chicago and Walter Dorn at Columbus. When his German relatives admonished him to hold his tongue about current affairs, he wrote back saying that he knew well he would be put into a concentration camp upon his return to Hitler's *Reich*. In May 1933, the Nazi director of the Reichsarchiv, Albert Brackmann, terminated Kehr's work contract. For years a chronically sick man, the thirty-year-old scholar succumbed to a heart defect in Washington, shortly after his arrival.[42] Kehr died as a transient scholar. Yet, despite his own cynicism, it would not be far-fetched to assume that he could have been persuaded, by his American friends and German sympathiziers, to become a permanent refugee historian in America, had fate allowed him to live.

Hajo Holborn's political locus reportedly was more to the left than that of Valentin, but probably not as radically so as Kehr's. Surely his beginning scholarship, while profound, did not have the ideological, thematic, or the methodological edge of Eckart Kehr's early work. This student of Friedrich Meinecke had become interested in Bismarck's foreign policy and subsequently, after his appointment to a Heidelberg lectureship in 1926, in humanism and the Reformation. In 1929 he produced a biography of Ulrich von Hutten.[43]

39 Letter as printed in Radkau and Geiss, eds., *Imperialismus*, 268. Also see Wehler, *Sozialwissenschaft*, 236–7; Schleier, *Geschichtsschreibung*, 507–16.
40 Gilbert, *European Past*, 84.
41 Wehler, *Sozialwissenschaft*, 239–40; Schleier, *Geschichtsschreibung*, 517–25.
42 Wehler, *Sozialwissenschaft*, 240–1; Schleier, *Geschichtsschreibung*, 525–8; Radkau and Geiss, eds., Appendix, *Imperialismus*, 265–78, 267.
43 Max Braubach, in *Hajo Holborn. Inter Nationes Prize 1969* (Bonn, 1969), 169.

By that time, a large-scale project got under way that undoubtedly sharpened his awareness of the critical times in which he lived: a thorough examination of the genesis of the Weimar republic. He soon was to publish in the SPD's journal *Gesellschaft*.[44] His democratic sensitivities were further reinforced when in 1931 the twenty-nine-year-old scholar assumed the Carnegie-funded chair at the left-politicized Deutsche Hochschule für Politik in the capital. There he met lecturers who were fundamentally of like mind, such as Eckart Kehr and Veit Valentin. In February 1933, already under Hitler, he published an outspoken defense of the Weimar constitution and of academic freedom; at the same time he prophesied that the Nazis would eradicate democracy.[45] Although there is no record that he was suspended from his Hochschule duties by the law of April 7, 1933, it seems obvious that such statements and his ties to the Social Democrats suggested to him the need to review his position in Hitler's dictatorship. "I was an outspoken republican, of which there were not so many – particularly at my age," he said later. Already the beneficiary of American institutionalized generosity, Holborn emigrated to the United States in the fall of 1933, so that he could "remain true to himself and his profession," as he communicated to his Berlin friend and colleague Dietrich Gerhard. By 1934 Holborn was teaching at Yale, ultimately to become Sterling Professor of History and president of the American Historical Association.[46]

The fact that Holborn's wife Annemarie was Jewish must have lent a decisive impetus to his decision for the Free World.[47] Jewish historians in Germany were forced from their positions, and so were "Aryans" with Jewish spouses. But depending upon what category these persons fell into, not all of them had to go immediately. Some so-called privileged Jews were able to hold out longer if they were

44 Ibid.; Dietrich Gerhard, "Hajo Holborn: Reminiscences," *Central European History* 2 (1970):12–13.

45 Hajo Holborn, *Weimarer Reichsverfassung und Freiheit der Wissenschaft* (Leipzig, 1933), esp. 24–5. Also see Gerhard, "Holborn," 12–13; Coser, *Refugee Scholars*, 282–3; Heiber, *Frank*, 154; Leonard Krieger and Fritz Stern, "Editors' Introduction," in Krieger and Stern, eds., *The Responsibility of Power: Historical Essays in Honor of Hajo Holborn* (New York, 1967), xii.

46 Braubach in *Hajo Holborn*, 170; dust-jacket biography for Hajo Holborn, *A History of Modern Germany: The Reformation* (New York, 1967) (first quotation); Gerhard, "Holborn," 14 (second quotation). On the circumstances of the dissolution of the Hochschule für Politik from a subjective vantage point, see Ernst Jäckh, "Die 'alte' Hochschule für Politik 1920–1933," in Jäckh and Otto Suhr, *Geschichte der Deutschen Hochschule für Politik* (Berlin, 1952), 5–32.

47 See Heiber, *Frank*, 185; Amy Sims, "Intellectuals in Crisis: Historians under Hitler," *Virginia Quarterly Review* 54 (1978):255.

covered by the "Hindenburg" exemption clauses. Among other things, these stipulated that those Jews who had served actively in World War I were not to be dismissed under the civil-service law of April 7, 1933, but could remain at their posts until further notice. After the Nuremberg Blood Laws of September 1935, no Jewish civil servants (including, of course, professors and state archivists) were allowed to stay on, and after Kristallnacht, in November 1938, life itself became hazardous in Germany for them.[48] From this it follows that Jewish historians who benefited from the exemption and hence remained in their jobs after the summer of 1933 must have been old enough to have served their country in war. Moreover, politically it means that they must have been reliable to the point of "defending the national state without reservation," and so they must have tended to the bourgeois center or even to the right.[49]

This was indeed the case with the four representatives of the second group of refugee historians, the nonleftist Jewish group. These were Drs. Dietrich Gerhard and Gerhard Masur and Professors Ernst Kantorowicz and Hans Rothfels.

Dietrich Gerhard, born in 1896, had fought in World War I. A student of Meinecke's, he became a specialist in European history, particularly that of England and Russia from the sixteenth to the nineteenth century. In the mid-1920s he served as a subeditor for *Historische Zeitschrift*, and in 1932 he was appointed lecturer at Berlin University and the Deutsche Hochschule für Politik. Although not yet immediately affected by Nazi legislation, Gerhard decided on his own volition to take steps to leave the *Reich*. Through the assistance of British friends he traveled to Edinburgh to give a guest lecture and was able in this way to secure for himself an invitation as visiting professor at Harvard, in the autumn of 1935. Ambassador Dodd was instrumental in this. Eventually Gerhard received tenure at Washington University in St. Louis.[50]

Gerhard Masur was five years younger than Dietrich Gerhard, too young to have been conscripted for the Great War but old enough to have joined the pre-Fascist free corps Brigade Erhardt after Germany's surrender. Yet another student of Meinecke's, he became a

48 Uwe Dietrich Adam, *Judenpolitik im Dritten Reich* (Düsseldorf, 1979), 51–232, esp. 64.
49 Quotation from paragraph 4 of the law of April 7, 1933, according to Rühle, *Reich*, 113.
50 *List of Displaced German Scholars*, 42; "Dietrich Gerhard," in Strauss and Röder, *Dictionary*; Peter Walther, "Von Meinecke zu Beard? Die nach 1933 in die USA eingewanderten deutschen Neuhistoriker," Ph.D. diss., State University of New York at Buffalo, 1989, 327–30.

lecturer at Berlin University in 1930. He concentrated on the modern history of political ideas and ecclesiastical history. Masur is one of the few refugee historians who has related the stages of his harassment by the Nazis in his memoirs. Such oppression included offensive acts against his father, a Berlin notary, and insults to himself, chiefly by "Aryan" colleagues. Masur writes that he remained in Germany "against better knowledge." He was banking on his nationalistic past, hoping that "the regime would run out of steam and that I would then be needed for the reconstruction." Such sentiments express naïveté rather than calculating opportunism; it is clear that Masur took the Hindenburg exemptions at face value. Nonetheless, in early 1935 Hans Rothfels, who had been talking to officials in the *Reich* education ministry, warned Masur of his impending dismissal, a warning that later was reiterated by Theodor Eschenburg. After Masur became the target of attacks by his brown-uniformed dean, he decided to emigrate, leaving in October 1935. Via Switzerland he went to Colombia, and thence to the United States.[51]

Professor Ernst Kantorowicz, the medievalist at Frankfurt, had served both as a volunteer in World War I and in the worst of the free-corps fighting – against Poles in Posen, Spartacists in Berlin, and the Bavarian Soviet Republic in Munich. As a graduate student in Heidelberg, this scion of a wealthy entrepreneurial family from Prussian Poland became a follower of the mystic-poet Stefan George, and largely as a consequence of George's influence he published, in 1927, still only thirty-two years old, his soon-to-be famous biography of Emperor Frederick II.[52] Kantorowicz became an adherent of the invisible, mystical *Reich*, and, although the *Reich* idea increased his nationalism, his eclectic aestheticism predestined him for opposition both to the egalitarianism of Weimar and to nazism, on elitist grounds.[53] The success of his book on Frederick II led the youthful

---

51 *List of Displaced German Scholars*, 43; Gerhard Masur, *Das ungewisse Herz* (Holyoke, Mass., 1978), 155–73 (quotation 162); "Gerhard Masur," in Strauss and Röder, *Dictionary*.
52 Yakov Malkiel, "Ernst H. Kantorowicz," in Arthur R. Evans, Jr., ed., *On Four Modern Humanists: Hofmannsthal, Gundolf, Curtius, Kantorowicz* (Princeton, 1970), 156–92; Josef Fleckenstein, "Gedächtnisrede" in *Ernst Kantorowicz zum Gedächtnis* (Frankfurt am Main, 1964), 11–27, 12–13.
53 See Ralph E. Giesey, "Ernst Kantorowicz: Scholarly Triumphs and Academic Travails in Weimar Germany and the United States," *Leo Baeck Institute Yearbook* 30 (1985):191–202, 198; and the treatment of the *Reich* idea in Kurt Sontheimer, *Antidemokratisches Denken in der Weimarer Republik. Die politischen Ideen des deutschen Nationalismus zwischen 1918 und 1933*, 4th ed. (Munich, 1962), 280–306. On George and elitism, see George L. Mosse, *The Crisis of German Ideology: Intellectual Origins of the Third Reich* (New York, 1964), 209–12.

scholar to a Frankfurt adjunct professorship in 1930; he was granted a full chair in 1932.[54]

Then in the spring of 1933, hurt by the excesses of even the early dictatorship – its open anti-Semitism and crusade against homosexuals – Kantorowicz applied for a leave of absence. When it was granted, he retired to Berlin. Using the capital as his base, he traveled much abroad and prepared his exodus from Germany, but not before he had lived through the Kristallnacht of November 9 and 10, 1938, hidden, in the Berlin villa of his "Aryan" friend Count Albrecht Bernstorff. Via Oxford he arrived in America, to resume his teaching first at Berkeley and finally at the Institute for Advanced Study in Princeton.[55]

Professor Hans Rothfels' case is the most problematic one among those four, for a number of reasons. First, he was the most nationalistic of these scholars and, in the end, the one most reluctant to leave his fatherland. Second, with the possible exception of Kantorowicz, Rothfels was, academically speaking, the most impressive, during three phases of his long career: a beginning one in Weimar and Third Reich Germany, an intermediate one in the United States, and then a final one in the German Federal Republic. And third, he was most important in the eventual reconstruction of post-Hitlerian Germany (something Masur claims to have wanted to do but never managed): in his pace-setting interpretation of the resistance to Hitler (written while he taught at the University of Chicago);[56] in his collaboration with democratic authorities to found the Munich Institute of Contemporary History, expressly as a politically reeducative institution; and as a teacher to a whole generation of pioneering West German scholars, both before 1939 and after, among whom merely Theodor Schieder, Werner Conze, and Hans Mommsen shall be mentioned.[57]

54 Josef Fleckenstein, in *Ernst Kantorowicz zum Gedächtnis*, 16; Friedrich Baethgen, "Ernst Kantorowicz," *Deutsches Archiv für Erforschung des Mittelalters* 21:1 (1965):6.

55 Josef Fleckenstein, in *Ernst Kantorowicz zum Gedächtnis*, 17–19; Malkiel, "Ernst H. Kantorowicz," 200–12. Also see [Yakov Malkiel], "Ernst H. Kantorowicz," *Romance Philology* 18 (1964):1–15. The medievalist's letter of resignation, dated April 20, 1933, is printed in Giesey, "Ernst Kantorowicz," 197.

56 Hans Rothfels, *The German Opposition to Hitler* (Hinsdale, Ill., 1948). The tenor of this book fully accords with Rothfels' fundamental nationalism. He implicitly argues that because there was resistance to Hitler, this vindicates the German conservatism whence nazism sprang. This conservatism always was separate from nazism. One of the earliest critics of this point of view was Rothfels's own student Hans Mommsen. Here, see the critique by Iggers, *Geschichtswissenschaft*, 345–6.

57 Iggers, *Geschichtswissenschaft*, 357–8. In the context of his supervisory work at the Institut für Zeitgeschichte, a personal reminiscence may be permitted. As a young scholar in the 1970s, I submitted articles for publication to *Vierteljahrshefte für Zeitgeschichte*, the institute's

Hans Rothfels was born in 1891; he had lost a leg while serving at the front in World War I. In his early conversion from the Mosaic faith to Christianity, one may see the desire to reject his Jewish heritage and emphasize, instead, a Prussian nationalism; yet, while this point has some validity, it cannot be stretched too far, for this practice, understandably, was fairly common among assimilative German Jews.[58] There is still disagreement concerning the depth of Rothfels' commitment to the idea of Weimar: While his student Werner Conze emphasizes his commitment, the East German historian Hans Schleier flatly denies it.[59]

But even Conze concedes that for Rothfels the concept of a strong German nation-state, with secure foreign-political and military moorings, was paramount.[60] Rothfels, this brilliant pupil of Meinecke, after a lectureship in Berlin assumed a full chair in modern history at the University of Königsberg in East Prussia, in 1926.[61] Even then, among German nationalists, Königsberg was regarded as the *Reich*'s bastion against marauding Slavdom, and there can be no doubt that Rothfels fully identified with this image.[62]

Schleier maintains that after Hitler's coming to power Rothfels collaborated with several Nazi agencies from this, his bastion of Königsberg – even with the SS.[63] Be this as it may, it is now obvious that he became involved in preparatory intellectual warfare against Slavdom under the firm control of Nazi Albert Brackmann, early on in the regime. In a provocative volume edited by Brackmann in 1933, Rothfels urged an "organic reconstitution" for the formerly Prussian and, after Versailles, Polish territories, "according to the

official journal. While these pieces eventually were accepted for publication, this was never done without Rothfels's own meticulous comments, sometimes in the margins of the manuscripts I had sent in. As long as he was among the living, Rothfels took his mentor's duties very literally.

58 Characteristically, Rothfels in 1918 married Hildegard Elizabeth Consbruch, who, like him, had converted (Werner Conze, "Hans Rothfels," *Historische Zeitschrift* 237 [1983]: 317).

59 Ibid.; Schleier, *Geschichtsschreibung*, 108. It is nevertheless interesting that the American historian Oscar Hammen, as late as 1941, when Rothfels had to be viewed preeminently as a victim of Nazi terror, ascribed to him the desire to serve the state above all, "even in the most personal affairs, so that it could assume the attributes of power in fulfilment of its historic mission" ("German Historians," 171).

60 Conze, "Hans Rothfels," 317–18.

61 *List of Displaced German Scholars*, 43.

62 Burleigh, *Germany Turns Eastwards*, 22–4. See Iggers, *Geschichtswissenschaft*, 309–10; Faulenbach, "Historiker," esp. 235–6; Conze, "Hans Rothfels," 330.

63 Schleier, *Geschichtsschreibung*, 108.

maturity of the people living there and the degree of their cultural achievement," in order to prevent certain chaos.[64] But significantly, Rothfels was not invited to join the official German delegation attending the Seventh International Historical Congress in Warsaw in August 1933.[65] This latter affront was a sign of changes to come. As a heavily privileged Jew (World War I front-line service; one serious war injury) Rothfels was allowed to maintain his chair but only until the end of 1934. He was then removed to Berlin, under the false promise of a comparable position, and henceforth eked out a pitiful existence in the capital under demeaning circumstances. When Rothfels was capriciously arrested and briefly imprisoned in November 1938, it must have been clear to him what time the clock had struck. Rothfels succeeded in sending his children to England in early 1939, and he and his wife followed, just as the war broke out.[66] Whereas Conze says that this was done with the aid of English friends, Schleier contends that "Nazi authorities" helped him.[67] After difficult years in England and the United States, Rothfels received a full chair at Chicago in 1946. When he returned to a professorship at Tübingen in 1951, he was one of very few German-Jewish scholars to be repatriated to their homeland.

In contrast to Hans Rothfels, not one among the leftist Jewish historians came back to Germany after 1945, at least not to resume his career.[68] In this third group, Arthur Rosenberg might be said to have been diametrically opposed to Rothfels, for to the extent that the Königsberg professor was national-conservative, Rosenberg was radical-Marxist, at least for an important phase in his life. In fact, after considering all of the refugee historians affected by the Nazi regime, it would be interesting to test the hypothesis that the more conservative one was, the longer one tended to stay in Nazi Germany, and the more leftist, the sooner one wanted to leave. Arthur Rosenberg, for instance, had been a Reichstag delegate for the Communist party (KPD) in the mid-1920s, and, thus exposed, he fled the *Reich* to Switzerland in March 1933.

Born in 1889, Rosenberg had become a lecturer in ancient history

---

64 Hans Rothfels, "Das Problem des Nationalismus im Osten," in Albert Brackmann, ed., *Deutschland und Polen. Beiträge zu ihren geschichtlichen Beziehungen* (Munich, 1933), 269. See Burleigh, *Germany Turns Eastwards*, 63–4.
65 Burleigh, *Germany Turns Eastwards*, 63–4.
66 Conze, "Hans Rothfels," 330–41.
67 Ibid., 341; Schleier, *Geschichtsschreibung*, 108.
68 Hans Rosenberg returned as an emeritus and died near Freiburg in the spring of 1988.

at the University of Berlin in 1914, and by 1930 he was an adjunct professor there, without regular salary. Typically, because of his political past (he had left the KPD in 1927) he had never obtained a full chair, even before 1933. Because he had published a history of Bolshevism, the Nazis had ample grounds for hunting him down soon after the *Machtergreifung*. From Switzerland he first went to Liverpool, later to start a teaching career at Brooklyn College, in New York, in October 1938. Arthur Rosenberg died in relative obscurity in 1943.[69]

The next victim deserving recognition here is Gustav Mayer. Not quite as far to the left as Rosenberg but a committed democratic socialist, Mayer became the biographer of the German labor movement. Among this group of refugee scholars, he was atypical, in two respects: first, he was by far the oldest historian considered in this study; second, although he left Germany, he never reached America. He considered taking refuge in the United States, in March 1933, but then dismissed the thought, because he believed that the Nazis "would not touch the universities."

Mayer was born in 1871 into an established Jewish family in the eastern Prussian provinces. His doctorate on Lassalle as a national economist dates from 1893, at Basel. This introduced him to the labor movement. But at that time, as a Jew, he found too many impediments to a university career, and so he joined the staff of the liberal newspaper the *Frankfurter Zeitung*. Supported by his wife's independent fortune, Mayer became a private scholar in Heidelberg and Berlin from 1906 to 1916, never losing sight of the ultimate goal of a regular university position. In this period Mayer published widely on German social democracy, Johann Baptist von Schweitzer, Friedrich Engels, and the pre-1848–9 revolutionary currents. Mayer's efforts, somewhat belatedly in 1915, to secure his *Habilitation* under Meinecke, were, typically, sabotaged by Dietrich Schäfer and Georg von Below. But in 1922, now under the republic, Mayer was accorded an adjunct professorship at Berlin, which he held till 1933, always battered by the right-conservatives. He became an immediate target of the Nazis' discriminatory policies and fled to London, where he led a difficult life until his death in 1948.[70]

---

69 *List of Displaced German Scholars*, 43; Cuno Horkenbach, ed., *Das deutsche Reich von 1918 bis Heute* (Berlin, 1930), 735; Wehler, *Sozialwissenschaft*, 263–5.
70 Gustav Mayer, *Erinnerungen: Vom Journalisten zum Historiker der deutschen Arbeiterbewegung* (Zurich, 1949), 358–74 (quotation 362); *List of Displaced German Scholars*, 43; Wehler, *Sozialwissenschaft*, 249–54.

Munich-born George Wolfgang Hallgarten was a close friend of Eckart Kehr and quite as convincingly leftist.[71] A young man of inherited wealth, Hallgarten accomplished his doctorate at Munich University under Karl Alexander von Müller, Michael Doeberl, and Hermann Oncken – overcoming some obstacles, for those were conservative teachers and Hallgarten's dissertation dealt critically with German–Polish relations in the nineteenth century.[72] Hallgarten had trouble publishing his dissertation, which did not appear until 1928, when the author was already twenty-seven years old.[73] He became the *enfant terrible* of the closed caste of German historians, not only because of his openly vented leftist views and his Jewish background but also because of a certain insensitivity in dealing with his senior colleagues and his somewhat undisciplined way of doing historical research.[74] Still well off financially, and nowhere near his *Habilitation* and a university post, Hallgarten left Germany for France in August 1933, having been harassed by the Nazis and knowing that the pursuit of an academic career in the Third Reich was futile.[75] In his memoirs Hallgarten has touchingly described how, after his arrival in the United States in 1937, despite his acquaintance with Charles A. Beard and his marriage into an established American family, he could never enter the historical profession as a regularly tenured scholar.

Another friend of Eckart Kehr from the Meinecke seminar was Felix Gilbert, a descendant of Felix Mendelssohn-Bartholdy. A student of the Renaissance and nineteenth-century diplomatic history, he was half-Jewish. Gilbert was four years younger than Hallgarten and a committed socialist, which startled even the enlightened Meinecke.[76] During the last years of the republic, Gilbert knew for sure that in the "atmosphere of pervasive academic conservatism" *Habilitation* would be difficult, if not impossible. Since after the Nazi seizure of power *Habilitation* closure was looming, Gilbert decided,

---

71 Hallgarten has related the circumstances of their first contact in *Als die Schatten fielen. Erinnerungen vom Jahrhundertbeginn zur Jahrtausendwende* (Frankfurt am Main, 1969), 166–7.
72 Ibid., 138–9; Schleier, *Geschichtsschreibung*, 458–61.
73 Schleier, *Geschichtsschreibung*, 453, 461.
74 Hallgarten's memoirs, *Als die Schatten fielen*, attest to all of this. One of Hallgarten's problems as a historical craftsman was that he simply could not make a point succinctly. I once observed him taking twenty minutes to state a question after someone's presentation at a historical conference. His second book, for purposes of *Habilitation*, had swollen to 1,730 pages of manuscript by mid-1933 (Schleier, *Geschichtsschreibung*, 465).
75 See Hallgarten, *Als die Schatten fielen*, 153, 179, 183, 185, 188; Schleier, *Geschichtsschreibung*, 465–6; Heiber, *Frank*, 92; Joachim Radkau, "George W. Hallgarten," in Wehler, ed., *Deutsche Historiker* (Göttingen, 1980), 107–8.
76 Gilbert, *European Past*, 75; Coser, *Refugee Scholars*, 286; *List of Displaced German Scholars*, 42.

in the fall of 1933, to leave for England and later for America, where he first went to Scripps College in California and finally to the Princeton Institute for Advanced Study.[77]

Like Gilbert, Hans Rosenberg was half-Jewish and married to an "Aryan," and he was not as radically leftist as the older Arthur Rosenberg. His year of birth was 1904; his parents were solidly middle-class. He grew up in Cologne and then, as a student of history, "fell under Friedrich Meinecke's spell" in Berlin. His main concern at first was liberalism in Germany and Western Europe. Yet increasingly he was moving to a social history of ideas, and that alone would have made him suspect in the eyes of venerable Weimar-republican historians. After *Habilitation* Rosenberg took up the position of lecturer at Cologne University in the winter semester of 1932–3. His teaching privileges were abrogated by the law of April 7, however, and Rosenberg and his wife left for London in the summer of 1933. After relocating in the United States in 1936, he found employment first at Illinois College, in Jacksonville, then at Brooklyn College, and finally at Berkeley. In a manner of speaking, he became the father of modern German social history – an émigré's accomplishment that was matched only by the post-1945 success of Hans Rothfels.[78]

The last protagonist to be considered in this sketch is perhaps the most tragic figure of them all. Her name is Hedwig Hintze. As a Jew, a leftist, and a woman professional, she was thrice at disadvantage in the Third Reich. Significantly, few historians even today have bothered to concern themselves with her biography – surely a reflection of unmitigated modern gender prejudices. The daughter of wealthy Munich parents, she had married Otto Hintze, her teacher, and become a specialist in the French Revolution. Such a subject was anathema to any self-respecting German chairholder. After *Habilitation*, Hedwig Hintze became a lecturer in Berlin. In 1933, after the loss of this post, she retired to France. Thereafter she rotated between Berlin and various places abroad. In August 1939 she left Germany forever and went to Holland. She received an offer to be associate professor of history at the New School of Social Research in New

---

77 Gilbert, *European Past*, 71 (quotation); personal communication by Professor Gilbert to me in Washington D.C., December 2, 1988; *List of Displaced German Scholars*, 42.
78 Coser, *Refugee Scholars*, 289 (quotation); Wehler, *Sozialwissenschaft*, 267–71; Heiber, *Frank*, 168–9, 185. In addition, see the judicious evaluations of Rosenberg's life and work in Gerhard A. Ritter, "Hans Rosenberg 1904–1988," *Geschichte und Gesellschaft* 15 (1989): 282–302; Winkler, "Ein Erneuerer," esp. 553–5.

York in 1941, but she never saw the United States. As Jews were being deported from Holland to the extermination camps of Eastern Europe, she took her own life on an undetermined day in 1942.[79]

---

79 *List of Displaced German Scholars*, 42; Schleier, *Geschichtsschreibung*, 272–402; Peter Walther, "Emigrierte deutsche Historiker in den Vereinigten Staaten, 1945–1950: Blick oder Sprung über den grossen Teich?," in Christoph Cobet, ed., *Einführung in Fragen an die Geschichtswissenschaft in Deutschland nach Hitler 1945–1950* (Frankfurt am Main, 1986), 42–3.

5

"Uphill Work": The German Refugee Historians and American Institutions of Higher Learning

KAREN J. GREENBERG

If there is one word to describe the story of the scholarly migration, that word is "cooperation." The successful integration of the refugee scholars into the American academic environment relied upon the unified efforts of four protagonists: funding agencies, American institutions of higher learning, the Emergency Committee in Aid of Displaced Foreign Scholars, and the individual refugee scholars themselves. In the public eye, the Emergency Committee assumed the lead role in the concerted activities of those groups. But if the Emergency Committee had the most visible role, it did not have the greatest influence upon the outcome of the migration. That role was occupied by the nation's institutions of higher learning and influenced in its direction by the behavior of the refugee scholars. The committee's allocation of funds depended entirely upon the application, usually from a university president or other high-ranking official, for the presence of a particular refugee scholar. The Emergency Committee, the additional sources of funding, and the futures of the refugee scholars thus took their cues from the decisions made by American faculties and supported by American university and college administrations. The migration of the refugee historians, then, needs at the outset to be viewed within the context of the relationship between the universities and the larger migration of refugee scholars.

When the American institutions of higher learning approached the possibility of bringing refugee scholars to their campuses, they expressed two motivations. According to American professors and administrators, the proposed migration could accomplish twin goals. In the words of President Marion Edwards Park of Bryn Mawr College, it would, if handled correctly, be an event that "kills two

Unless otherwise indicated, all translations are by the author.

birds."[1] The two birds, proverbially slain with one stone, were, first, the enhancement of higher learning in America, and second, the rescue of a number of professors who had lost their positions.

Park's optimistic assertion, made in 1933, reflected a couple of telling assumptions, ones which lay at the center of the overall effort to bring refugee scholars to American campuses. First, it assumed that Americans were deeply enough involved in an international community of scholarship to develop reliable opinions about the nature and quality of the work produced by individual professors in Germany. For scientists and for many social scientists, such assumptions made sense. During the 1920s formal contacts between American and German individuals and institutions had thrived. Physicists and mathematicians had participated in international seminars and had worked together at German research facilities. Sociologists, economists, and political scientists had often met at conferences and in print – for example, in the creation of the *Encyclopedia for the Social Sciences.* An early and pronounced interest by the Rockefeller Foundation in the refugees reflected that reality. The foundation had, in its own words, expended "considerable amounts" – over $4 million – upon the creation of an international community of scholars and scientists.[2] Accordingly, officials of the Rockefeller Foundation and faculty throughout the United States felt confident in these fields in determining which of the refugees deserved an accolade such as "top-notcher," "first-class," and "one of the best minds."[3]

A second assumption apparent in President Park's statement was that the American academy could rely upon the refugees to improve higher education in the United States by addressing existing weaknesses. In the fields of natural science and in many of the social science fields, professors often expressed an eagerness for exposure to the theoretical areas of inquiry in which the German refugee scientists were strong.

1 Marion Edwards Park to the Rockefeller Foundation, July 11, 1933, Rockefeller Foundation Archives (hereafter *RFA*), RF 1.1, Series 200D, Folder 1580, Rockefeller Archive Center, Tarrytown, N.Y. are by the author.
2 J. V. Sickle to E. E. Day, May 12, 1933, RFA, RG2, Series 717, Box 91, Folder 725.
3 Particularly revealing on this point was the attempt of the Rockefeller Foundation to rate the scholars by assigning them grades ranging from A to B –, Rockefeller Foundation Report to Edward R. Murrow, August 22, 1933, RFA, RG2, Series 717, Box 92, Folder 731. For assessments of the excellence of the refugee historians, see for example, Stephen Duggan to Otto Springer, February 5, 1944, Papers of the Emergency Committee, New York Public Library, New York City (hereafter *PEC*), Box 90, "Rothfels, Hans"; John Whyte to Betty Drury, July 29, 1939, PEC, Box 30, "Rosenberg, Arthur": and Frederic Woodward to Stephen Duggan, June 15, 1939, PEC, Box 17, "Kantorowicz, Ernst."

The refugee historians, to American minds, fitted neither of Park's criteria – at least not initially. They did not belong to a formal international community; their research projects had not attracted a great deal of money from American foundations; few of them were personally known by leading American historians. Moreover, Americans were not sure just how the refugee historians could be used to enhance the study of history in the United States. Often, upon surveying the credentials of an ousted historian, Americans commented that because his subject matter was already represented, he was an unlikely choice for the few slots to be filled by refugee scholars. Such was the case with Ernst Kantorowicz, for example, at Johns Hopkins.[4] That institution similarly referred to the possible addition of Hans Rosenberg as a mere "luxury."[5] He did not, therefore, receive an invitation from that university. Seldom did Americans consider, during the early years of the migration, the question of the methods of the refugee historians as distinguishing and desirable scholarly characteristics.

Perhaps owing to their failure to meet President Park's criteria, the refugee historians received very little attention during the formative years of Emergency Committee and institutional policies regarding the refugee scholars. The relatively few historians dismissed in Germany during those early years further inhibited American attention to the historians as a group. One revealing sign of that lack of interest was the fact that the historians, for the most part, were not invited to leave Europe for the purpose of joining American faculties. Seldom did they come on the nonquota visas available to college professors who had the offer of positions in this country arranged ahead of time. Ernst Kantorowicz and Arthur Rosenberg, for example, came on visitor's visas, as did many others. The historians did not appear on the early lists drawn up by faculty groups at Columbia, Yale, Harvard, and elsewhere, groups intent upon bringing refugees to their campuses.[6] Their stance outside of Park's categories

---

4 Isaiah Bowman to Bernard Flexner, March 17, 1939; Frederic Woodward to Stephen Duggan, June 15, 1939, PEC, Box 17, "Kantorowicz, Ernst."
5 Kent Roberts Greenfield to the Emergency Committee, November 6, 1935, PEC, Box 30, "Rosenberg, Hans."
6 See, for example, L. C. Dunn to Frank Fackenthal, August 11, 1933, Leslie Clarence Dunn Papers, Columbia University Central Files, Low Library, Columbia University, New York City; T. B. Appleget to Sir William Beveridge, June 8, 1933, RFA, RG2, Series 717, Box 91, Folder 727; L. P. Eisenhart to S. Duggan, June 7, 1933, PEC, Box 122, "Princeton University; and L. C. Dunn, "Memorandum to the Executive Officers," undated, Leslie Clarence Dunn Papers (microfilm), Butler Library, Columbia University, New York City.

placed the historians among the group of scholars which Harlow Shapley, an astronomer at Harvard and a leading figure in the rescue of German scientists, described under the rubric "culture," a category for which placement, in his words, amounted to nothing if not "uphill work."[7]

That struggle took on particular poignancy in the decisions which affected the refugee historians once they were in the United States and had made known their intention of finding places in the nation's colleges and universities. Language and social skill – often mere paper concerns for eminent scientists whose language was the international one of mathematics and for social scientists whose reputations often counseled patience on the part of hiring institutions – had a greater impact on the fate of the refugee historians. Chancellor Gray of American University interviewed Hajo Holborn and concluded that the latter's English would be "inadequate" for the fall term.[8] Sidney Fay, at Harvard, considered Felix Gilbert "perhaps overmodest and a little lacking in self-confidence."[9] The vice-president of the University of Chicago warned against Kantorowicz's appointment, partly on the grounds that his English was only "moderate," though it "probably would improve."[10]

Discussions about the desirability of hiring individual refugee historians often revolved around the role of research in American institutions. American inclinations to hire the refugee historians defied the pronouncements of British professors, who wrote to America regarding them. A common refrain in that correspondence was the assertion that historians of evident talent as writers and researchers did not belong in the United States. Holborn, for example, was described as "better suited in English research institutions than in a teaching post in America."[11] Similarly, Felix Gilbert was considered more appropriate for appointment to a British research facility.[12] Americans were sensitive to the possibility of disappointing research-oriented scholars. Isaiah Bowman, the president of Johns Hopkins, expressed dismay that the university library had only

7 Harlow Shapley to Stephen Duggan, March 23, 1944, PEC, Box 1, "Baron, Hans."
8 Edward R. Murrow to E. H. Wilkins, March 26, 1934, PEC, Box 15, "Holborn, Hajo."
9 Sidney Fay to Betty Drury, January 24, 1940, PEC, Box 11, "Gilbert, Felix."
10 Telegram from Mr. Woodward to Abraham Flexner, March 26, 1938, PEC, Box 17, "Kantorowicz, Ernst."
11 Walter Adams to Stephen Duggan, January 26, 1934, PEC, Box 15, "Holborn, Hajo."
12 Academic Assistance Council memorandum regarding Felix Gilbert, October 5, 1934, PEC, Box 11, "Gilbert, Felix."

"scanty material in Dr. Kantorowicz's particular field."[13] The president of Illinois College believed that Hans Rosenberg, given his "standards of excellence," would be "much happier in a metropolitan center."[14] The Emergency Committee designed policy to address the issue by attempting to encourage relationships between large, research-oriented universities and the refugee historians.

Despite these obstacles, the refugee historians did quite well for themselves. Their success is largely attributable to their determination to help one another and to the impression they were able to make, personally and professionally, upon their new intellectual home.

As if in compensation for the lack of an extensive network of associations within the American universities, the refugee historians were determined to take care of themselves. Holborn led his colleagues in that determination. He visited the Emergency Committee often, both on his own behalf and on that of others, such as Hans Baron and Veit Valentin.[15] Hans Kohn, who considered himself, in this country, a historian, did likewise for many. Kohn and Holborn also wrote letters for their German-born colleagues. Even as Felix Gilbert arrived in the United States, Holborn alerted a number of individuals and institutions to Gilbert's special qualities as a historian. "I would not hesitate to prophesy that Gilbert will be recognized before long in this country," wrote Holborn, as one of the "most promising younger German historians."[16]

Not only did the historians assist one another, but they also demonstrated a commendable patience in the face of decisions which threatened their careers. Hans Rothfels insisted before the Emergency Committee that Brown University was not merely extending "charity" to him in allowing him to teach there but was doing the best it could to keep him on.[17] Ernst Kantorowicz expressed " disappointment," in 1941, when the University of California still had not found a permanent post for him, but he assured the Emergency Committee that a professorship would probably fall vacant within a few years. "An advantage is in-dwelling in every disadvantage," he wrote in appreciation of his leisure time for writing.[18] At Yale, Hol-

13 Isaiah Bowman to Bernard Flexner, March 17, 1939, PEC, Box 17, "Kantorowicz, Ernst."
14 H. C. Jaquith to Hans Rosenberg, June 12, 1937, PEC, Box 30, "Rosenberg, Hans."
15 Hajo Holborn to Henry Allen Moe, February 2, 1943, PEC, Box 1, "Baron, Hans."
16 Hajo Holborn to John Whyte, May 4, 1937, PEC, Box 11, "Gilbert, Felix."
17 Hans Rothfels to R. Hubbard, June 7, 1944, PEC, Box 90, "Rothfels, Hans."
18 Ernst Kantorowicz to Bernard Flexner, May 4, 1941, PEC, Box 17, "Kantorowicz, Ernst."

born repeatedly attempted to forestall Emergency Committee attempts to place him elsewhere. Hans Baron and Hans Rothfels refused to complain about salaries commensurate with those of tutors.[19]

More than either their unified front or their patience, what endeared the refugee historians to the American academy was the quality of their work. Far from presenting a problem, language turned out to be an eminently surmountable obstacle for those refugees. Holborn's progress with his English was commended after his first year here.[20] Felix Gilbert's facility with the new language was described by his colleagues at Claremont as "not only adequate but admirable."[21] The social skills of the refugee historians also earned them praise. Hans Rosenberg and his wife made themselves graciously receptive to students in the Illinois College community.[22] Holborn impressed the Yale faculty and administration with his exceeding charm.[23]

Most important, the refugee historians turned out to be good teachers and admirable scholars. Gilbert, Holborn, and Hans Rosenberg received special notice as teachers.[24] Within a few years of their arrival in the United States, the refugee historians also earned praise for their unique approach to the study of history. Gilbert was praised by faculty and students for being "unusually widely read in literature and philosophy."[25] While Illinois College specifically mentioned its admiration of Hans Rosenberg's "cosmopolitan point of view,"[26] Hans Baron was recognized as offering "the kind of subject" – cultural history – "which is not fully represented at the present in American universities."[27] Letters of recommendation from recog-

19 Memorandum, John Whyte, December 14, 1935; James R. Angell to Stephen Duggan, February 26, 1936; PEC, Box 15, "Holborn, Hajo"; Betty Drury to John Whyte, May 20, 1937, PEC, Box 11, "Gilbert, Felix."
20 Charles Seymour to Edward R. Murrow, April 23 1935, PEC, Box 15, "Holborn, Hajo."
21 William Ament, letter of recommendation for Felix Gilbert, February 19, 1937, PEC, Box 11, "Gilbert, Felix."
22 H. C. Jaquith to John Whyte, November 12, 1936; H. C. Jaquith to Hans Rosenberg, June 12 1937, PEC, Box 30, "Rosenberg, Hans."
23 Charles Seymour to Edward R. Murrow, April 23, 1935, PEC, Box 15, "Holborn, Hajo."
24 William Ament, letter of recommendation for Felix Gilbet, February 19, 1937, PEC, Box 11, "Gilbert, Felix"; Charles Seymour to Edward R. Murrow, April 23, 1935, PEC, Box 15, "Holborn, Hajo"; H. C. Jaquith to Hans Rosenberg, June 12, 1937, PEC, Box 30, "Rosenberg, Hans."
25 William Ament, letter of recommendation for Felix Gilbert, February 19, 1937, PEC, Box 11, "Gilbert, Felix."
26 H. C. Jaquith to Hans Rosenberg, June 12, 1937, PEC, Box 30, "Rosenberg, Hans."
27 Walter Kotschnig to Francis Keppel, January 22, 1935, PEC, Box 1, "Baron, Hans."

nized authorities in the United States reflected growing appreciation for the refugee historians. Hans Baron's application for a Guggenheim Fellowship in 1943 was supported by glowing letters from A. O. Lovejoy, Carl Becker, Roland Bainton, Sidney Fay, and others.[28] Typically, refugee historians were recommended by leading academics such as Conyers Read of the University of Pennsylvania and Charles Beard as scholars with "profound insights" representing the "highest order of scholarship."[29]

The question remains, however, What were the sources of funding? The relationship of the institutions to the funding of the refugee historians illustrates further the developing American admiration for those scholars. Perhaps owing to the lack of a formally established international network between the refugee historians and the American academic community, the historians did not attract funding specifically designated for their field. When the Rockefeller Foundation funded Hajo Holborn and Hans Kohn, for example, it did so as an extension of its 1920s policies, not as a precedent to funding other historians. Occasionally, as in the case of Kantorowicz and the Oberlaender Trust, one of the foundations that had agreed to provide matching grants for the Emergency Committee provided funds for a historian. Most commonly, however, support for the refugee historians came from the universities themselves. Although the universities insisted that they could not afford such expenditures, they found ways to gather the sums necessary to contribute to the salaries of the refugee historians. This was true of the actions of institutions toward refugee scholars in general, but it was particularly pronounced in the cases of the refugee historians. Thus, for Ernst Kantorowicz and Felix Gilbert, for example, institutional money matched Emergency Committee funds.[30] Brown University established a special fund for the support of Hans Rothfels.[31] New York City's colleges even made it a principle to accept a scholar only if they could put up much, if not all, of the salary themselves. Arthur Rosenberg benefited specifically from that policy, one which college administrators deemed to have a "corking record."[32]

28 Hans Baron to the Emergency Committee, March 30, 1943, PEC, Box 1, "Baron, Hans."
29 Conyers Read, letter of recommendation for Felix Gilbert, March 8, 1940, PEC, Box 11, "Gilbert, Felix"; Charles Beard, letter of recommendation for Arthur Rosenberg, PEC, Box 30, "Rosenberg, Arthur."
30 Financial Support Charts, Emergency Committee Scholars, PEC, Box 185, "Support Charts."
31 Laurens H. Seelye to Betty Drury, May 9, 1943, PEC, Box 90, "Rothfels, Hans."
32 John Whyte to Betty Drury, July 29, 1939, PEC, Box 30, "Rosenberg, Arthur."

Nor was that all. The institutional appreciation of the refugee historians extended to the policies of the late 1930s and early 1940, as the war in Europe, the increasing numbers of refugees, and America's own entry into war hastened refugee scholar programs to their end. Often, as institutions and organizations announced the curtailment or cessation of their activities, refugee historians were excepted. When, in 1939, the University of California moved toward its official decision, made in 1940, to end its involvement with refugee scholars, the authorities were willing to make a "very small number" of exceptions, including one for Kantorowicz.[33] Brown defied Emergency Committee suggestions that Hans Rothfels be advised not to enter the country but remain in England instead.[34] Yale insisted, though the authorities there also announced an end to involvement with the refugees, that it would eventually find the funds for Holborn to occupy a permanent post there.[35] In 1940 a number of historians won attention in the ambitious program of the New School for Social Research and the Rockefeller Foundation to bring one hundred more refugee scholars to American shores.

In the case of the refugee historians, it appears that the challenge of "uphill work" was successfully met. The transformation of their struggle into a success resulted largely from the historians' own ambition and perseverence, from their ability to impress and educate their American audiences, students and colleagues alike, and from their apparent lack of resentment of low salaries and ad hoc contracts. Despite initial misgivings on the part of their hosts, when it came to the refugee historians, Americans could rest content in the knowledge that they had indeed slain the proverbial two birds at which they had aimed.

33 Sproul to Charles Liebman, June 12, 1939, PEC, Box 17, "Kantorowicz, Ernst."
34 Stephen Duggan to Waldo G. Leland, December 1, 1938; Thomas B. Appleget to Stephen Duggan, October 15, 1940, PEC, Box 90, "Rothfels, Hans."
35 James R. Angell to Stephen Duggan, May 24, 1937, PEC, Box 15, "Holborn, Hajo."

6

Everyday Life and Emigration: The Role of Women

SIBYLLE QUACK

Normally, women are mentioned all too infrequently in a volume such as this one. It appears that the refugee historians were nearly exclusively men. Nevertheless, questions arise which cannot be answered only by reflecting on "the historians" – the men – alone: How were refugee German academics able to survive the very first years of immigration? Who within the family provided the necessary income? Who made language instruction and occupational retraining possible? Who took care of the children, shopped for food, paid the rent, and so forth? While these questions appear to be of little relevance to theory, to the arts and sciences, they in fact constitute the very precondition for intellectual productivity. It is fitting that the émigré women be mentioned here, if only initially as the men's assistants – as the midwives, so to speak, of academic productivity in the field of history. To be truthful, a special volume devoted to the role of women in emigration would be necessary to really do the subject justice.

I am concerned here with the role of women in German-speaking, university-educated academic refugee families in the United States in general. I do not believe that the families of refugee historians differed significantly from the families of other academic refugees. However, it is striking that a relatively large number of émigré professors of history were able to obtain positions in the United States quite early on, in particular through the assistance of the Emergency Committee in Aid of Displaced Foreign Scholars. Thus they generally were not confronted with complete unemployment, in contrast to the émigré doctors and lawyers. Nevertheless, one cannot assume from occupational designations such as "Teacher at XYZ College" that the refugee families were actually able to live on these salaries.

Unless otherwise indicated, all translations are by the author.

Here, too, it often was undoubtedly the woman's job which made it possible for the family to survive. One of the women I interviewed – who was married to a professor of history, later at the Friedrich Meinecke Institute, and who herself held a doctorate in political economy – kept the family afloat by working as a secretary in New York City. She and her husband later started a language school in New York, which she continued to run on her own after her husband obtained a position as a college professor. Without giving any further examples here, I would like to venture the hypothesis that the role of the women in the families of refugee historians did not differ greatly from the role of the women in other refugee academic families. Wives and sisters – and occasionally aunts and mothers – enabled families to survive the first years of exile and in fact often made professional reintegration of the men possible in the first place.

Let me briefly discuss a few general observations I made in the course of my research project on German-Jewish émigré women in the United States after 1933, taking some who settled in New York City as an example.[1] I will start with a few comments on the backgrounds of émigré women from the academic milieu, women who were married to academics or who came from university-educated families. I must add that most of my interviewees were born during the *Kaiserreich*.

1. The wives and sisters of the academics who are the subject of this essay often had a university education themselves, or at least a higher secondary school education. Many were "university-educated housewives." It is striking that the Jewish women and girls were more highly educated than their Christian counterparts.

Because of the middle-class status of German Jews, a high percentage of Jewish girls attended the Höhere Töchterschule in the cities, and even in rural areas of Germany; this percentage greatly exceeded their proportion in the general population. For example, approximately 32 percent of the Jewish girls in Prussia attended the Mittelschulen and höhere Mädchenschulen in 1906, compared with 4.59 percent of the Gentile girls.[2] When German universities finally began to admit women during the first decade of the twentieth century,

---

1 See the author's research report in *Bulletin of the German Historical Institute* 4 (Spring 1989): 37–41.
2 See Arthur Ruppin, "Jüdische Schulkinder in preussischen Schulen," *Zeitschrift für Demographie und Statistik der Juden* 5 (1909):141.

Jewish women were highly represented among the first generation of female students in Germany.

Coincidentally, the daughters of upper-middle-class and university-educated families generally received foreign-language instruction above and beyond that offered in the schools. Many of the women who later emigrated had foreign-language skills which they had acquired in the course of lengthy stays in countries such as England, for example, either during their schooling, after completion of their *Einjähriges*, or after passing their *Abitur* examination. I mention this point primarily because it has sometimes been claimed that émigré women adjusted more easily to the new language than émigré men; this "fact" has usually been attributed to the greater adaptability of women in general or to their supposed ability to be more able to accept their language weakness.

However, even if these Jewish girls and women in Germany received a university education, they tended to become housewives after they got married. To be sure, there were exceptions. But professional working mothers were rare. The same, of course, was true of Christian women as well.

The living standard of the university-educated families under discussion here was quite high. Servants were the order of the day, sometimes even three: a maid, a cook, and a nanny. The housewife was generally interested in cultural affairs and often was also active in social-welfare organizations, such as the Jewish welfare institutions or the Jüdischer Frauenbund. I am not entirely sure whether the Jewish religion played such an important role in the frequently quite assimilated families, with the consequence that the women were more strongly committed to their traditional role – responsibility for the domestic sphere – than their Christian counterparts. At any rate, the gulf between academic education and subsequent housewifely activity, in the case of Jewish women, remains striking.

For the most part, these women shared the fate of all women in Germany during the *Kaiserreich*: ignorance with regard to offering opportunities to women in politics and education. During the Weimar republic, a different generation of women came to maturity, women who would have enjoyed more options and better prospects for the future had Hitler not driven them from the schools and universities.

2. In most cases, the distribution of responsibilities within the family shifted while the refugee families were still in Germany, prior to emigration.

We all know how drastically the lives of Jewish families changed when Hitler came to power. The situation of Jewish women was fundamentally altered as well. It is very important to recognize that during the Nazi period an exchange of gender roles took place within Jewish families in Germany, an experience which proved very important for the men and women who later emigrated. It was not always, as is often believed, emigration itself which changed the distribution of work and the relationship between the sexes. It has frequently been noted that Jewish women – and the wives of politically persecuted Gentile men, as well – stepped into the breach after their husbands had lost their positions and provided for their families while they were still in Germany.

We know what an important role the Jewish welfare organizations played during this period. It was primarily women who worked in these organizations, as care-givers, nurses, or social workers.

Furthermore, Jewish women were subjected to tremendous psychological pressure through the inhuman actions of the Hitler regime, for they saw and heard, through their children, what was taking place in the schools, on the street, and in public. They suffered with their children, attempted to help them, and sought solutions which would preserve human dignity.

A large number of women émigrés took courses which prepared them for emigration. Courses in the following subjects, for example, were taught at Jewish institutions: sewing, cooking, baking, the making of chocolate, hat making, child care, and nursing. Courses stressing typing and secretarial skills were particularly popular and proved extremely useful after emigration.

Women took care of the preparations for emigration, which included procuring visas, standing in line at embassies and consulates, and filling out applications. It is my impression that the very decision to emigrate was quite often instigated by the women – often against their husbands' wishes.[3]

The women in those families forced to experience the Reichskristallnacht in Germany were saddled with a tremendous burden. It is important to discuss their role in this context. The Reichskristallnacht made an indelible impression on all who lived through it. For most Jewish men it meant deportation to concentration camps; for the women it meant destroyed homes, terrified and emotionally

---

3 I got this impression from numerous interviews and memoirs. Claudia Koonz, in *Mothers in the Fatherland: Women, the Family, and Nazi Politics* (New York: St. Martin's, 1987), 347–83, comes to the same conclusion.

shocked children, and uncertainty concerning the fate of their husbands, fathers, and brothers. What women accomplished during
these days and weeks – in order to survive, get their children out of
the country, obtain their husbands' release from concentration
camps, procure visas, break up their homes – has yet to be matched
and is mentioned all too seldom. It also shows how tired, how exhausted these people must have been by the time they finally reached
the countries to which they had emigrated.

It was essentially a "normal occurrence" in emigration for the
women to find jobs first. The refugees were aided by a network of
social organizations in the United States, especially in New York
City. Some had been established by American Jews long before;
others had been founded in the 1930s by German Jewish refugees. I
have insufficient space to speak about organizations such as the National Council of Jewish Women, which helped a large number of
refugees. In the 1930s, the council extended its Service to the Foreign
Born. It took care of housing, employment, English instruction, legal
aid, and many other problems which refugees encountered. Of
course one must also mention the Self Help agency, founded in 1936
(a large social agency still in operation in New York City); the Blue
Card, an institution which collected money for refugees; and the
kindergartens run by the group called Help and Reconstruction. All
these organizations were originally established by both men and
women, but women were especially active in staffing them. Six men
and thirty-seven women, for example, worked or volunteered for
Self Help in 1940.[4] They provided immediate advice and aid to in-
coming refugees. At that time, Self Help functioned mainly as an
employment service.

It soon became clear that women were far more employable than
men. Many of them worked as domestics, and a large number as
live-in housekeepers. A lot of professional men, especially academics,
could not find jobs in the beginning. Some were able to find unskilled work. Women, on the other hand, generally found unskilled
work immediately. It was they who secured the family's existence
through the entire period of instability. They often changed jobs
during this time, while their husbands either were trying to find
jobs in the academic field, passing language examinations, or being
retrained.

4 See "Selfhelp of Émigrés from Central Europe: Einige statistische Angaben, 10. April 1940,"
  in *Self Help Papers* (deposited in the Self Help office in New York City).

The following is a good example: A woman doctor from Berlin ended up peeling potatoes in someone else's kitchen so that her husband, also a doctor from Berlin, could receive training that would enable him to practice medicine again. The tragedy was that she herself was never able to practice medicine again. For years she held jobs as a cleaning woman, nurse, and in other nonprofessional jobs.[5] In this manner the refugee women supported their families.

That, however, was not all. They were also responsible for caring for the children and supervising their households, while the men were being retrained or tried to find a job. In the course of my research I have often heard émigré women talk about their husbands, half laughing, half crying, explaining that they did not know how to help with the housework, did not wash dishes or clean house, and often were not even able to do the shopping. Rarely did these women fail to add that their sons and sons-in-law are much better in that respect today. In the words of the wife of a lawyer from Germany, "He just couldn't. He simply had two left hands." The wife of a man who later became a professor of history, the woman I mentioned at the beginning of this essay, spoke of American friends of hers who repeatedly voiced their amazement at the behavior of male refugees from Germany.

The first and truly hard years of exile, the time during which the groundwork was laid for a new life in the host country, in the new home, were largely mastered by the émigré women. After America entered the war, things changed somewhat. More jobs were available, for men as well as for women, and many refugee men worked for the army.

By no means, however, did this mean an end to the refugee families' worries and struggle for survival. Kindergarten and day-care, for example, became scarce as American women also entered the job market. The already hectic daily routine of the refugee women, struggling under the burden of two full-time jobs, was further complicated by the problem of figuring out what to do with their young children while they were at work. Refugee organizations, self-help groups, and institutions were often able to provide some assistance to these beleaguered women.

It has been said that the German-speaking academic émigrés in the United States ultimately attained roughly the same social status they

5 *Das Tagebuch der Hertha Nathorff. Berlin–New York. Aufzeichnungen 1933–1945*, ed. Wolfgang Benz (Frankfurt am Main, 1988), esp. 165–8.

had enjoyed in their countries of origin. One must add: Thanks to the help of the women. In their lives we can observe a development which proved fundamentally different from their former lives in Germany, namely a trend toward nonacademic occupations: from attorney to social worker, from teacher or doctor to nurse, from university-educated housewife to bakery worker, secretary, or masseuse. In many cases these women continued to work even after their families had settled in and their husbands had returned to their academic professions; more than a few of them worked later on as volunteers – in Jewish institutions, for example.

7

The Special Case of
Austrian Refugee Historians

FRITZ FELLNER

If we are to discuss the special case of Austrian refugee historians, we must consider those factors which placed these Austrians in an extraordinary position. Certainly the question of Austrian national identity, independence, and sovereignty forbids the tacit incorporation of the German-speaking Austrian historians into the general topic of this volume. Yet I think there are even more important reasons for treating the Austrians as a special case, namely (1) the time and type of exodus for Austrian scholars, which differed from that of German scholars; (2) the peculiar fashion in which historical research on the so-called Austrian exile has treated this subject.

Regarding the first reason, the exodus of scholars from the Austrian Republic, which had come into being in 1918 and was later annexed by Germany in 1938, did not occur as a result of the seizure of power by the National Socialists in Austria but instead was brought about far earlier, immediately after the collapse of the Habsburg monarchy. This exodus can – admittedly in a simplified fashion – be categorized into four phases.

First, the depressed economic situation and the intellectual climate in Austria and in Austrian universities in the 1920s caused some of the leading Austrian academics to emigrate either to the United States or to the Weimar republic before 1930. Political or racial persecution or acute personal distress were not responsible for this exodus; rather, the attractiveness of better career opportunities, both financial and intellectual, become motivating factors. Josef Redlich, Josef Schumpeter, and Hans Kelsen are examples of this first phase.

Second, the creation of the *Ständestaat* (corporate state) and the February civil war in 1934 forced a significant number of Marxist intellectuals to leave the country, or, alternatively, they themselves to go. These individuals were mainly young Marxist intellectuals, not yet professionally established – students or young Ph.D.s who in the years to come would take up academic careers in the Anglo-Saxon countries and, to a lesser degree, in France. In this context, it must be noted that National Socialist academics with established positions, such as Hans Uebersberger, or young academics who saw no chance of pursuing a career in the ideological climate of the *Ständestaat* also left Austria between 1934 and 1938 in order to continue their already partly established careers in the Third Reich. Immigration of Catholic scholars who fled the Third Reich to Austria partially compensated for this loss of the academic talent of Marxists and German nationalists who left Austria, but only for a brief period.

Third, in 1938 a twofold exodus of scholars from Austria occurred. On the one hand, a small number of prominent Catholic academics, who had held positions in the Austrian corporate state, left, making brief intermediate stops in France and later emigrating to the United States. On the other hand, some Jewish academics, who either still held positions in the universities (particularly in cultural institutions) or had recently been barred from other professional activities, were forced to leave. This group of intellectuals made up the major contingent from Austria of those scholars whom we refer to as "refugees" in this volume.

Fourth, it should not be forgotten that although we are concentrating upon the persecution of scholars between 1934 and 1945, a significant number of young intellectuals left Austria for the Federal Republic of Germany and the United States between 1945 and 1960, for reasons similar to those of their colleagues in the 1920s, namely, the lack of material and personal rewards and the dominance of a conservative intellectual climate in Austria. The impact of this post-1945 exodus has not yet been fully discussed or realized, because our interest in Austria's past has focused on pre-1945 history.

Now let us examine the present conditions and standards of historical research dealing with Austrian intellectuals in exile. In Austria, research on the exiles is not included as part of the history of scholarship but instead is treated as a secondary aspect of political history. More precisely, it is included as a part of the history of Austrian resistance and of Austrians' engagement with and struggle for the country's liberation. Whenever Austrian historians take up the topic of academic exile, they do not address the question of the difficulty of integrating exiled or emigrated scholars into another country or assess the chances of new career possibilities, nor do they ask about the influence or effect that the emigrants may have had on a field of research or in new areas of specialization. Instead, only the political consequences for Austria are considered of central importance to research in exile history. Two works are typical of this approach: *Politik im Wartesaal* (Politics in the waiting room), an excellent book by Helene Maimann, discusses Austrians in exile in Britain; Franz Goldner has analyzed political emigration from Austria between 1938 and 1945 into those countries which accepted these refugees from the Third Reich.

Another symptom of this tendency is the fact that in 1977, at the international symposium for research on Austrians exiled between 1934 and 1945, held in Vienna, only two short lectures discussed Austrian scholars and artists in exile, and these were presented on the last day of the conference. In the printed proceedings of the conference, these talks, which dealt only with scientists and musicians, were put in the appendix.

Between 1985 and 1987, the Viennese Institute for Science and Art sponsored a series of lectures which, for the first time, presented a comprehensive collection of documented research and research results on the exiles. These lectures were supplemented by interviews and laid a solid foundation for research on the exodus of scholars between 1930 and 1940. However, the title of the book which emerged from these lectures and presented the researchers' conclusions to the public demonstrated that the *Fragestellung*, the starting point of research, was once again an introverted focus upon Austria. This book is entitled *Vertriebene Vernunft* (Scholarship driven out). It emphasized the fact that Austria had lost many of her most talented scholars and artists through their exile. Questions such as what the countries of destination had gained from these émigré scholars, what effect these Austrian scholars had on further developments in their areas of specialization, or what influence they gained in the countries which accepted them, were not even asked. In a special section devoted to the historians, Günter Fellner gave a survey which emphasized the Marxist point of view. Ordinarily, the historians are never addressed in this context. Up to now, the work of Gerald Stourzh on exiled historians and political scientists, written in 1965, has been unsurpassed. It reflects his personal experiences in American history and political science departments in the 1950s. Presently, Joseph Eppel is preparing a volume on Austrian emigration to the United States for the *Dokumentationsarchiv des Österreichischen Widerstands*. Whether Eppel will analyze the impact of Austrian scholars in America remains to be seen.

The fact that little attention has been given in exile research to specialists in the humanities – and in particular, the almost total neglect of the historians – has its roots for the most part in the character of Austrian historiography before 1938. With few exceptions, Austrian historiography had a German-national orientation. Even the few Jewish historians, like Heinrich Friedjung or Ludo Moritz Hartmann, perceived themselves as part of German historiography, particularly when they researched Austrian history. In addition, Austrian historiography was not Marxist oriented and was more conservative than other sciences in its *Weltanschauung* and methods.

Moreover, the Austrian historical profession, organized in some respects as a *Zunft* (guild), employed very few Jews. This was the result of complicated interactions that cannot be discussed fully within the framework of this essay but that cannot simply be explained by the catchword "anti-Semitism," although that was no doubt a contributing factor.

The distinctive qualities of the Austrian refugee historians who came to the United States can also be explained from the character of Austrian historiography before 1938. The number of historians of Austrian origin who lived in the United States after 1938 was relatively high. However, a quantitative comparison with the number of historians who came from other German-speaking countries is difficult, because the statistical data, as well as their own understanding of their national identity, are rather imprecise. This task is made even more difficult by the rather far-reaching claim of Austria to be the homeland of these scholars.

Those Austrians – and here I use the term in its narrowest sense, namely, for those originating from the territory of the Austrian Republic – who left the country between 1938 and 1970 can be clearly categorized into three groups:

a. Historians who had practiced their profession in their home country before their emigration or exile. This would include those working either at a university, high school, or archive. This group is relatively small in number; in fact only three individuals come to mind: Friedrich Engel-Janosi, who received a *venia legendi* for history from the University of Vienna in 1929 and was a guest professor at the University of Rome in 1937–38; Eric Kollmann (who spelled his name Kollman after he came to the United States), history professor at a Vienna high school, who in the 1930s taught at the Ottakring Volkshochschule, and Gerhart Ladner, a graduate of the Institute of

Austrian Historical Research, who began his career as a researcher in medieval history. A few other names from fields related to history, like history of art and political science, could be added to this list, but I do not want to run the risk of being blamed for omitting one name or the other in the short amount of space available.

b. The second group is somewhat larger. It includes historians who practiced other professions before emigrating to the United States but whose specialty was such that finding a position in their professional field in the United States was extremely difficult, because of the very different structure of their fields. New opportunities arose for some of these individuals – opportunities which were more difficult to come by than these few sentences imply. For many exiles, an inclination toward historical research suddenly became a primary career possibility. Robert Kann must be the first person mentioned whose "second" career became of academic importance on both sides of the Atlantic; also in this category are Eduard März, who returned to Austria, and George Kent, Alfred Diamant, and Kurt Steiner, all of whom remained in the United States. Kurt Steiner specialized in political science, a field from which a number of additional individuals could be named.

c. The third group is the largest one. This includes all those who left Austria as children, before completing their education, and who went on to finish their studies in the United States and made a career in history after 1948. I do not want to mention any names in this group, for I feel that to name anyone would be unfair to those left unnamed. This group includes those who were born between 1919 and 1924, now scattered throughout the United States. They represent a very important element of the historical profession in the United States today.

d. Finally, a fourth group might be added: the children of Austrians who had been driven out of Austria, children born after 1935, who grew up as Americans and entered academic careers dealing with research or teaching in non-Austrian, or even non-European, history.

The members of the first two groups – those historians who emigrated from Austria and those Austrian emigrants who became historians after settling in the United States – attempted to return to Austria in 1945. The difficulties that arose, however, and prevented them from returning are too numerous and complex to discuss. Only two historians were able to reestablish themselves in Austria, and then only many years later: Engel-Janosi and Eduard März. Two others – Robert Kann and Gerhart Ladner – remained wanderers between the two continents. The third group I have mentioned became Austrian-Americans. To research the impact they have had on historical scholarship in the United States would be a particularly interesting topic.

In 1965, Gerald Stourzh made a first attempt to survey the scholarly achievements of German-speaking emigrants in the field of the social sciences in a bibliography published in volumes 10 and 11 of the *Jahrbuch für Amerikastudien*. From the point of view of 1988 and against the background of the Austrian debate on Austrian national identity, one is surprised to see that Stourzh included Austrians in the list of German scholars. One of the most urgent tasks facing historians is to continue Stourzh's bibliography up to the late 1980s. The updating of the bibliography could demonstrate what a large number of scholarly works in the field of history was published by historians of Austrian descent. A survey of the teaching positions held by these men and women would give credit to the impact of the group of historians of Austrian descent who finished their education and made their scholarly careers exclusively in the United States.

Giving due consideration to the fact that such a bibliography and list of teachers so far is incomplete, it can nevertheless be stated that the members of the groups just mentioned regarded it as their preeminent task to devote their scholarly activities to research in the history of their home country (the land of their birth) and to improve knowledge and understanding of the history of Austria in the United States. The history of Central Europe and of the Habsburg monarchy was established as a special branch of historical scholarship in the United States by Arthur J. May, S. Harrison Thompson, and R. John Rath in the 1930s. With the support of May, Thompson, and Rath, historians who emigrated to the United States from Austria founded in American universities schools of historians who succeeded in establishing Austrian history as a part of the curriculum in many colleges. The research work accomplished by the Austrian emigrant historians, in quantity as well as in quality, had the result, that since 1950 the amount of research in the United States and the number of American publications dealing with the history of the Habsburg empire and the two Austrian republics has been equal to the work done in Austria. Austrian emigrants have received full recognition as scholars in the fields of literature, political science, sociology, history, musicology, history of art, and economics. Austrian emigrant scholars are – to use a term from the Spanish civil war – a fifth column, working within their respective fields in the interest of securing Austrian history its proper place.

SELECTED BIBLIOGRAPHY

Günther Fellner. "Die Emigration österreichischer Historiker. Ein ungeschriebenes Kapitel in der Zeitgeschichte ihres Faches." In Friedrich Stadler, ed., *Vertriebene Vernunft. Emigration und Exil österreichischer Wissenschaft. Internationales Symposium 19. bis 23. Oktober 1987 in Wien.* 2 vols. Vienna, 1988. 2:171–91. (This essay was published after this manuscript was completed.)

Franz Goldner. *Die österreichische Emigration 1938–1945.* Vienna, 1972.

Helene Maimann. *Politik im Wartesaal. Österreichische Exilpolitik in Grossbritannien 1938–1945.* Vienna, 1975.

Wilhelm Schlag. "A Survey of Austrian Emigration to the United States." In Otto Hietsch, ed., *Österreich und die angel-sächsische Welt: Kulturbegegnungen und Vergleich.* Vienna, 1961. 139–96.

Friedrich Stadler, ed. *Vertriebene Vernunft. Emigration und Exil österreichischer Wissenschaft. Internationales Symposium 19. bis 23. Oktober 1987 in Wien.* 2 vols. Vienna, 1988.

Gerald Stourzh. "Die deutschsprachige Emigration in den Vereinigten Staaten: Geschichtswissenschaft und politische Wissenschaft." *Jahrbuch für Amerikastudien* 10 (1965):59–77.

Gerald Stourzh. "Bibliographie der deutschsprachigen Emigration in den Vereinigten Staaten: Geschichte und politische Wissenschaft." Pt. 1, *Jahrbuch für Amerikastudien* 10 (1965):232–66; pt. 2, *Jahrbuch für Amerikastudien* 11 (1966):260–317.

"Zur 30. Wiederkehr der Befreiung Österreichs: Internationales Symposium zur Erforschung des österreichischen Exils von 1934 bis 1945 vom 3. bis 6. Juni in Wien." Unpublished manuscript.

8

Schicksalsgeschichte: Refugee Historians in the United States

CATHERINE EPSTEIN

To date, the research agenda of emigration studies has been dominated by the study of professionally successful academic refugees and their intellectual contributions to their host countries. Following this trend, research on German-speaking émigré historians in the United States after 1933 has centered on well-known historians who published extensively and held prestigious academic positions. About fifteen refugee historians have become household names to members of the American and German historical professions. Hajo Holborn, Felix Gilbert, and Hans Rosenberg, to name but a few of the most notable refugee historians, have been celebrated with *Festschriften*, academic honors, media interviews, and serious analyses of their historical works.

Researchers' focus upon the famous refugees has in many cases allowed the literature on emigration to become a literature of celebration. Anthony Heilbut's *Exiled in Paradise* is exclusively concerned with the brilliant and colorful émigrés whose names are virtually synonymous with the 1933 wave of emigration; not surprisingly, pictures of Albert Einstein, Hannah Arendt, and Bertolt Brecht grace the cover of his book.[1] Lewis Coser, in his book *Refugee Scholars in America*, has short biographies of some fifty outstanding refugee scholars.[2] Included are four of the best-known refugee historians: Hajo Holborn, Felix Gilbert, Hans Rosenberg, and Paul Oskar Kristeller. Coser also writes on two economic historians: Alexander Gerschenkron and Fritz Redlich. As a first, important step toward widening the circle of those émigrés studied, Herbert Strauss and his colleagues recorded some eighty-seven hundred refugees in their *International Dictionary of Central European Emigrés*; however, this dic-

Unless otherwise indicated, all translations are by the author.
1 Anthony Heilbut, *Exiled in Paradise* (Boston, 1983).
2 Lewis Coser, *Refugee Scholars in America* (New Haven, 1984).

tionary is limited to those refugees who attained a certain degree of professional success.[3]

Similarly, the few studies devoted specifically to refugee historians also focus upon the most notable of these émigrés. Georg G. Iggers' informative essay describes the careers and influence of the best-known German-speaking historians who emigrated from Germany.[4] Peter Walther discusses the approximately twenty established historians of modern history who emigrated to the United States.[5] Finally, Heinz Wolf's *Deutsch-jüdische Emigrationshistoriker in den USA und der Nationalsozialismus* examines the luminaries of the "second generation" – those refugee historians who received their formal training in the United States.[6]

The emphasis on studying individuals who were professionally successful has resulted in *Beitragsgeschichte*, that is, the history of academic contribution. Scholars have been preoccupied with the question of what German scholarship lost and what host countries gained through the emigration of so many prominent academics after 1933. Students of the emigration have concentrated particularly upon *Wissenschaftstransfer*, or the transfer of ideas and methodologies via the academic migration.

Of course, *Beitragsgeschichte* is extremely important and should be a major focus of emigration studies. However, the exclusive interest in successful émigrés has glossed over the variety of *Schicksale*, the variety of experiences found in the emigration. One gains a more balanced and accurate picture of refugee historians' experiences when one examines the biographies of *all* the historians or historians-to-be who emigrated to the United States. I call this approach to emigration studies *Schicksalsgeschichte*: the examination of a large number of individual life trajectories.

I have identified some ninety "first-generation" individuals who eventually taught history or published extensively on historical topics in the United States. First-generation historians are those who came to the United States as adults after studying and working in

---

3 *International Biographical Dictionary of Central European Emigrés, 1933–1945*, ed. Herbert A. Strauss and Werner Röder (Munich, 1983).
4 Georg G. Iggers, "Die deutschen Historiker in der Emigration," in Bernd Faulenbach, ed., *Geschichtswissenschaft in Deutschland* (Munich, 1974).
5 Peter Th. Walther, "Emigrierte deutsche Historiker in den USA," *Berichte zur Wissenschaftsgeschichte* 7 (1984):41–52.
6 Heinz Wolf, *Deutsch-jüdische Emigrationshistoriker in den USA und der Nationalsozialismus* (Bern, 1988).

the German-speaking parts of Central Europe. These individuals received a Ph.D., or *Promotion*, in some field at a German-speaking university prior to emigration. While a *Promotion* in history by no means ensured an academic career in Central Europe, it was a first step toward professionalization, and as such opened some and closed other career paths. The same is true of those individuals who held advanced degrees in fields other than history; for them, becoming professional historians in the United States entailed a caesura in their professional lives . This group of first-generation historians includes historians of modern and medieval history; historians of the Jewish religion and other religions; historians of economics and law; historians of medicine and other sciences; and historians of Oriental and ancient peoples.

Literature on the emigration has described the circumstances facing refugee historians upon their arrival in the United States as, at best, difficult. Refugee scholars came to the United States in the middle of the Depression, when teaching jobs were scarce. They tended to know little English and next to nothing about American history, a subject none had formally studied. In addition, anti-Semitism was perceived as widespread in American academia.[7] However, both studies on the emigration and refugees' autobiographies have seemingly forgotten the harsh realities of the first decades which refugee historians spent in the United States: These years were often fraught with financial difficulties, un- or under-employment, and worries about friends and relatives abroad. Many refugee historians found their new homes in provincial academic communities, far from centers of émigré concentration. They fought their college administrations not only to earn a pittance but also for the privilege of teaching history rather than language. Other historians struggled for years to live and find work in New York City, often working in fields of history largely ignored by American historians. In addition, many refugees were forced to switch professions, only becoming historians after emigration. These are typical *Schicksale* of first-generation refugee historians. As one refugee historian, Guido Kisch, has written in his memoirs, "Not all émigré *Schicksale* [fates] could become apotheoses of success."[8]

Because prominent refugee historians emigrated as historians and

7 Hans Rosenberg, "Rückblick auf ein Historikerleben zwischen zwei Kulturen," in *Machteliten und Wirtschaftskonjunkturen* (Göttingen, 1978), 15–16.
8 Guido Kisch, *Der Lebensweg eines Rechtshistorikers* (Sigmaringen, 1975), 16.

remained in the profession in the United States, scholarly literature on the emigration has assumed that this was the dominant career pattern for all or most of these refugees. However, one might better label this career pattern the "classical case," since only about half of the refugee historians experienced it. *Schicksalsgeschichte* highlights a theme central to this essay: that is, that professional historians from Central Europe at the very least had to alter the style and content of their teaching and redirect their research; similarly, many other refugees who were established professionals in other fields first became historians through the circumstances of their emigration. In the following pages, I will outline first the *Schicksale* of those historians who had been historians in Central Europe; thereafter, I will turn to those historians who were at the beginnings of their careers as historians in Central Europe; and finally, I will address the group of émigrés who were professionals in other fields in Germany or Austria but who became historians here.

Thirty-four historians who eventually came to the United States were established to one degree or another as historians in the German or Austrian historical profession or were on the fringes of these historical professions in Central Europe. Twenty-five historians who held university positions in history emigrated to the United States; of these twenty-five, ten were full (*Ordinarius*) professors, five were associate (*ausserordentliche*) professors, and ten were lecturers (*Privatdozenten*). A further nine individuals were librarians, archivists, or researchers involved in historical work.[9] Of these, three did not come to the United States until after World War II; Gerhart Ladner spent the war years in Canada, Gerhard Masur in Colombia, and Raphael Straus in Palestine.

9 The ten professors include nine full (*Ordinarius*) professors in the regular German university system: Eberhard Friedrich Bruck, Ernst H. Kantorowicz, Guido Kisch, Richard Laqueur, Ernst Levy, Eugen Rosenstock-Huessy, Hans Rothfels, Richard Salomon, and Eugen Täubler. As indicated in the text, Ismar Elbogen was at the Lehranstalt (later Hochschule) für die Wissenschaft des Judentums. The associate (*ausserordentliche*) professors were Friedrich Engel-Janosi, Carl Landauer, Otto Neugebauer, Arthur Rosenberg, and Franz Schehl. The lecturers (*Privatdozenten*) were Hans Baron, Elias Bickerman, Ludwig Edelstein, Dietrich Gerhard, Hajo Holborn, Gerhart Ladner, Otto Mänchen-Helfen, Gerhard Masur, Hans Rosenberg, and Martin Weinbaum.
   The nine historians who were not in the university system include Aron Freimann, director of the Judaica Department at the Frankfurt Municipal and University Library; Raphael Straus, researcher on the history of Jews in Bavaria and editor of the journal *Zeitschrift für die Geschichte der Juden in Deutschland*; Theodor E. Mommsen, staff member of the *Monumenta Germaniae historica*; Selma Stern-Täubler, staff member of the Akademie für die Wissenschaft des Judentums; Helene Wieruszowski, librarian at the University of Bonn; Alfred Vagts, affiliated with the Institut für Auswärtige Politik in Hamburg; Ernst Posner and Sergius

Very few of these relatively established émigré historians belonged to the *Historikerzunft*. Since the German historical profession during the Weimar period was so nationalistic and anti-Semitic, the great majority of full professors were sympathetic to Hitler and thus both wanted and were able to retain their positions after 1933. Only three full professors of modern and medieval history came to the United States: Ernst Kantorowicz, Hans Rothfels, and Richard Salomon. The other full professors who emigrated held chairs in legal or ancient history. Finally, Ismar Elbogen, a professor at the Lehranstalt (later Hochschule) für die Wissenschaft des Judentums in Berlin, taught Jewish history.

Of the ten full professors, nine found teaching or research jobs in history in the United States; they had well-established reputations and were often world-renowned in their fields. Many of these nine did not have great difficulty finding positions, but in most cases their academic status suffered a dramatic decline in their new country. While some of these professors may have had difficulty in the United States because Americans were not interested in their specialties, others may have been disadvantaged by their age; having held full professorships, many of these men were well into or beyond middle age. For example, Eberhard Friedrich Bruck, a professor of legal history in Bonn, emigrated at the age of sixty-two; in the United States he became a mere research associate at the Harvard University Law School. Guido Kisch, a professor of legal history in Halle who was forty-two at the time of his emigration, had a terribly demoralizing time finding appropriate work in the United States; in his memoirs, Kisch describes at considerable length the difficulty of finding employment. Finally, Richard Laqueur, a professor of ancient history from Halle, spent twelve unhappy years in the United States; some of this time he worked as a packager in a large bookstore. Why Laqueur failed to find any kind of academic position remains something of a mystery.

Most of the associate professors, lecturers, and other individuals involved in the historical profession in Germany also found jobs in history soon after their emigration. While still in Vienna, Friedrich Engel-Janosi was invited to teach at the Johns Hopkins University. Similarly, Arthur Rosenberg became a professor of history at Brook-

Yakobson, archivists at the Preussisches Geheimes Staatsarchiv; and Veit Valentin, archivist at the Reichsarchiv.

lyn College in New York City after several years of teaching in Liverpool, England. Hajo Holborn and Dietrich Gerhard, both students of Friedrich Meinecke's, received calls to Yale University in 1934 and to Washington University in St. Louis in 1935, respectively. Theodor E. Mommsen, a staff member of the *Monumenta Germaniae historica* in Berlin, started his American university career at Johns Hopkins University in 1936. Ernst Posner, an archivist in the Prussian State Archives in Berlin, was instrumental in the development of the U.S National Archives; at the same time, he was a professor of history at American University in Washington, D.C., from 1939 on. However, Franz Schehl, an ancient historian from Graz, never found a university position; for a time he taught at the Priory School in Portsmouth, Rhode Island.[10] Thereafter, he seems to have disappeared from the academic world.

While more-or-less established historians found jobs in the United States with relative ease, they nonetheless often had to redirect their research or their teaching. This point was emphasized in several interviews which Radio Bremen conducted in 1962. Eugen Rosenstock-Huessy, a professor of legal history in Breslau, became known for his work on social philosophy in the United States. In his interview with Radio Bremen, he noted, "My emigration also meant that I took up a new field; Americans could not find any use for my original field."[11] In this same interview series, Carl Landauer was described in the following manner: "In Berlin he [Landauer] was an economic theoretician, but once in the United States he realized that economic theory was more advanced in America than in Germany. Because he couldn't do anything with his old speciality, he had to switch fields." Landauer added, "I started to work in an area somewhere between economics and sociology, in particular the history of socialism, which at that time was relatively unknown here."[12] Richard Salomon, an *Ordinarius* for Eastern European history and culture at the University of Hamburg, had written extensively in his field prior to his emigration. Once in the United States, where he taught at Kenyon College in Gambier, Ohio, for over twenty-five years, he turned to medieval and church history and published almost nothing on Eastern Europe in the remaining thirty-odd years of his life. In obituaries published in the United States, the earlier

10 Volker Losemann, *Nationalsozialismus und Antike* (Hamburg, 1977), p. 202, n. 111.
11 *Auszug des Geistes*, ed. Radio Bremen (Bremen, 1962), 106.
12 Ibid., 170.

Salomon was virtually forgotten, and he was remembered only for his work here.[13] Thus, while many refugees continued their occupation with relatively little career displacement, their scholarly production was nonetheless significantly affected by their emigration. We must reassess the balance sheet of German losses and American gains to account for the common phenomenon of refugee academics pursuing new, different scholarly activity in the United States.

The historians just described – the "classic" cases – make up less than half of the first-generation refugee historians who emigrated to the United States. The remaining refugees who became historians had either just received their doctorates or were well-established professionals in other fields. Younger academic refugees in the United States had in some ways more difficulty entering the historical profession than their older counterparts. They could not rely on some of the support mechanisms their older colleagues enjoyed, such as established contacts in the United States and/or the help of refugee aid committees. These committees, and professors and administrators of universities and colleges as well, feared that young European-trained academics would take jobs away from young Americans, spawning resentment of refugee scholars in general.

Many younger historians may have expected to get jobs in history relatively quickly. Perhaps counting on the reputation of German universities, they were no doubt disappointed when jobs proved either temporary or, as was often the case, never materialized at all. Of the twenty individuals who had received doctorates in history but who had little or no career experience, only five taught history continuously through 1945.[14] All the other young historians experienced career breaks of one sort or another. I have found that a number of refugee historians taught for a year or two in the late 1930s but then turned to other work, often war related.

Several refugee historians were drafted into the army: George W. F. Hallgarten, Golo Mann, and Peter Olden. Olden was drafted even though the president of the College of St. Teresa in Winona, Minnesota, where Olden taught, begged Olden's commanding officer for his discharge. Explaining that "it would be extremely difficult for us to fill his place here at the College," Sister Mary Aloysius

---

13 Fritz T. Epstein, "Hamburg und Osteuropa zum Gedächtnis von Professor Richard Salomon," *Jahrbücher für Geschichte Osteuropas* 15 (1967): 59–60.
14 These historians were Fritz Caspari, Frederick Henry Cramer, Paul Oskar Kristeller, Stephan Kuttner, and Bernard Dov Weinryb.

Molloy urged Captain Mask "to consider our request" for Olden's immediate discharge.[15] The letter proved to be of no avail, and Olden remained with the US Army and then the American government in Germany until the early 1950s. Olden was, however, an exception. Most younger historians were not considered indispensable to the teaching of history in the United States; on the contrary, they had considerable difficulty finding employment at all.

World War II created many new opportunities for academic refugees from Central Europe. Government agencies such as the Office of Strategic Studies (OSS) employed refugees at a time when the academic market was shrinking, since so many young, college-aged Americans were in the armed services or otherwise engaged in the war effort. At the same time, war-related work was a welcome and rewarding duty to the refugees; their unique language skills and firsthand knowledge of Germany allowed them to be useful to their new country's war effort. They could finally actively participate in the war against Nazi Germany. In addition, the work offered émigrés the opportunity to live in metropolitan areas such as Washington and New York. Seven first-generation refugee historians, including Felix Gilbert and Hajo Holborn, worked for the OSS at one time or another.[16] Others, such as Adolf Leschnitzer and Henry Pachter, worked for the Office of War Information in New York City. If refugee historians begrudged their time away from historical work at all, they no doubt realized that their experiences in the armed services and in government bureaucracy heightened their understanding of history. As Barry Katz suggests in Chapter 9 of this volume, those historians employed by the OSS came away with a better sense of *Realpolitik*, a sense later incorporated into their historical studies.

There is a large group of individuals who changed careers and became historians after their emigration. This phenomenon has received virtually no attention in the literature on the emigration, yet it is one of the more salient patterns of refugee biographies, typical not only of eventual historians but also of many other professionals. Generally those individuals who became historians had been lawyers, journalists, businessmen, secondary-school teachers, or rabbis. Like

15 Letter from Sister Mary Aloysius Molloy to Captain Mask, dated August 22, 1941. A copy of the letter was sent to me by the College of St. Teresa on January 29, 1988.
16 The other historians employed by OSS were Paul Alexander, Fritz Epstein, Eric Fischer, Henry Pachter, and Veit Valentin.

those young historians who had just received their doctorates, many of these refugees did not become professional historians until after the war. During the war they were often in graduate school or, like those young historians who had just received their doctorates, did government or free-lance work.

Refugee lawyers faced an almost impossible situation following their emigration. The system of law which they knew was completely different from the American system, and lawyers who wished to practice in the United States needed to be completely retrained. Not surprisingly, many lawyers could afford neither the time nor the expense of being retrained in the legal profession. Eight individuals with doctorates in law became history professors in the United States.[17] For some of these lawyers, factors other than the difficulty of entering the American legal profession may have influenced their career change. Some may have lost faith in the power of law after witnessing the travesty of a *Rechtsstaat* in their native countries. Robert A. Kann, a lawyer from Vienna who became a well-known historian of Austria in the United States, wrote, "One who sees a legal system, built up through hundreds of years of cultural life, destroyed with one blow, does not find it easy to turn to the laborious study of another legal system."[18] Many of the lawyers-turned-historians went to graduate school in the United States. For some, at least, the study of history was a welcome change. As Paul Alexander, a Byzantinist, wrote to his future wife, Eleanor in 1937, "So many refugees I know have had to retrain and do work that is hard and unsatisfactory, while I have changed to a profession that fulfills me and is, for me, far more satisfying than the study of law."[19]

One might have thought that lawyers interested in history would turn to legal history as their new field of expertise. In fact, only one lawyer who had practiced in Central Europe became a historian of law in the United States. Despite his precarious financial situation, Adolf Berger managed to complete his *Encyclopedic Dictionary of Roman Law* in 1953; during his twenty years in the United States he also taught part-time at the École Libre and at City College in New

---

17 Lawyers-turned-historians include Paul Alexander, Adolf Berger, John Hans Buchsbaum, Andreas Dorpalen, Rudolf Glanz, Fred Hahn, Robert A. Kann, and Hans Julius Wolff.

18 Robert A. Kann in an unpublished curriculum vitae for the Austrian Akademie der Wissenschaften, 1968. Mrs. Marie Kann of Princeton, N.J., sent a copy to me (quotation on p. 5).

19 Paul Alexander in a letter to his future wife, Eleanor Eyck. Eleanor E. Alexander, *Stories of My Life* (privately published, n.d.), 67.

York. Berger's situation, and the fact that he was the only one to become a historian of law in the United States, illustrates the difficulty refugee historians of law faced. These historians were specialists in Roman law, the system of law on which the German legal system is based; however, because the American legal system stems from other traditions, Americans were little interested in this legal specialty. Even well-established legal historians, a number of whom had been full professors in Germany, encountered serious difficulty in finding employment. Eberhard Friedrich Bruck took on a low-paying research position at the Harvard University Law School, and Ernst Levy taught modern European history courses, in addition to his seminars in legal history, at the University of Washington in Seattle. A young historian of law, Hans Julius Wolff, had a particularly difficult period in emigration. Wolff taught Roman and civil law at the University of Panama between 1935–1939 and then emigrated to the United States in 1939, hoping to find a position here. During the war years Wolff studied for a time and then did research during the day while working nights in a bakery to support himself. Although he finally managed to teach law and legal history between 1945 and 1952 at several midwestern universities, he accepted an invitation to return to West Germany in 1952 as a full professor of Roman and civil law at the University of Mainz; later he moved to the University of Freiburg.

Journalists also found it difficult to continue their profession in emigration; eight journalists became historians here.[20] Not only was language a barrier to their professional success, but the contacts they had made in Europe were largely irrelevant here. Felix Hirsch, political editor of the *Berliner Tageblatt*, and Frederick Heymann, an economics editor for the *Frankfurter Zeitung*, both became historians in the United States. For these two journalists, becoming historians was the fulfillment of a dream. As Hirsch himself wrote, "When I began my studies, . . . it was my dream to become a *historian*, and I never gave it up, even though the disastrous impact of the German inflation on my family's fortune forced me to postpone my plans till I came to the USA."[21] In a tribute to Heymann after his death, it was said that "in 1949 he began to realize an old dream. He commenced

20 The eight journalists included Ernst Breisacher, Frederick Ernest Gaupp, Frederick Heymann, Felix Hirsch, Hans Kohn, Carl Misch, Henry Pachter, and Werner Richter.
21 Hirsch wrote a personal statement now found in his file at the Research Foundation for Jewish Immigration, New York City. (Quotation on pp. 2–3.)

research on the history of the Hussite movement and the Bohemian Reformation."[22]

Other journalists, though, were more ambivalent about their academic careers. Carl Misch, a political editor of the *Vossische Zeitung* before his emigration, taught history for years at Centre College in Kentucky. In 1960, in a short autobiographical piece in *Aufbau*, he wrote, "Since 1947 I have been a Professor at a prestigious college in Kentucky where I teach European history. I enjoy my academic career, but still feel journalistic blood flowing in my veins."[23] In 1947, Misch considered becoming editor of a German newspaper in the French zone. However, the conditions under which he would have returned were not generous: His pay would have been in German marks; only he, and not his wife, would have received a double ration card; he would probably have had to give up his American citizenship; and he would not have been given political control of the newspaper. In addition, the current editor, Erich Dombrowski, reminded Misch that he could expect only a poorly heated single room, given the prevailing housing situation in Mainz. Dombrowski hastened to assure Misch that he would help in every way he could, so that Misch would not lead a "troglodyte existence."[24] Believing that Dombrowski did not really wish to have him as editor of the newspaper, Misch declined the offer. Refugees considering reemigration frequently faced similar situations and, like Misch, decided to remain in their new countries.

A number of businessmen became professional historians after their emigration to the United States. Among others, Friedrich Engel-Janosi, Hanns Reissner, and Fritz Redlich had been employed in business.[25] All of these men, however, had pursued serious historical research in addition to their business careers in Central Europe. While still in Vienna, Engel-Janosi chose less profitable ways of run-

22 Found in an unpublished tribute by John B. Toews, "Tribute to Professor Frederick G. Heymann, 1900–1983," 3. This tribute was sent to me by Frank J. Heymann on July 23, 1988.
23 Carl Misch, "Mein Werdegang," *Aufbau* (April 22, 1960).
24 Misch Collection, Folder 80.5-1-44, Archives, State University of New York at Albany.
25 Other businessmen-turned-historians include Ludwig Edelstein, Paul von Lilienfeld-Toal, and Arnold Wiznitzer. Another example of a historian working in his family business while pursuing historical research is Ludwig Edelstein. While helping to run his father's commercial house in the late 1920s and early 1930s, he researched several papers on ancient dietetics, the history of dissection in antiquity, and the Greek empirical school of medicine. See Harold Cherniss, "Ludwig Edelstein," in *Year Book of the American Philosophical Society* (1965), 132.

ning his family business in order to continue his historical research;[26] Nazi persecution of his business and restrictions imposed on capital export precluded a future business career; after he emigrated he became, with few regrets, a full-time historian. In his memoirs there are no remarks to the effect that he missed managing his business after his emigration. Fritz Redlich was very anxious to become a full-time historian before his emigration and described his years in the family business as lost time.[27] Other businessmen, such as Hanns Reissner and Arnold Wiznitzer, combined careers in banking and business with historical research, after their emigration. Reissner did not begin teaching history full-time until after he retired from the Bank Leumi; he then taught for some years at various institutions in metropolitan New York.

One medical doctor, Erwin Ackerknecht, became a historian of medicine through his emigration. His widow, Enid Ackerknecht, recently wrote, "He came to the United States in 1941. As a young doctor he had written a doctoral dissertation on a topic of medical history. But he became an historian of medicine only in the United States."[28] Like most refugee medical doctors, Ackerknecht would have had to return to medical school in order to receive a state license to practice. He turned to ethnology and the history of medicine, fields in which he was also well versed.

Rabbinical education included the completion of a dissertation, and students often wrote on some aspect of the history of the Jews in Germany. There are, therefore, a number of individuals who held Ph.D.s in history who had become rabbis in Central Europe but became professional historians in the United States.[29] Some of these rabbis had continued their historical research on Jews while still in Germany. Adolf Kober published extensively on the history of Jews in Germany during his tenure as rabbi in Cologne. After his emigration, he was a research fellow at the American Academy of Jewish Research in New York. Ernest I. Jacob combined a rabbinate in the Ozarks with teaching European history at Drury College in Springfield, Missouri. Thus, while historical research was not new to some of these rabbis, turning to research or teaching as a full-time occupa-

---

26 Friedrich Engel-Janosi, . . . *Aber ein stolzer Bettler* (Graz, 1974), 160.
27 Fritz Redlich, *Der Unternehmer* (Göttingen, 1964), 16.
28 Letter dated January 13, 1989, from Mrs. Enid Ackerknecht to the author.
29 Rabbis who became professional historians in the United States include Ernest I. Jacob, Adolf Kober, and Luitpold Wallach.

tion, or as a significant source of income, represented a caesura in their careers.

A number of secondary-school teachers became professors of history in the United States.[30] Several of these individuals – Robert Friedmann, Eric Kollman, and Bruno Strauss – found jobs as history professors far from metropolitan areas where the German-speaking émigré population was concentrated. All three of these men came from Vienna and Berlin; in the United States they respectively spent decades in Kalamazoo, Michigan; Mt. Vernon, Iowa; and Shreveport, Louisiana. Although their occupations did not change so dramatically, they became professionally active in very foreign environments.

The secondary-school teachers who became professors of history in the United States highlight an important aspect of the emigration and potential re-migration of refugee historians. While those émigrés who were secondary-school teachers before their emigration could have returned to Germany or Austria as *Gymnasium* teachers, they could not return as university professors. For émigrés who switched professions and who did not have a *Habilitation* from a German university, the traditional hierarchical structure of the German university system precluded their return as full professors of history after 1945. In a sense, some refugees actually benefited by their emigration, in·that they were able to pursue university careers in the United States. However, these careers were not transferable to West Germany after the war.[31]

For some refugees, the way they became historians was completely haphazard and, in a sense, arbitrary. The widow of Frederick Gaupp, originally a theater critic, writes, "In 1946 a complete stranger gave us guarantees to go to the USA, where a former inmate – [presumably of a prisoner of war camp] – invited us to Southwestern University in Georgetown, Texas. Here my husband taught history until he had to retire in 1970."[32] Erwin Ackerknecht, a medical doctor in

---

30 *Gymnasium* teachers who became professors of history include Eric Fischer, Robert Friedmann, Eric Kollman, Adolf Leschnitzer, Christian Mackauer, and Bruno Strauss.
31 Other factors, of course, also played a role in refugee historians' decisions not to return to Germany after the war. However, the decision about whether to return to a university position in Germany generally obtained only for those refugee historians who had held some kind of university position prior to their emigration. Hans Rothfels was the only historian to return to Germany as a full professor, in Tübingen, after the war. On the whole, refugee historians remained in the United States for personal reasons. See Winfried Schulze, *Deutsche Geschichtswissenschaft nach 1945* (Munich, 1989), 130–44.
32 Letter dated March 27, 1988, from Mrs. Ilse Gaupp to the author.

Germany, worked in the field of medical history immediately following his emigration. Later he became an ethnologist at the American Museum of Natural History in New York City. In 1945 he returned to the history of medicine. In a published interview, Ackerknecht remarked that "it is for entirely external reasons that I went back to medical history – I got a job, and this in a place where I could not continue any ethnological work."[33] Later in the interview Ackerknecht reiterated, "In the University of Wisconsin, the ethnologists regarded me as a colleague; I held seminars for anthropology students, read the journals and went to meetings. But I had to build up a Department of the History of Medicine, and then I shifted into that work on Virchow which also was partly history and partly anthropology."[34] The examples of Gaupp and Ackerknecht illustrate the arbitrary way in which the *Schicksale* of some refugees were decided; many refugee careers were creatures of American capriciousness.

The significance of many historians undergoing career changes lies both in the personal consequences for individual historians and in the more general consequences for their teaching and historical research. While, as we have seen, some historians were satisfied with their new careers, undoubtedly the process of changing careers, often in midlife, was very difficult. Often these men were forced out of a field in which they had been very successful; refugees who became historians had to begin at the bottom rung of a new career ladder. They probably worried about their chances of success and whether they would be able to support their families in their new profession. Career displacements surely created stressful situations for even the most hardy refugee historians. Unfortunately, no refugee historian has left a direct statement about the effects his career change had on his personal and professional life.

On a more general level, the significance of so many emigrants changing careers and becoming historians suggests that the issue of loss and gain, so popular among historians of the academic emigration, must be rephrased. This question is generally posed as a zero-sum game: American scholarship benefited from what German scholarship lost. However, the emigration of historians, at least, suggests that this phenomenon was more complicated than a simple

---

33 "Introduction: An Interview with Erwin H. Ackerknecht," in Erwin H. Ackerknecht, *Medicine and Ethnology*, ed. H. H. Walse and H. M. Koelbig (Bern, 1971), 11–12.
34 Ibid., 13–14.

loss–gain dichotomy; German and Austrian losses differed from
American gains. Where Germany lost a journalist or Austria a lawyer, the United States won historians who had backgrounds in journalism or law. At the conference on refugee historians held at the
German Historical Institute in Washington, D.C., in December
1988, Franz Michael, a specialist in Chinese history, emphasized that
he felt he had brought something very special to the study of Chinese
history in the United States. He credits his interdisciplinary approach
to Chinese history to his background: education at a humanistic
secondary school in Germany, training as a lawyer, and many travels
during the 1920s and 1930s. Similarly, Robert A. Kann once wrote,
"I do not know whether I was a good lawyer, but I can say that
legal methodology, especially that of Kelsen and Verdross, had a
permanent influence on the way I think and on my historical
work."[35]

A number of woman historians emigrated to the United States.
Their *Schicksale* in general differ from those of their male counter-
parts. The experiences of only two of the women historians, Selma
Stern-Täubler and Helene Wieruszowski, have been amply docu-
mented in works on the emigration. Selma Stern-Täubler emigrated
with her husband, Eugen Täubler, to Hebrew Union College in
Cincinnati, where she eventually became the first archivist of the
American Jewish Archives. Helene Wieruszowski held a professorship for years at Brooklyn College, where her colleagues Emmy
Heller and Charlotte Sempell also taught, on a less regular basis.
Erika Spivakovsky never held a teaching job, but she published several books and many articles; she was a fellow of the Radcliffe Institute for Independent Study for some years. The reasons why most
of these women did not become full-time professors of history are
many: In some cases, the need to support their families immediately
after emigration meant that these women could not allow themselves
the luxury of finding jobs in history; in other cases, American administrators resisted hiring women historians; finally, some of these
women may have chosen to be housewives first and historians second. In her obituary of Emmy Heller, Wieruszowski wrote, "As the
wife of a Jewish doctor and the mother of three children, she could
not devote herself entirely to her academic work and thus had to
struggle for a career in her new, foreign surroundings."[36] More

35 Robert A. Kann, curriculum vitae, 3.
36 Helene Wieruszowski, "Emmy Heller," *Deutsches Archiv für Erforschung des Mittelalters* 15
   (1959): 612. The original German sentence reads, "Als Frau eines jüdischen Arztes und

pointedly, Charlotte Sempell recently wrote, "I became adjunct professor in 1947, i.e. in the beginning I was only an instructor at the fabulous pay of $3.25 an hour. [I] stayed in [the] evening because I had two young children, [and] later the opportunities shrank and at [*sic*] that period, the fifties, a married woman in a male-dominated field like history had no chance."[37]

Some women who may have wished to become historians and who held doctoral degrees in history from German universities were unable to do so in the United States. Edith Lenel, the last student of Hans Rothfels to receive a Ph.D. in Königsberg, said in an interview that she did not look for a job in history after her emigration because she thought it hopeless.[38] Having just completed her dissertation, she had neither a publishing record nor teaching experience. In addition, she was not fluent in English. In the mid-1930s, she spent a year as Hans Kohn's research assistant at Smith College. After the war, Lenel became a librarian at Montclair State College, later a German teacher, and eventually chairperson of the German department. In the interview, she said that she would have liked to have done historical research, particularly on Francis Lieber, the German-American political scientist. On several occasions she asked for scholarships from the college to go to California, where Lieber's papers are preserved, but was told that the college could only fund studies of teaching methodologies. Lenel's teaching schedules were also such that she had virtually no time for her own interests. Offered little opportunity to pursue historical research, she did not make her mark as a historian, although she did publish one article based on Lieber's archives in *Historische Zeitschrift* in 1965.[39] It is, of course, impossible to know how many other refugee academics shared Lenel's experiences.

Why did so many refugees choose to become historians in the United States? A number of émigrés who were unable to pursue university careers in Weimar Germany because of their political leanings and/or their Jewish origin used the opportunity provided by emigration to (re)enter a career closed to them in their native countries. The most notable example of this is Veit Valentin. In 1916, in a famous academic scandal, Valentin was forced to renounce his *venia*

Mutter dreier Kinder musste sie ihre Lebensarbeit dem Berufskampf in der Fremde opfern."

37 Letter from Charlotte Sempell to the author, dated April 24, 1989.
38 Interview with Edith Lenel in Newtown, Pa., on August 22, 1988.
39 Edith Lenel, "Barthold Georg Niebuhr und Wilhelm von Humboldt. Briefe im Nachlass von Franz Lieber," *Historische Zeitschrift* 200 (1965):316–31.

legendi – his right to lecture – because of his liberal political opinions. After a successful career as an archivist, Valentin was dismissed from the Reichsarchiv for political reasons in 1933. He emigrated first to England and then to the United States; unlike in Weimar Germany, he was able to teach in both countries, although he never found a permanent teaching position in the United States.

Emigrants who were Jewish, or of Jewish origin, may well have wished to become professional historians in Germany. However, they knew that as Jews they had little chance of receiving the call to a full professorship in modern history. Unwilling to remain on the fringes of the German historical profession, they turned to professions such as law or journalism in which they could attain influence. Alternatively, some liberal Jews may have felt that the interwar German historical profession was too stodgy and uninteresting; rather than commit themselves to careers in this profession, they turned to fields where their liberal aspirations could better find expression.[40]

Perhaps the major reason why so many refugees became historians in the United States is that the American historical profession proved relatively open. The success refugee historians had in finding jobs in the United States rested both on external factors and their own achievements. After the Second World War, a number of factors coincided which allowed for the creation of jobs in history in general, and for the refugees in particular. Interest in European history, particularly German history, intensified as scholars attempted to understand the factors underlying the recent, catastrophic developments in Europe. The onset of the Cold War reinforced this interest, as historians struggled to make clear the sources of international tension.[41] The new world-power role of the United States demanded that Americans have a broader education in European and other histories. The GI Bill provided the wherewithal for war veterans to go to college, and as a result many new academic jobs opened up. All these factors contributed to the expansion of the historical profession; teaching European history became a very plausible way to earn one's living.

Refugees especially benefited from this expansion. Since European and some other specialized histories were not strong points of the

40 Michael Groth, *The Road to New York: The Emigration of Berlin Journalists, 1933–1945* (Munich, 1988), 87–8.
41 David H. Pinkney, "American Historians on the European Past," *American Historical Review* 86 (1981):1–20, 3.

American educational system, small colleges needed to find persons outside of traditional American academic channels to teach European history; refugees were readily available to fill this void. Because the college system was less rigid in the United States, individuals who had not previously been academics were given jobs in European history. Colleges and universities justified hiring émigrés on the grounds that they could convey European history to their students not only through lecturers and books but also through their personal experiences. Finally, the awe with which many Americans viewed the German educational system no doubt helped many well-educated refugees who were not professional historians nonetheless fill college and university jobs in history. Thus the historical profession provided a *Sammelbecken*, or catchall, profession for German-speaking refugees unable to continue in other professions.

Although American colleges and universities clearly needed teachers of European history, the émigrés, of course, contributed to their own success. Their high level of education, or *Bildungsgrad*, was such that they could step into the college classroom and teach history. They became known for their hard work in the classroom and in committees and for their often quite substantial publishing records. Their success also hinged on their unusualness among their American colleagues; their European backgrounds, cosmopolitanism, and even their accents made students pause to consider wider horizons. Many years after his graduation, a student of Carl Misch at Centre College in Kentucky wrote to his former professor, "I think you know, but the matter can stand expression, that the courses which you taught had great and lasting worth in my education. I particularly enjoyed the course in Modern European History which you taught with a flavor of personal experience coupled with the perspective of the scholar and historian."[42] Misch was labeled "a campus legend" in an article in a local newspaper.[43] Eric Kollman, on his retirement after twenty-eight years of service at Cornell College in Iowa, was honored with a piece in the school newspaper entitled "A Story of Dedication" in which he was credited with the "ability to stimulate thought and questioning among his students – to bring them to the point of being able to 'wonder.' "[44] Kollman, who wrote on modern

42 Letter from Donald D. Harkins to Carl Misch, dated May 16, 1961. Found in the Misch Collection, Box 2, Folder 4, at the Leo Baeck Institute, New York City.
43 David Madden, "No Time to Weep," *Courier-Journal Magazine* (May 14, 1961), 40.
44 Vicki Ellis, "Eric Kollman: A Story of Dedication," *Cornellian* (March 29, 1973), 3.

Austria, could almost certainly have found a more prestigious academic position, but he chose to remain at Cornell College, in part as an expression of thanks to the college for having given him employment in his time of need.

While many first-generation refugee historians ended up working in colleges in provincial, small-town communities, not all refugee historians found such a prospect attractive. In an interview published after his death, Henry Pachter explained why he did not try to get a small-town college job in the early 1940s: "We still weren't sure how the war would end. I considered myself a political animal who had to go back to Germany to help, no matter what kind of regime would follow the Nazis. So, let's say I didn't rush into American life. In a small town I would have had to become American, adjusted to the academic rat race."[45] After the war, Pachter remained in the United States and chose to work in the field of market research so that he could live in New York City. Teaching history in the American heartland never appealed to him, because life in small college towns "gets too personal. You have to know everybody. You have to go to every party. If not, you are defined as an enemy. In New York you can lose yourself."[46] In the 1950s Pachter found a teaching position at the New School for Social Research, and he later taught at other universities in the New York metropolitan area. While many refugee historians were willing to teach history at small colleges, Pachter was not alone in wishing to avoid this *Schicksal*. Surely some refugees chose not to become historians precisely because they did not wish to move away from New York City or other metropolitan areas; such émigrés, who had background in history, in turn became professionals in other fields.

The examination of all the different life trajectories of refugee historians, *Schicksalsgeschichte*, captures the multifaceted experiences of a generation in the emigration. The *Schicksale* of refugee historians were much more diverse than is generally thought; an examination of these many *Schicksale* highlights aspects of the emigration of refugee historians often ignored in the copious literature on the academic emigration. For better or worse, the emigration dramatically altered the lives and careers of all refugee historians. The *Schicksale* of refugee historians also shaped their contribution to higher education in the

45 Henry Pachter, "The Radical Émigré in the Metropolis," in Bernard Rosenberg and Ernest Goldstein, eds., *Creators and Disturbers* (New York, 1982), 122.
46 Ibid., 132.

United States. Because so many refugee historians began their work in history relatively late in life and then often had very heavy teaching loads, their main influence lay in their interaction with and their ability to inspire American students; in short, in their teaching. This is true of historians at small colleges and large universities, in provincial and urban settings. The extent to which students of refugee historians have praised their former teachers – in conversations with me, in correspondence found in archives, and in published tributes – suggests that refugee historians often made their contribution in very personal yet unmeasurable ways. While most refugee historians did not achieve more than local fame, their stories – their *Schicksale* – nonetheless belong to the history of German-speaking refugee historians in the United States after 1933.

9

German Historians
in the Office of Strategic Services

BARRY M. KATZ

There is a perverse sense in which modern physics was the great beneficiary of the regime that expelled the physicists from Germany, and we all know the story of how they exacted a terrible revenge. The same may be said, *mutatis mutandis*, of historical scholarship and of the German historical scholars driven out of Europe in the 1930s. The historians' Manhattan Project was the Research and Analysis Branch of the wartime Office of Strategic Services (OSS). Although the impact of the refugee historians on World War II would prove to be somewhat less explosive, the analogy is profoundly suggestive, even slightly inspiring. Like their counterparts in the physical sciences, the humanist scholars of OSS were given an unprecedented opportunity to contribute to the anti-fascist struggle, not in spite of their academic training but precisely on the basis of it.

The groundwork of America's first central intelligence agency was laid by a presidential order of June 1941 in which President Roosevelt created an office charged with the collection, evaluation, and distribution of foreign intelligence. Although OSS became most famous for the overseas exploits of its "operational" branches, Gen. William Donovan, who directed the organization throughout its brief lifetime, always acknowledged that the heart of America's first intelligence agency lay in its essentially academic functions of research and analysis.

These operations were overseen by the distinguished Harvard

Bibliographic note: Information in this essay is drawn from my own study of academic scholars in OSS, *Foreign Intelligence: Research and Analysis in the Office of Strategic Services, 1942–1945* (Cambridge, Mass., 1989), and is based upon materials in Records of the Office of Strategic Services, RG 226, National Archives, Washington, D.C. For a somewhat different perspective, see Alfons Söllner, *Zur Archäologie der Demokratie in Deutschland,* 2 vols. (Frankfurt am Main, 1986): vol. 1, *Analysen von politischen Emigranten im amerikanischen Geheimdienst, 1939–1945;* Bradley F. Smith, *The Shadow Warriors: OSS and the Origins of the CIA* (New York, 1983), and Robin Winks, *Cloak and Gown: Scholars in the Secret War, 1939–1961* (New York, 1987), each has an informative chapter on the R & A Branch.

University historian William L. Langer, who, with the assistance of the American Council of Learned Societies and Librarian of Congress Archibald MacLeish, set about immediately to recruit a professional staff drawn from across the social sciences. Over the next twelve months academic specialists from fields ranging from geography to classical philology descended upon Washington, bringing with them their most promising graduate students, and set up shop in the headquarters of the Research and Analysis (R & A) Branch at Twenty-third and E Streets and in the new Annex Building of the Library of Congress.

By mid-1942 Langer's recruiting drive had attracted a faculty that could rival any university: The Economics Division was to produce five future presidents of the American Economic Association; two future Nobel laureates contributed to the work of the agency, as did most of the founders of the postwar discipline of Sovietology. Of its forty professional historians, no less than seven would rise to the presidency of the American Historical Association – a fact that scarcely accounts for the neglect of the R & A Branch in the scholarship on World War II, on the roots of American intelligence, and, most significantly, perhaps, on the leading currents of modern intellectual history.

In spring 1943, as the tide turned in favor of the Allies, the directors of the R & A Branch began a fresh recruiting drive whose results were, if anything, even more astonishing. Although there was express resistance in the government to the employment of enemy aliens, William Langer recognized that the community of refugee scholars in America sheltered yet another reserve army of skilled experts, fluent in the European languages, attuned to the intricacies of European party politics, sensitive to cultural nuance, and alert to points of strength, vulnerability, and potential resistance in Germany and German-occupied countries.

Walter Dorn and Eugene N. Anderson, two American-born but German-trained historians, spearheaded the recruitment of what became, quite literally, a staff of "foreign intelligence" experts who were hired with greater concern for their intellectual acumen than for political uniformity: social theorists Franz Neumann, Herbert Marcuse, and Otto Kirchheimer of the neo-Marxist Institut für Sozialforschung in Frankfurt; Hamburg art historian Richard Krautheimer; jurist Henry Kellerman and political scientist John Herz; economists Walter Levy and Paul A. Baran; and, of course, Hajo Holborn and Felix Gilbert, the two outstanding representatives of a tradition of German historiography with its roots in Meinecke, Burckhardt, and Ranke. Altogether, perhaps only two dozen German émigrés found refuge in OSS (mention should also be made of Paul Alexander, Annemarie Holborn, and Inge Neumann), but their presence was felt in a manner quite disproportionate to their numbers. Surveying his cosmopolitan domain, Eugene Anderson was heard to remark that "in the Central European Section the *lingua franca* is broken English."

Even if we narrow the discussion to German-speaking historians, we can do little more here than mention the nature of their contribution to the prosecution of the war and the preparation for peace. Hajo Holborn, among the first of the refugee historians to be drawn into intelligence work, served as one of three special assistants to William Langer, with particular responsibility for the Civil Affairs program, to which the R & A Branch was a major contributor. The tasks assigned to R & A covered research on issues ranging from specific Nazi laws to be abrogated to the means of maintaining technical services during the immediate posthostilities period, and it fell largely to Holborn to coordinate this wide-ranging research program and to provide a direct liaison between the R & A Branch and the army. Holborn was widely respected for his encyclopedic knowledge of German affairs but less so for his administrative gifts; his postwar book *American Military Government* (1947) gives little indication of the trials and tribulations of the historian who had descended from reflection on the historical process to participation in it.

While Holborn shuttled back and forth between OSS headquarters and the Pentagon, his old friend and colleague Felix Gilbert moved steadily eastward. Starting in Washington, Gilbert worked with other Central Europeanists on political and psychological warfare, through the end of 1943. Like any good historian, however, he longed to get closer to his sources and was grateful to be transferred to the OSS outpost in London in February 1944 and then to Paris. Finally, in the spring of 1945, he advanced into the heart of occupied Germany, where, from headquarters in an abandoned champagne factory outside Wiesbaden, he monitored the revival of political, cultural, and intellectual life. While he strove, in his official communications, to observe the canons of intelligence reporting – to be objective, informative, and concise – the historian's hand is evident in every memorandum he wrote.

When Peter Gay sought a concise description of the artists and intellectuals who carried the spirit of Weimar with them into exile, he could do no better than to borrow from Franz Schoenberner the suggestive image of "the insider as outsider." The wartime experience of Holborn, Gilbert, and other refugee academicians in the heart of America's first central intelligence agency suggests just the reverse image, however: that of the *outsider as insider*. It should not be surprising, then, that as much as their historical training shaped their contribution to the work of the R & A Branch, their three-year sabbatical with OSS left its mark on subsequent academic historiography. There is convincing evidence to this effect.

First, the German émigrés gained in the R & A Branch an education in contemporary *Realpolitik* and an insight into the unvarnished process by which the political decision later studied by historians are made. The results of this immersion into the real world of military and diplomatic history can be seen in many places but perhaps nowhere better than in the essays that comprise the classic *Makers of Modern Strategy*, which Professor Stern has aptly described as "an OSS operation *in mufti*."

Second, the R & A Branch served as one of the important sites of the cross-fertilization of European and American scholarly discourse that was one of the few fruitful legacies of the Hitler years. The presence of the *geistesgeschichtliche* Europeans helped to deepen the theoretical level of historical scholarship in the United States. Conversely, the émigrés themselves fell under the influence of senior American scholars of the professional caliber of William Langer, Crane Brinton, Bernadotte Schmitt, and many others, who imparted to them the social scientific perspectives whose roots had sunk so much more deeply into the historical profession in the United States than in Europe.

Finally, the German-speaking historians contributed decisively to the postgraduate education of a generation of younger American scholars who had been drawn from graduate school or a depressed wartime job market into OSS: Leonard Krieger, Gordon Craig, H. Stuart Hughes, Franklin Ford, Carl Schorske, and countless others gained from them an extraordinary postgraduate education during their years of apprenticeship in the R & A Branch. Indeed, my own indebtedness to them suggests that even a third generation has been the beneficiary of the German-speaking historians of the Office of Strategic Services.

10

The Refugee Scholar as Intellectual Educator: A Student's Recollections

CARL E. SCHORSKE

More subjective than many of the other essays in this exploration, the shards of memory that follow offer at best a worm's-eye view of the presence and impact of the émigré historian. Mine is the perspective of a student of yesteryear looking up, not of the historical scholar of today looking back. If this attempt at *Rezeptionsgeschichte* based on personal recollection alone has any justification here, it is twofold: First, that it may point to the swiftly changing context of American political and academic culture of the 1930s and 1940s in which the professional influence of the émigrés was exercised. Second, that it may remind us of the power of the émigrés in the formation of the American student's mental outlook in areas lying well beyond purely professional historical education.

I

We sometimes forget how much time passed before émigré scholars secured a foothold in American colleges and universities. Even among those who left Germany immediately after Hitler's seizure of power, many spent some years in France or England before finally reaching our shores. Such was the case with all those who became my respected older friends and informal mentors: Fritz Epstein, Felix Gilbert, Hajo Holborn, Herbert Marcuse, and Franz Neumann. Of course, once they reached these shores their often painful search for a position in a depressed academic market further retarded the construction of new careers, the securing of the very institutional foundations of their influence. Today we think of the success stories – of the *illustri* from Germany scattered widely across America's academic map. But from the student point of view, the likelihood of exposure to German influence before World War II was slim indeed.

140

At Columbia College, where I roamed widely as a humanities major, I never heard of an émigré teacher during my undergraduate years. After graduating in 1936 I went on to graduate school at Harvard. During my time I studied at Harvard (1936–41), the history department never appointed even a temporary lecturer from the German-speaking émigré community. Gaetano Salvemini, to be sure, taught in the department, but the pittance that supported him as lecturer was not from the university budget.

Harvard boasted the presence of Sidney Fay, who taught what was a rarity in any university in those days: a specialized course in German history. In the depressed academic market of the late 1930s, there could hardly have been a place for another native German historian, the field that counted most for me. My teacher, William Langer, told me at the time of his sense of impotence in the face of urgent letters from German scholars requesting assistance in finding jobs. On one occasion he reported having contributed to a success: the placement of Hans Rothfels at Brown University. He also tried to help George Wolfgang Hallgarten to find a publisher for his rich, if somewhat chaotic, manuscript entitled *"Vorkriegsimperialismus."* Failing in his efforts, Langer arranged for Hallgarten's typescript to be duplicated and deposited in four or five major libraries in the United States; he also wrote an extensive review article to call the attention of the profession to the manuscript's substantive importance.

I studied at Harvard with only two émigré scholars, neither one in history: C. J. Friedrich in political theory and Karl Viëtor in German literature. While both enriched my knowledge and understanding, I never felt that either opened up a new way of thinking such as I might have felt if I had studied with Kantorowicz, Cassirer, or Panofsky. In hindsight, it does not seem to me that in the strongly traditional field of modern European history the German émigrés revolutionized American thinking as much as they did in physics or in the social sciences.

There was, however, one historian who in fact helped me to a new understanding of German history during my graduate years: Fritz T. Epstein. Epstein never had an appointment in the Harvard history department. I came to know him in 1938, a year after his arrival in Cambridge after three years in England. Shy, modest to a fault, in quite desperate economic straits, as he tried, with only marginal bibliographical and research positions, to support his family of four, Epstein became a personal guide and counsellor to almost all of the Harvard graduate students interested in German or Russian history. Carl Gustav Anthon, Hans Gatzke, Klemens von Klemperer, Frederick Barghoorn, and, later, Robert Byrnes are among those who would count themselves forever in Epstein's debt.

Epstein was an *érudit* to the marrow of his bones. His synthetic and constructive power, like that of most *érudits*, had its limits, but his command of what was going on in contemporary historical scholarship in Central and Eastern European history was alert, sensitive, and breathtakingly comprehensive. Once he had discovered the intellectual interests of his young associates, Fritz would deluge them with bibliography lists, clippings, or reviews from European newspapers and academic journals, to speed and enrich their work. He also had a quality of gentle guidance in private discussion that opened up perspectives and lines of exploration to which one had been blind.

Epstein's mixture of gifts – bibliographical command, infinite generosity, and a subtle pedagogical capacity for widening the intellectual horizons of his student friends – acquired particular importance because of the context of political and academic culture in the late 1930s. In the increasingly agitated atmosphere of Fascist expansion, we students were drawn to scholarly problems that found little or no place in the formal course offerings of the Harvard history department. The mainstream of American historical thinking about Europe since 1815 had centered on a Wilsonian problematic of nation-state politics and its international ramifications and control. Both of Harvard's major professors in modern European history, Sidney Fay and William Langer, focused their work in different ways on the coming of World War I and a critique of the simplistic anti-German ideology that deeply colored America's view of it. The international scene of the late 1930s, however, with its great, volatile triad of social and political systems – communism, fascism, and capitalist democracy – and disturbing combination of domestic upheaval and international aggression, raised a new set of concerns not easily dealt with in the Rankean perspective of our teachers.

To address such problems, which could not be dealt with in our formal work, the graduate History Club at Harvard organized separate self-directed seminars, jocularly called, in the leftist jargon of the day, "cells." In the cell to which I belonged, we explored not only how the rise of communism and fascism was affecting the course of events but also how professional historians were responding. Frederick Barghoorn took on the exploration of Russian historiography since the revolution; I worked on the German historians' confrontation, both intellectual and institutional, with the Nazi movement and the German state. For me and my colleagues, these inquiries were not merely a matter of awareness of the terrible drama of *Gleichschaltung*, of the problems of moral responsibility and value conflicts raised by the examples of Russian and German scholarship. They also led to deeper questions concerning the forms of historical meaning making and the vulnerability of the historian's intellectual procedures, in his search for truth, to the impact of political and social forces. Thus our interest in political-professional struggles in Germany, such as Hermann Oncken's against Walter Frank or the struggle for control of *Historische Zeitschrift*, opened up the problem of historical relativism and how relativism served as a vehicle of accommodation to Nazi domination over historical thought. The problems of the very nature of historical thought, raised thus acutely in Germany, seemed life-and-death questions to us as we defined our vocation and its ethic. But they were not, as I have suggested, part of our training or of the consciousness of our instructors. Our teachers knew well how to pursue *Quellenkritik*, but a sociointellectual and philosophical critique of historical work as itself a historical product was hardly part of their consciousness of their mission as scholars, let alone as teachers. Fritz Epstein, the marginal émigré, guided us to the intellectual battlefields and burned-over areas of Germany and Russia where this new consciousness could be cultivated.

That so many of my generation of American historians should have entered as fully into intellectual history (of course, with a political import) as our finest teachers had into diplomatic history reflects the rude shock with which we were awakened from our positivistic Enlightenment slumbers by observing the impact of totalitarian power on German and Austrian – or, for a few, Russian – history and historians. We would doubtless have turned toward the more problematized German historical thought eventually, without benefit of the Epsteins and the Holborns. But their presence certainly speeded and clarified the process of finding a new historical-critical consciousness, in the face of the loss of our positivistic innocence and our Wilsonian optimism.

II

My second and far more extensive encounter with scholars of the German emigration began in 1942 in the Office of Strategic Services

(OSS). It is often said that the OSS was a second graduate school for its young American participants. Crucial to that fact was the important presence of émigrés in the Research and Analysis (R & A) Branch. They are assumed to have been the "faculty," whereas the Americans were the "students." I have some doubts about this metaphor. Not all of the émigrés were old, nor were all the Americans young. Both groups, trained to individual, academic scholarship, had to adapt themselves to the demands of purposive, policy-oriented research. All were thus plunged into a kind of intellectual work where neither age nor cultural background offered a clear advantage. The model of graduate training ill suited the demands of the functions to be learned and performed for a government at war. Conversely, the OSS, with its central concern with predictive description, was particularly ill suited to the methods stressed in our graduate schooling in history, which had emphasized the otherness of the past and the importance of complex multi-factoral analysis.

My own experience leads me to think that the émigrés in OSS contributed less to the development of us natives as scholarly professionals than is usually assumed, and much more to our cultural formation. They contributed to making intellectuals out of us young academics by broadening our horizons and multiplying our awareness of the existential implications of ideas – philosophical and literary, as well as social and political. But once again, it was the changing world that set an agenda for the American intelligentsia that made the European mental equipment both relevant and attractive.

The function of the R & A Branch – to follow all currents of social and cultural life in Nazi-occupied Europe – provided a setting in which deeper intellectual issues could surface. The emergence of the multifaceted resistance movement was particularly demanding of rich cultural as well as social categories for adequate political analysis. Thus it raised questions about religious communities – not only institutional and ecclesiological but also theological ones – when we explored the dynamics of religious resistance to the Nazis. As the result of one of my endless discussions with him about the possible strength of Catholic resistance, Otto Kirchheimer introduced me to the neo-Augustinian theology of Adam Przywara. I was thus impelled to read Przywara and to enter a new world of discourse which came to have great importance later, when his follower, Cardinal Bea, played a determining role founding the program of Vatican II. Herbert Marcuse became engrossed in the French left-Catholic periodical *Esprit*. It was he who also insisted that I read *Les temps modernes* and opened my eyes to nascent existentialism as a new response to the conditions of occupation with wide implications for the liberal heritage. Paul Baran, a Russian émigré Marxist economist of extraordinary intellectual incisiveness, first introduced me to the work of Lukacs. At the margins, where, through burgeoning friendship, intellectual exchange had its least immediate political relevance but often its deepest impact, Franz Neumann awakened my interest in Burckhardt's *Weltgeschichtliche Betrachtungen*, Marcuse made me reconsider *Parsifal*, and Felix Gilbert enticed me into Friedrich Hölderlin's poetry with two beautifully printed volumes of the *Hymns* and the *Elegies*.

Was this another graduate school? – Not like any I have experienced. Peculiarly at OSS, the line between goal-oriented discussions interpreting wartime Europe intellectual play, between collegial work and conviviality, was often impossible to draw. We Americans were being culturally Europeanized by events, just as Europe was about to be Americanized. The general conditions of American-European cultural relations were being drastically altered by the war itself, and these set the frame for the influence exercised by the European scholars. In this sense, the question of the influence of the German émigrés seems somewhat *mal posée*. The émigrés, for their part, were being Americanized by their participation in American government and politics, as the war against nazism was being transmuted into the Cold War against communism. The young American academics and the German refugee scholars were educating each other, out of an almost unconscious common necessity, as the New World became old and the Old World new in the cultural and political integration of the two.

PART III

In this part of the volume we return to what Catherine Epstein calls *Beitragsgeschichte*, the history of academic contributions and their influence. Kenneth D. Barkin (Chapter 11) begins with a general statement on the role of the refugees in the American historical profession after 1950. Then Otto Pflanze, Hanna Schissler, and Robert Lerner (Chapters 12–14) provide case studies of four important scholars: the modern historians Hajo Holborn and Hans Rosenberg, and the medievalists Ernst Kantorowicz and Theodor E. Mommsen. The result is a record of scholarly accomplishment and deep personal inspiration that continue to shape the way many Americans write and think about European history.

Amid this celebration of achievement, Barkin sounds a cautionary note that is worth underscoring: In comparison to the refugees' impact on subjects such as physics or art history, their influence on history was limited. While among the historians there were many fine scholars and inspiring teachers, one looks in vain for figures comparable to Einstein or Panofsky, whose work redefined their disciplines. The refugee historians' influence was deep but narrow; it transformed the way Americans studied the German past, but – with a few notable exceptions – it had relatively little impact on the American profession as a whole. Thus this chapter in the relationship between German and American historiography is very different from the one described by Ernst Schulin in Chapter 1: In the late nineteenth century, Germans had taught Americans how to be historians; after 1945, the refugees taught Americans how to be historians of modern Germany.

Why this should be so becomes clear when we remember that, in history, professionalization is inseparable from nationalization. To a far greater degree than in most other disciplines, the intellectual and

147

institutional foundations of historiography are nationally defined. (That this is especially true for the study of modern history helps to explain why the refugees' greatest impact has been on scholarship in earlier historical periods.) The refugees' importance, therefore, came from the way in which they were able to introduce American students to the traditions of German national historiography. It is as ambassadors of this foreign academic culture, rather than as members of an international community of investigators, that the refugees' role in the United States can best be understood.

11

German Émigré Historians in America: The Fifties, Sixties, and Seventies

KENNETH D. BARKIN

During the Christmas holidays of 1960, I returned to my home in Brooklyn from Brown University, where I had just begun my graduate training in German history with Klaus Epstein. It happened that the American Historical Association's annual convention was being held in New York that year, and, as a fledgling historian, I decided to take the subway to Manhattan to get a better sense of the profession that I hoped to enter. I was especially interested because my thesis director was serving on a panel at the conference, and I wanted to see him in action. The main paper at the session concerned German academia in the 1920s and its role in the demise of the Weimar republic. Fritz Ringer, a young Harvard historian, delivered a stinging indictment of the politics of German scholars; this address later appeared in book form as *The Decline of the German Mandarins*. Epstein was critical of Ringer's conclusions, but what engraved that session deeply in my memory was the participation of the audience during the discussion. One after another, scholars with thick German accents arose to attack Ringer for his condemnation of their own *Doktorvater* or an *Ordinarius* whom they had known. Ringer had not, after all, attended lectures in the twenties or conversed with these *Ordinarien* during their *Sprechstunden*. Pandemonium ensued as arguments arose among shouting members of the audience, with each other and with members of the panel. Carl Schorske, in his role as chair, repeatedly and fruitlessly banged his gavel to restore order. Franklin Ford of Harvard stormed out of the session. Only later did I learn that he had been Ringer's *Doktorvater*. When Schorske finally got the audience to quiet down – and, I should add, sit down – he announced that there would be no further questions or comments about Ringer's paper.

Unless otherwise indicated, all translations are by the author.

149

I drew two conclusions from my jarring experience. First, German history was a serious – an intense – enterprise, which easily aroused combativeness and passion. Nothing subsequently has changed my mind on this score. Second, I made a vow not to speak about any subject after 1918, in order to avoid finding myself in the vulnerable situation in which Ringer had unwittingly placed himself with his all-too-contemporary topic. That vow I have kept until today. I take some comfort in Franz Neumann's judgment that the emigration was so complex a phenomenon and its participants so varied, despite surface appearances, that few convincing generalizations can be made about it. In his view, they did not constitute a cohort.[1]

Some five years later, I attended another convention in Washington and ventured to the *Bierabend* where German historians, with their weapons checked at the door, meet socially. I bumped into a young German historian, Klaus Schwabe, whom I had gotten to know in Freiburg some years earlier. When we left later he turned to me and said, "Tonight I feel that for the first time in my life I have actually experienced the atmosphere of the Weimar republic." Casting a glance back I could see Holborn, Hans Rosenberg, Fritz Epstein, Dietrich Gerhard, and George Hallgarten – all with groups of younger men around them eagerly following their every word. This also convinced me that the discipline I had chosen was singular. The masters had been active protagonists in the saga of twentieth-century German history in a way that was not true of the masters of British or French history in this country. It was inconceivable that a visitor to a French or British social gathering at an American Historical Association convention would have left feeling he had experienced Paris in the twenties or Stanley Baldwin's England. Moreover, this feeling had overwhelmed Schwabe in Washington, D.C., in the sixties, not in Hamburg or Berlin.

The literature on the intellectual migration from Central Europe to the United States is already a formidable one. It includes secondary works by H. Stuart Hughes, Joachim Radkau, Helge Pross, and Mar-

---

1 "Thus there is no comparison possible with the flight of Greek scholars from the Byzantine Empire in the fifteenth century. The extraordinary diversity of European refugee scholars makes it virtually impossible to determine their contribution with precision. . . . The influences are too subtle, too diffused, to be easily identified or measured." Franz Neumann, "The Social Sciences," in F. Neumann, Henri Peyre, Erwin Panofsky, Wolfgang Köhler, and Paul Tillich, eds. , *The Cultural Migration: The European Scholar in America* (Philadelphia, 1953), 23.

tin Jay.[2] Countless articles have been written, the most recent by Volker Berghahn. Émigrés such as Neumann and Erwin Panofsky have analyzed the migration themselves, and autobiographies have appeared from the pens of George Hallgarten and Felix Gilbert.[3] Looking over a list of those who had received graduate training in Central Europe before embarking for North America, one cannot help noticing the sizable number of names of historians who did not find a place in American academia.[4] We should not forget these scholars who were unable to make the transition from one university system to another. Others such as Valentin, Hallgarten, and Vagts did not attain academic positions, which seemed to weaken the impact of their writings. Given the parlous state of American universities in the thirties, it is remarkable how many did go on to fruitful and productive careers. The international agencies offering assistance to German scholars record helping nineteen historians, or 6 percent of the total placed in regular jobs.[5] Thus, the number of historians migrating was modest, and of these only two, Kantorowicz and Hans Rothfels, had held chairs for modern or medieval history, and one other, Hajo Holborn, had had a senior position at the Carnegie-sponsored Deutsche Hochschule für Politik. The vast majority were thus young and not settled into a *Beamtenleben* as the holders of history chairs. Since they were predominantly Jewish in background and/or politically liberal democrats, they were a very small and unrepresentative segment of the historical profession in Germany. They tended to come from the newer universities such as Frankfurt, Hamburg, or Cologne and, of course, had studied in Friedrich Meinecke's seminar in Berlin. In short, they were, with an exception or two, on the periphery – not part of the historical mainstream of German historians in the twenties.

2 H. Stuart Hughes, *The Sea Change* (New York, 1975); Joachim Radkau, *Die deutsche Emigration in den USA* (Hamburg, 1971); Helge Pross, *Die deutsche akademische Emigration nach den Vereinigten Staaten. 1933–1941* (Berlin, 1955); Martin Jay, *The Dialectical Imagination* (Boston, 1973); and idem, *Permanent Exiles: Essays on the Intellectual Migration from Germany to America* (New York, 1985)

3 Felix Gilbert, *A European Past: Memoirs, 1905–1945* (New York, 1988); George Hallgarten, *Als die Schatten fielen* (Frankfurt, 1969).

4 For example, Ismar Elbogen, Edgar Rosen, Selma Stern-Täubler, Alfred Vagts, and Veit Valentin.

5 Of the 335 scholars who applied for jobs to the Emergency Committee in Aid of Displaced Foreign Scholars 110 were social scientists, and of these 19 were historians, compared to 33 economists and 33 law professors. Gerald Stourzh, "Die deutschsprachige Emigration in den Vereinigten Staaten: Geschichtswissenschaft und politische Wissenschaft," *Jahrbuch für Amerikastudien* 10 (1965):59–77, 64–95.

We are concerned here with university-trained historians rather than all academic émigrés, and with the historians' impact in the United States in the fifties, sixties, and seventies. It is generally assumed that their impact was enormous, as was the case in physics, music, political science, and psychology. In order to establish whether this was so, we should ask some precise questions. We should differentiate their impact on German history in this country from their impact on all historians, the majority of whom were preoccupied with North America or Great Britain. We should even inquire as to their impact on the educated American public – let us say all of those who had some graduate training. Perhaps it would be fruitful to cast our eye on allied disciplines such as art history and political science, to gauge the influence of these disciplines, as compared with history, on American thinking about the past. After all, historicism in Germany was not confined to the discipline of history; its influence was to be found in most humanistic and social science disciplines. Should we, for instance, accept the artificial German boundaries that would mark a Schmoller, Sombart, Schumpeter, or Wilhelm Abel as *Nationalökonomen* or *Wirtschaftshistoriker*, belonging to another discipline entirely?[6]

The United States was thought to be a scholarly backwater in the 1930s but not quite a tabula rasa. Americans had trooped to Germany since early in the nineteenth century to experience the wonders of German scholarship in theology, history, philosophy, and economics. Henry Adams, John Motley, Josiah Royce, Simon Patten, and Richard Ely had all made the ritual pilgrimage and returned convinced of German intellectual primacy. The American Economics Association was modeled on the Verein für Sozialpolitik. Herbert Baxter Adams found much support for his belief that American liberties were to be traced back to the Saxon forests. In the twenties, the young Talcott Parsons returned from Germany with the mission of making his countrymen aware of Max Weber's critical contributions to history and sociology. Moreover, Germans and other European scholars had regularly served as visiting professors at American universities. Before World War I, the University of Wisconsin had had a revolving professorship set aside that brought a German scholar

---

6 All of these scholars were considered economists in Central Europe, although their major works were historical (and often historicist) in character. Abel is evidence that social and economic history had not completely disappeared in the twenties and thirties.

to the campus each year.[7] About 9 percent of the faculty at major universities before World War I were not American citizens.

German history, nevertheless, was not well established at American universities in the thirties. A survey of articles in the *American Historical Review* shows that 80 percent of those published in the interwar years focused on Britain and America. A few articles are to be found about German diplomatic history, and less than a handful on Prussia. Bernadotte Schmitt of Chicago and Sidney Fay of Harvard were the major authorities on Germany, and their interest in the postwar era was similar to that of their counterparts in Germany: to establish who was really responsible for the origin of World War I.[8] The study of German history in the United States suffered from the wave of anti-German hysteria during and after World War I, in which the German language disappeared from high schools and textbooks were rewritten to make the Hessian mercenaries employed by the British the main villains of the American Revolution. These cleansed texts were still in use in my own high school in the midfifties, where the only foreign languages offered were French, Spanish, and Latin. Historians in America were about as conversant with German history as their German colleagues were knowledgeable of the North American past. There was one exception, the maverick American social scientist Thorstein Veblen, whose *Imperial Germany and the Industrial Revolution*, published in 1915, articulated many themes that were to reappear in the scholarship of the émigrés.[9]

The three decades following World War II witnessed the solid establishment of German history as a critical part of the curriculum of every major university. The contraction that had characterized American higher education came to an end in the late 1950s. Demand for historians outstripped supply for a good ten years. In addition, the pervasive anti-Semitism that had marked America's major private

7 See Moritz Julius Bonn's *Wandering Scholar* (London, 1949), for an account of his year (1914) as a visiting professor at Wisconsin.
8 S. B. Fay, *The Origins of the World War* (New York, 1928); Bernadotte Schmitt, *The Coming of the War* (Chicago, 1930).
9 As early as 1915, Veblen had compared Germany to Japan and wrote, "Germany combines the results of English experience in the development of modern technology with a state of the other arts of life more nearly equivalent to what prevailed in England before the modern industrial regime came on. . . . The case of Germany is unexampled among Western nations both as regards the abruptness, thoroughness and amplitude of its appropriation of this technology, and as regards the archaism of its cultural furniture." Thorstein Veblen, *Imperial Germany and the Industrial Revolution* (New York, 1915), 83.

universities between the wars receded in the early fifties. Both Herbert Gutman and Carl Schorske say they were advised that a career in history would be very difficult for a Jew, or even for someone with one Jewish parent.[10] The distinguished black historian, John Hope Franklin, who entered graduate school at Harvard in the late thirties recently expressed his surprise not at the hostility to blacks, which he had been prepared for, but at the virulent anti-Semitism, which came as a shock. In a memoir he noted, "The most traumatic social experience I had there [Harvard] was not racist but anti-Semitic. . . . When I suggested the most active, brightest graduate student for president [of the Henry Adams history club], the objection to him was that although he did not have some of the more reprehensible Jewish traits, he was still a Jew."[11] The émigrés may have, in fact, played a significant role in weakening anti-Semitism. The increasing tolerance allowed émigrés to move up the academic ladder and also meant they could train younger émigré Jews and American Jews for posts at the university level.

As self-conscious heirs of the Rankean tradition, their first contribution was an emphasis on the importance of original unpublished sources in scholarly research. Felix Gilbert, recalling his own training, recently wrote, "Meinecke's seminars provided a rigorous training in historical methodology. They focused on the art of interpretation. We usually discussed a single document or treatise like the French Charter of 1814, or Machiavelli's *Prince* and subjected the meaning of each sentence, almost each word, to scrutiny and discussion."[12] As an undergraduate at Brooklyn College in the fifties, I enrolled in the mandatory Western Civilization course, which had been organized in part by Hans Rosenberg. Every week we had to read five documents carefully and be prepared to discuss them in depth. It not only gave us a firm grounding in historical analysis but, in my own case, introduced me to the Kathedersozialisten I was subsequently to choose as my dissertation subject. There is no substitute for this kind of training, and to the extent that Americans

---

10 Carl Schorske, "A Life of Learning," in Charles Homer Haskins Lecture, American Council of Learned Societies Occasional Papers, no. 1, April 23, 1987; David A. Gerber, ed., *Anti-Semitism in American History* (Urbana, 1986); also, Lewis S. Feuer, "The Stages in the Social History of Jewish Professors in American Colleges and Universities," *American Jewish History* 71 (1982):432–65.
11 John Hope Franklin, "A Life of Learning," in Charles Homer Haskins Lecture, American Council of Learned Societies Occasional Paper no. 4 (April 14, 1988).
12 Gilbert, *A European Past*, 70.

have made a contribution to the study of German history in the postwar decades, it is owing in part to the émigrés' emphasis on the rigorous analysis of primary sources. There is, of course, an irony here, since by leaving Germany they had cut themselves off from the sources for their own research. If their scholarly output was not enormous, one has to remember that for two decades, in the prime of their careers, they had no access to the documents that they considered critical for serious scholarship.[13] Also, one should not forget that teaching loads were enormous in those days. The fifteen hours a week that Hans Rosenberg had to spend in the classroom would be considered a form of indentured servitude by my colleagues, who spend approximately one-third of that in scheduled classes.

One hears a good deal these days about professors as role models. The Central European historians unwittingly embodied certain values and a cultivation that was not common, then or now, in American academe. They had received a comprehensive education in the *Gymnasium* for nine years. Their preparation in languages and paleography was daunting. The breadth of their knowledge was intimidating. Trained as an intellectual historian under Meinecke, Gerhard Masur could write a learned book dealing with Van Gogh, Gauguin, Gide, Galsworthy, and Oscar Wilde. Felix Gilbert could gracefully move from the *Quattrocento* to the twentieth century, with a sojourn in the American republic, and begin his European textbook with references, in the first pages, to Ibsen, Beardsley, Mann, Shaw, and Richard Strauss.[14] I remember my bafflement when I discovered that Arthur Rosenberg, whose *Birth of The Weimar Republic* had convinced me that I should concentrate on modern Germany, was, in fact, an ancient historian casting a glance at his own era.

Apart from this breadth of learning, many of the émigrés conveyed a sense of *Gravitas* – of intensity – about their subject. Studying German history, one sensed, was different from studying French or British history, in that it was a calling – a *Beruf* – that required seriousness of purpose and a prodigious capacity for work. Wit and irony had little place in an enterprise that was concerned with *Truth*.

13 It is surprising, however, that none of the émigrés used the captured Nazi documents that were housed in Washington in the fifties and sixties.
14 Gilbert's range as a historian is daunting. He has written one of the major texts on twentieth-century Europe, as well as a significant analytical work on Renaissance Florence and a monograph on U.S. foreign policy in the eighteenth century. *The End of the European Era: 1890 to the Present* (New York, 1970); *Machiavelli and Guicciardini* (Princeton, 1965); *To the Farewell Address* (Princeton, 1961).

Those who did not have the prerequisites were best advised to leave immediately. In my own experience there was a luncheon with Hans Rosenberg in Berkeley in the early seventies. I walked into his musty office in the basement of Dwinelle Hall to find an over-stuffed arm-chair and the walls covered from ceiling to floor with bookshelves containing aging volumes by scholars such as Hartung, Schnabel, and H. Ritter von Srbik. I was greeted with the words, "Sit down, Mr. Barkin, and I will tell you what I think of everything that you have written." Later that afternoon I said to a friend that although I was only thirty-one, I had already been through Judgment Day, and it was the God of the Old Testament that I had encountered. Whether history is, as one theorist has written, the last refuge of failed theologians I am not sure, but preparing to be a German histo-rian in the fifties and sixties required qualities very much like those required for the taking of clerical orders.

When academia began to expand rapidly in the sixties, the émigrés, with Holborn at Yale, Rosenberg at Berkeley, and Gerhard at Wash-ington University, were able to supply a well-trained generation of young German historians for the expanding campuses (as is well known, Holborn produced fifty-five doctorates at Yale alone). Moreover, since the dollar–mark exchange rate was very favorable to the Americans, the vast majority of these young scholars had spent at least a year, and often two years, doing research at German archives. The names Theodore Hamerow, Otto Pflanze, Peter Gay, Leonard Krieger, and Arno Mayer will give you some idea of the quality of the generation produced in the forties and fifties. Most important, the canon of critical works in the liberal-democratic his-toriographic tradition had been passed on to these fledgling histori-ans. The works of Ziekursch and Kehr, for instance, were probably read more by Americans than by German *Doktoranden* in the decades after the Second World War. To take Kehr as an example, I had read his major articles before Hans-Ulrich Wehler brought out an edition in 1965. Naumann, Weber, and Hintze were also part of my required reading. When I went to Freiburg in 1963, I felt that I had entered a different historical universe. The major series of lectures during the sixteen-week fall quarter were devoted to *Preussische Aussenpolitik 1858–1867.* Ultimately, I found myself most comfortable in the *Semi-nar für Agrarpolitik*, where the shelves were lined with works on the social and economic history of agriculture.

Thus, the émigrés were able to ensure that German history would become an accepted part of the American university curriculum by producing a talented *Nachwuchs*. Their own commitment to a liberal-democratic interpretation of German history meshed well with the democratic values of young, educated Americans of the postwar era. It is interesting to note that the émigrés who rapidly returned to Germany were, generally, nationally minded conservatives such as Hans Rothfels or Marxists like Theodor Adorno and Max Horkheimer. In both cases, America could not readily supply an appreciative audience for their ideas. Those in the left-liberal tradition did return as guest professors, and this led to a useful exchange of ideas. One reason that it has become commonplace for Americans to publish in German journals and for Germans such as Mommsen, Winkler, and Stürmer to publish in America is, no doubt, the links developed by the émigrés with their German colleagues during this period.[15] I think it is not unfair to say that the United States became second only to Germany in studies of the Central European past, and when one remembers that in the midsixties Berkeley could boast Hans Rosenberg, Wolfgang Sauer, Carl Schorske, Raymond Sontag, and Gerald Feldman in the history department and Reinhard Bendix and Leo Loewenthal in the social sciences, one may wonder if there was any better place to train young German historians.

We should now turn to the discourse that the émigré historians created about the last two centuries in Germany. It is well to keep Neumann's injunction in mind. While the vast majority were liberal democrats, there were exceptions, such as Hans Rothfels, whose *German Opposition to Hitler* (which we all read) sought to preserve what was salvageable of the national-conservative tradition. The question that preoccupied the émigrés and their students was, "Why did radical fascism come to power in Germany?"; nor should the question have been any different. German historians did not have the luxury of the leading French scholars, who could write tomes on the peasants of Languedoc, or British scholars, who could wax eloquent about the rise of the gentry or its failure to rise. For German scholars to have done that in 1950 or 1960 would have been to engage in escapism – to open themselves to the charge of apologetics. If

15 That one regularly reads articles by German scholars in American journals and by Americans in some German journals such as *Geschichte und Gesellschaft* is graphic evidence of the role played by the émigrés in breaking down the interwar isolation that characterized German historical scholarship.

contemporary German historians can choose to write about village *Spinnstuben* or urge us to become missionaries in rowboats, it is because the big question was addressed for a good three decades.[16]

The Nazi period itself was, on the whole, ignored by historians, which left the field open to Franz Neumann, whose *Behemoth* became the book most read by scholars, while William Shirer's rather shallow *Rise and Fall of the Third Reich* became a best seller.[17] The émigrés and their students concentrated their attention on Weimar and Imperial Germany. And here the operative principle was that Germany had diverged from the liberal-democratic evolution that marked British, French, and American history. There might be disagreement about the timing of the divergence or about its character, but few doubted the singularity of modern German history.

As is well known, *Geistesgeschichte* became a main avenue to explain the divergence. Meinecke's seminar had schooled his disciples in Dilthey, and even Felix Gilbert, who was drawn to Italian history, wrote his dissertation on Droysen. It has been fashionable for some time to denigrate intellectual history, to treat it, as one historian has written, as the *Spätblüte des Historismus*.[18] This cynicism is unwarranted and seems to apply solely to studies of liberal and conservative intellectuals. Works on Lukacs or Gramsci receive a special dispensation and are often thought to be at the cutting edge. There are many works by the émigrés and their students that could be cited, but the most characteristic would be Hans Kohn's *Mind of Germany*, published in 1960. In his preface, Kohn wrote, "The present work wishes to provide a tentative reply to the one question on which much of the fascination of German history rests: how the alienation of Germany from the west came about."[19] Thus, Kohn assumes Germany's divergent course from the outset. He justifies his concentration on *Geistesgeschichte* by stressing that "in Germany, the anti-intellectuals were not the mob, but men frequently of refined taste

16 I do not mean to criticize social history or *Alltagsgeschichte* but merely to point out that in the aftermath of the Third Reich German scholars did not have the option of writing history with the politics left out. One might even wonder if the French were not engaging in escapism, after Vichy and the decline of French power over two centuries, by their preoccupation with the *longue durée*. Many of the *Annales* scholars were ex-Communists who were, perhaps, fleeing the complexity of modern history.

17 Franz Neumann, *Behemoth: The Structure and Practice of National Socialism, 1933–1944* (New York, 1944). Neumann's superb book has yet to be translated into German.

18 Hans-Ulrich Wehler, "Geschichtswisssenschaft Heute," in *Stichworte zur 'Geistigen Situation der Zeit'*, 2nd ed., ed. J. Habermas (Frankfurt, 1979).

19 Hans Kohn, *The Mind of Germany* (New York, 1960), ix.

and great erudition." Basically, he sees German intellectuals as having abandoned Enlightenment principles and the sage wisdom of Goethe. Chapters on Father Jahn, Arndt, Wagner, Nietzsche, and Rilke document the departure from liberal-democratic Western traditions. Holborn more or less agreed in his multivolume *History of Germany*, in which he wrote of a, "deep cleavage [that in the age of Hegel] was opened between Germany and Western Europe such as had never existed in any earlier century of European history."[20] Other books in this genre include those by Fritz Stern, Leonard Krieger, George Mosse, Klemens von Klemperer, and Klaus Epstein.[21] They all share an implicit belief in the importance of ideas and the conviction that intellectual history provides a vehicle for understanding the failure of democracy to take root in Germany. Within the framework of *Geistesgeschichte* there was room for significant variation. While Kohn centered his attention on major intellectuals, Stern and von Klemperer dissected the thought of authoritarian thinkers of the second rank, whose impact they found to be widespread. George Mosse's *Crisis of German Ideology* sought to analyze popular culture, an arena he considered to be alive with anti-Semitism and antidemocratic ideals.

A problem with this approach that many of the émigrés and their students adopted was, as the citation from Kohn demonstrates, that Germany was posited as having a unique intellectual history, without this contention ever being fully established by comparisons with other European nations. Britain and France also had their share of anti-Semitic, illiberal thinkers, and in the case of the former, education at all levels was more restricted than it was in Germany. This difficulty also marred the aforementioned work of Ringer, who subsequently came to the conclusion, many years later, that the German university and school system were surprisingly open, given the authoritarian political structure.[22]

It should also be noted that intellectual history was not entirely new to the American scene, although the biographical approach as

20 Hajo Holborn, *A History of Modern Germany, 1648–1840* (New York, 1964), Chap. 17, pp. 510–31.
21 Fritz Stern, *The Politics of Cultural Despair* (Berkeley and Los Angeles 1961); Leonard Krieger, *The German Idea of Freedom* (Boston, 1957); George Mosse, *The Crisis of the German Ideology* (New York, 1964); Klemens von Klemperer, *Germany's New Conservatism* (Princeton, 1957); Klaus Epstein, *The Genesis of German Conservatism* (Princeton, 1966).
22 Fritz Ringer, *The Decline of the German Mandarins* (Cambridge, Mass., 1969). Also see Ringer, *Education and Society in Modern Europe* (Bloomington, 1979).

influenced by Dilthey was not widespread. More common was the study of unit ideas, as exemplified by Arthur O. Lovejoy's *Great Chain of Being* (1936).[23] Lovejoy had studied in Paris, not Germany, although he had been very much influenced at Harvard by Josiah Royce, who had studied in Germany. It is interesting to note that the editorial board of the *Journal of the History of Ideas* (1940) included Crane Brinton, Perry Miller, J. H. Randall, J. Salwyn Shapiro, and Louis B. Wright – all Americans. For those who believe that the émigrés introduced intellectual history to the Americans, I suggest they read Perry Miller's *New England Mind in the Seventeenth Century* (1939), a work of monumental scholarship and analysis.

Another way of tackling the big question was to concentrate on the progressive forces and the reasons for their failure. Thus the Social Democratic party (SPD) was analyzed by Carl Schorske, Peter Gay, Joseph Berlau, and Richart Hunt.[24] At a time when few historians in Germany (G. A. Ritter being an exception) were concerned with the history of the Left, the émigrés turned the attention of their students to the SPD under the empire and the Weimar republic. The tenor of these scholarly works was critical. The Social Democrats were taken to task for their repeated failure to tame the Junker-dominated state. During World War I they had cooperated with the Hindenburg-Ludendorff dictatorship. The revolution of 1918–19 was adjudged to be unsuccessful, and in a memorable phrase Ebert was denounced as the "Stalin of the German Revolution," or, in effect, the architect of a German Thermidor. Ironically, younger American scholars applied a litmus test of Marxist orthodoxy and found the SPD wanting. Recently numerous reassessments of socialism and the German revolution have been published in the Federal Republic; these studies build on a foundation that was laid by the émigrés and their progeny.

Social and economic studies of German history did not come to the forefront until the late sixties. To be sure, both Kehr and Hallgarten had convincingly sought to integrate economic interest groups into their analyses of the *Kaiserreich*, but the former had died shortly after arriving in the United States, and the latter had not attained a

---

23 Arthur O. Lovejoy, *The Great Chain of Being* (Cambridge, Mass., 1936). Also see Daniel Wilson, *Arthur O. Lovejoy and the Quest for Intelligibility* (Chapel Hill, 1980).
24 Carl Schorske, *German Social Democracy, 1905–1917* (Cambridge, Mass., 1955); Peter Gay, *Eduard Bernstein and the Dilemma of Democratic Socialism* (New York, 1952); A. Joseph Berlau, *The German Social Democratic Party, 1914–1921* (New York, 1949); Richard Hunt, *German Social Democracy, 1918–1933* (New Haven, 1964).

professorship at a major graduate institution. Their work was read but had few imitators. Theodore Hamerow's 1955 dissertation, which was directed by Holborn, on the social and economic history of *Vormärz* and the revolution of 1848 stands out for its early attempt to assess the importance of artisans, peasants, and workers in the revolution's initial outbreak and ultimate failure.[25] The word failure should perhaps be put in quotation marks, since a quite recent British émigré to Reagan's America states that the revolution was, in fact, a marked success. For the shift toward economic studies of the *Kaiserreich*, we are indebted to Hans Rosenberg. At Brooklyn College and at Berkeley, Rosenberg urged his students to consider socioeconomic explanations of Germany's failure to establish a viable democracy. As Kehr had turned his attention to the vested interests of the elite groups, Rosenberg followed with his cutting analyses of the Junkers. In the postscript to his 1958 *Bureaucracy, Aristocracy, and Autocracy*, he wrote of "the long protracted counterrevolution in Germany [that] was brilliantly executed by the old ruling groups" and attributed the fall of republican democracy in the thirties to the [conservative] alliance with the Captains of big industry which went back to the 1870s."[26] For Rosenberg, National Socialism was no "traffic accident" in German history, nor did he condone the idea of discontinuities in history that became popular in the early years of the Federal Republic. Although his name is associated with an antipathy to *Geistesgeschichte* – a rejection of Meinecke – he in fact agreed with the other émigrés when he wrote, in his illuminating postscript,

German philosophers and historians since Hegel and Ranke played a notable part in the corrosion of liberalism as a public way of life. By proudly magnifying the developing chasm between "The German Mind" and the western European Enlightenment, the most politically influential spokesmen of the German intelligentsia furnished a pompous ideological foundation for the departure from the basic values of Western liberal democratic thought.[27]

Rosenberg is of course most renowned for his *Grosse Depression und Bismarckzeit*, which was foreshadowed by articles on the same subject twenty-five years earlier. With one deft stroke, he changed the nature of discourse about Imperial Germany.[28] We learned a new vocabu-

---

25 Theodore Hamerow, *Restoration, Revolution, and Reaction* (Princeton, 1958).
26 Hans Rosenberg, *Bureaucracy, Aristocracy, and Autocracy* (Cambridge, Mass., 1958). 233.
27 Ibid., 234.
28 Hans Rosenberg, *Grosse Depression und Bismarckzeit* (Berlin, 1967). It should be pointed out that there were quite a few footnotes in this work to American social science scholar-

larly of *Juglars, Wellen, Konjunktur*, and of course the name Kondratiev became almost a household word. Rosenberg wove together social, economic, and political history, convincing us that the timing of unification, just three years before the outbreak of the "Great Depression," augured poorly for the nation's liberal evolution. Political and constitutional controversies gave way to issues of economic security and welfare legislation.

Where some had looked to the failure of socialism, Rosenberg (and Holborn) charted the demise of liberalism as the key to the survival of Germany's authoritarian elites. He posited a linkage between the Great Depression, protectionist collectivism, and the abandonment by many liberals of a commitment to a liberal Germany fully integrated into the Western economy. His own assessment was unambiguous: "If one considers the internal and external political effects of agricultural policy up to National Socialism, the shift in 1879 proves . . . to have been one of the most erroneous decisions of German, and, therefore of European history in the nineteenth century."[29] Thus, Rosenberg introduced us not only to Kondratiev but to the defeated and submerged tradition of Richter, Brentano, Naumann, and Ziekursch. He diverged from those who posited a "German mind" by resurrecting an authentic left-liberal tradition that avoided the Scylla of conservative nationalism and the Charybdis of orthodox Marxism.

It is not common in the literature on the emigration to separate the Austrians from the Germans or to consider the impact of economic historians. I think this is an error. Alexander Gerschenkron, Joseph Schumpeter, and Friedrich von Hayek all had a significant impact on how educated Americans interpreted the German past. Schumpeter migrated to Harvard in 1930, and Gerschenkron, who was Russian by birth, did all of his university degrees in Vienna before leaving in 1938 for Berkeley and subsequently Harvard. Von Hayek was a visiting professor in the interwar period and later went to Chicago. Thus, all three were in major American universities and had the opportunity of influencing the next generation of economic historians. Moreover, the three were incredibly productive in exile, perhaps because the subdiscipline of economic history did not have a Rankean foundation and thus was not tied to primary sources. In 1986, the

---

ship. It may well be that Rosenberg was more influenced by American economic history and theory than is commonly thought.

29 Ibid., 182.

three had a total of twenty-three books in print in English, of which Schumpeter, who had died in 1950, had authored nine. When one stops to reflect on these Austrians, their success and influence is perhaps not so difficult to comprehend. They came out of a different tradition from that of the Germans – one that was more theoretical, and less historicist, in orientation. They were less reserved in their support for capitalism and a laissez-faire internationalist policy. Their advocacy of entrepreneurial capitalism blended well with the neo-classical revival that marked postwar American social science. Indeed, they may have helped bring about the revival, as their fellow Austrian Karl Popper spurred a positivist renaissance in philosophy.

For our purposes, it is of interest that they all used German history as a negative example – an instructive case of failure due to the rejection of market capitalism by the Left and Right. Schumpeter attributed the evils of the twentieth century, as has his recent disciple Arno Mayer, to the survival of the aristocratic mentality into the twentieth century. For Schumpeter (as for Fritz Redlich) the industrial entrepreneurs were heroes of the modern era, knights worthy of our esteem. Imperialism, he told an enthralled American audience, should be weakest in the most capitalistic and least aristocratic of societies – the United States – and this, he concluded, was in fact the case.[30] On the title page of Gerschenkron's much-read 1944 study, *Bread and Democracy in Germany*, were the words *Latifundia perdidere Germaniam*. Parallel to Rosenberg, Gerschenkron emphasized, "The agricultural crisis of the last quarter of the nineteenth century presented Germany with her great democratic opportunity. The crisis threatened to shatter the economic position of the Junkers and to do away with their existence as a coherent social group. This golden opportunity was missed."[31] He went on, in his celebrated "Economic Backwardness in Historical Perspective," to argue that the Anglo-American path to modernization was the model but that other nations – latecomers – would have to use temporary substitutes for the free market, in order to amass the capital for modernization. Once these substitutes had achieved their purpose, he stressed, they would wither away and, by implication, the Anglo-American model would reemerge, after a short detour.

30 Josef Schumpeter, *Capitalism, Socialism, and Democracy* (New York, 1942), and *Imperialism and Social Classes*, tr. Heinz Norden (Oxford, 1951).
31 Alexander Gerschenkron, *Bread and Democracy in Germany* (Berkeley and Los Angeles, 1943), 67.

The ideas of Friedrich von Hayek are rarely discussed by historians, although his *Road to Serfdom* was a best seller in America, serialized by *Reader's Digest* for its millions of subscribers.[32] It is a book about Germany. Hayek's attack on all planning and government intervention in the market echoes the early Mill. For Hayek, the pedigree of nazism was not Jahn or Arndt but Fichte, Rodbertus, and Lassalle. In practice, socialism always leads to totalitarianism, Hayek warned, whatever its ostensible compassion for the weak. The Germans, with their strong tradition of both a left- and a right-wing critique of capitalism, were the *bête noir* of the book. He concluded, "The Germans know that what they still regard as the British and American traditions and their own new ideals are fundamentally opposed and irreconcilable views of life."[33] All of this was music to American ears in the postwar era. The Austrians reinforced Rosenberg's critique of the Junker elite and spread the message to a much larger audience. It is curious that three economic historians who came to maturity under the Habsburg empire and its successor state have served as a Greek chorus, warning Americans of the dangers of Continental ideas and paying homage to fundamental American values. In a sense their message, like that of the historians, harks back to Ernst Bloch's cryptic comment about *das gleichzeitige des ungleichzeitigen*. Modernization had to be across the board. A semifeudal military, a reactionary-minded landed elite, and an artisanry still in the thralls of a small-town guild mentality were not supposed to share the historical stage with steel tycoons, stock-market speculators, and an industrial working class responding to the sirens of Marxism. Ultimately, the message of the émigrés was clear. Germany, the land of historicism, had brought too much historical baggage into the twentieth century. The research agenda of the fifties, sixties, and seventies was to explain this conundrum.

This manner of posing the problem was not entirely novel. Naumann had wrung his hands in *Demokratie und Kaisertum* over Germany's entering the modern world led by Junkers and priests, hand in hand. Veblen had diagnosed Imperial Germany as an unstable chemical compound of modern and feudal elements in his 1915 *Impe-*

---

32 Friedrich von Hayek, *The Road to Serfdom* (Chicago, 1944). The dedication reads, "To Socialists of all Parties."

33 Ibid., 218. The Austrian economic historians may have been of critical importance in the neoclassical wave that was to spread after World War II. A decade earlier, in the midst of the Depression, classical economics had lost many of its adherents.

rial Germany and the Industrial Revolution. What was novel was that this analysis now became the conventional wisdom in America.

The question naturally arises whether the émigré historians had a significant impact on the entire discipline of history such as, say, Hannah Arendt and Hans Morgenthau had on political science, Erwin Panofsky on art history, or Erik Erikson on psychology. In each of these cases, and others that could be cited, the works of these authors became required reading for everyone in their respective disciplines. An article in the *Review of Politics* in 1987 began with the line "Arendt's *Origins of Totalitarianism* is one of the great books in modern political science."[34] A recent work in art history contains the statement "In the history of modern art history, the primary event is undoubtedly the work of Erwin Panofsky."[35] One could even go farther and venture to argue that the writings of the leading émigrés in a variety of humanistic and social science disciplines were required reading for all well-educated Americans. In some respects, it was more the social scientists than the historians who had the greatest impact on the general American view of the European past. Arendt, Naumann, Erich Fromm, and von Hayek all penned academic best sellers. One reason for the outpouring of books on the transatlantic emigration is the consensus that whole disciplines were transformed by the émigrés. In the case of history, this did not happen. I am skeptical whether there was a historian's equivalent of Arendt's book on totalitarianism or Panofsky's *Studies in Iconology.*

Colin Eisler assessed the reasons for the enormous influence of the German art historians as follows: "Unafraid of value judgments, prepared to go out on a limb more readily than the cautious and accurate factually oriented scholars in America, the European art historian tended to present his material in a more speculative, sometimes more adventurous and stimulating manner than was the custom here."[36] These sentences, which express the very antithesis of the Rankean tradition, could well apply to the political scientists and psychologists but not to the historians. The reason lies in the state of the discipline in Weimar Germany.

While many disciplines experienced a surge of creativity in Wei-

---

34 John Stanley, "Is Totalitarianism a New Phenomenon? Reflections on Hannah Arendt's *Origins of Totalitarianism," Review of Politics,* 49 (Spring 1987): 177–207.
35 Michael Ann Holly, *Panofsky and the Foundations of Art History* (Ithaca, 1984), 10.
36 Colin Eisler, "Kunstgeschichte American Style: A Study in Migration," *Perspectives in American History* 2 (1968):544–629.

mar, the historians, to use American imagery, drew the wagons around in a circle to protect the old historicist verities. The *Staatsfrömmigkeit* that had characterized professional history under the *Kaiserreich* changed little after war, revolution, and inflation, as Bernd Faulenbach has convincingly demonstrated.[37] If anything, World War I increased the insularity of the German historical guild. They seemed unaware of the work of their foreign contemporaries – Marc Bloch, Lucien Febvre, R. H. Tawney, Lewis Namier, G. D. H. Cole, and Charles Beard. Politically and methodologically, conservatism was the order of the day. How many of us would turn to the Weimar writings of Fritz Hartung, Erich Brandenburg, Hermann Oncken, or even Friedrich Meinecke for insights about modern German history? I suspect we are more likely to read their works to understand the mentality of the Weimar *Bildungsbürgertum.*

One reason for the modest influence of the émigré scholars is the small number who migrated (some two of fifty professors) compared with other disciplines. History, which had taken on the aura of an official discipline under the empire, was less open to Jews and those on the political left and center than newer disciplines such as art history. There were fewer "rootless cosmopolitans" to be purged. As Rudolf Vierhaus reminded us some years ago, there was no violent collision between the Nazis and the historical guild.[38]

The second reason is that the émigrés were trained in a pristine historicist methodology that was under siege in other Western nations. Their *Doktorväter* were obsessed with state-centered politics and biography. Thus, unlike the art historians or philosophers, the émigré historians had no exciting new message to bring to their American counterparts. They might have echoed Mephistopheles, in Goethe's *Faust*: "Grau, teurer Freund, ist alle Theorie,/Und des goldenen Lebensbaum ist grün." Even Felix Gilbert could open the second chapter of his 1970 textbook, *The End of the European Era*, with the ominous words "Generalizations in history are dangerous."[39] Indeed, economic history was far better established in the

---

37 Bernd Faulenbach, *Ideologie des deutschen Weges; Die deutsche Geschichte in der Historiographie zwischen Kaiserreich und Nationalsozialismus* (Munich, 1982); also Georg Iggers, *The German Conception of History* (Middletown, Conn., 1968); Bernd Faulenbach, *Geschichtswissenschaft in Deutschland* (Munich, 1974); and G. Iggers, *New Directions in European Historiography* (Middletown, Conn., 1975).

38 Rudolf Vierhaus, "W. Frank und die Geschichtswissenschaft," *Historische Zeitschrift* 207 (1968):619.

39 Gilbert, *The End of the European Era* (New York, 1970), 36. The next line is "When closely examined, historical events and developments almost invariably reveal aspects which are individual and unique."

United States, with Beard, Arthur Schlesinger, Sr., Arthur Cole, and Herbert Heaton.[40] In his *Grosse Depression*, Hans Rosenberg warmly praised the scholarship of Alvin Hansen, Wesley Mitchell, and Simon Kuznets – all Americans who had published earlier works on business cycles. The application of the theory of alternating waves to German history was novel, but many attempts had already been made to apply it to American history. As early as 1912, James Harvey Robinson, the prominent Columbia University historian who had a Ph.D. from Freiburg, had called for a new social science history in which advances in anthropology, economics, psychology, and sociology would be incorporated into the writing of history. He suggested that it was time to change *wie es eigentlich gewesen* to *wie es eigentlich geworden ist*.[41] While many of the émigrés rebelled against their conservative training, the nature of the revolt was determined by the orthodoxy of the older generation. Rebels also, then as now, understood that there were few vocational options for them in a small historical guild that amounted *in toto* to about one hundred fifty positions.

There is one notable exception – one area of history in which the Central European contribution was and is enormous: the study of Renaissance Italy. In 1983, Gene Brucker wrote a review essay in the *American Historical Review*. He began with the assertion "Since World War II the historiography of Italian city states in the late medieval and Renaissance periods has been dominated by foreigners, particularly by English and American historians. . . . No obvious connection can be drawn between the tradition of prewar scholarship, which was predominantly German and Italian, and the Anglo-American monopoly since 1945"[42] Gilbert, in his memoirs, recounts his surprise at the lack of serious attention paid to Renaissance Italy by British and American scholars in the thirties and forties.[43] The

---

40 Charles Beard, *An Economic Interpretation of the Constitution* (New York, 1913). Also by Beard see *The Economic Basis of Politics* (New York, 1922); Arthur M. Schlesinger, *The Colonial Merchants and the American Revolution, 1763–1776* (New York, 1918); Herbert Heaton, *Yorkshire Woollen and Worsted Industries* (Oxford, 1920), and *Economic History of Europe* (New York, 1936); Arthur H. Cole and W. Smith, *Fluctuations in American Business, 1790–1860* (Cambridge, Mass., 1935); and Cole, *Wholesale Commodity Prices in the United States, 1700–1861* (Cambridge, Mass., 1938).

41 James Harvey Robinson, *The New History* (New York, 1912), 62. Among the disciplines that Robinson felt the historian ought to be conversant with were anthropology, sociology, political economy, comparative religion, social psychology, animal psychology, geography, and climatology.

42 Gene Brucker, "Tales of Two Cities: Florence and Venice in the Renaissance," *American Historical Review* 88: 3 (June 1983): 599–616.

43 Felix Gilbert, *A European Past*, 172.

sharp change noted by Brucker coincided with the intellectual migration from Central Europe.

Renaissance scholarship had a long and noble tradition in Central Europe. Indeed, to some extent the very concept of the Renaissance was a product of the German historical imagination. So many volumes on this subject appeared in Imperial Germany that F. F. Baumgarten coined the term *Renaissancismus* in 1917. Among the names that immediately come to mind are those of Burckhardt, Dilthey, Goetz, von Martin, Brandi, and von Pastor.[44] But studies of the Renaissance did not come solely from the pens of historians. The art historians Wölfflin, Worringer, and Panofsky and the philosophers Cassirer and Kristeller had all made significant contributions to the study of Italy in the *Quattrocento*. Disciplinary boundaries fell by the wayside in Renaissance scholarship, and that may be the key to *Renaissancismus* American-style. The reigning icon of Renaissance studies was Burckhardt – a dissenter from the historicist tradition – rather than Ranke, its founder. It should not be forgotten that Meinecke, in his last public lecture in 1948, at the age of eighty-four, wondered, to his credit, whether German scholars had paid too much attention to Ranke and too little to Burckhardt.[45]

The primacy of Anglo-Saxon scholarship is due to the combined emigration of philosophers, art historians, and two notable historians, Hans Baron and Felix Gilbert. Baron's *Crisis of the Early Italian Renaissance* (1955) and Gilbert's *Machiavelli and Guicciardini* (1965) were two landmark works that stirred great interest in early Italian history when they appeared. Both are studies in intellectual history that show the marked influence of Dilthey. They both go beyond Meinecke in seeking to place their subjects in the specific culture and events of contemporary Florentine history. Unlike American intellectual historians, with their emphasis on unit ideas, both Baron and Gilbert use a biographical approach and emphasize the evolution of ideas over time. These two works were read, re-read, and discussed. They kindled a new interest in civic humanism and Renaissance historiography.

44 On the German tradition of Renaissance scholarship, see Wallace K. Ferguson, *The Renaissance in Historical Thought* (Boston, 1948). Also Hans Baron, *The Crisis of the Early Italian Renaissance*, 2 vols. (Princeton, 1955). Baron's was one of the two most impressive books that I read in graduate school, the other being Perry Miller's previously mentioned book on the New England mind.
45 Friedrich Meinecke, *Ranke und Burckhardt*, Vorträge und Schriften der Deutsche Akademie der Wissenschaften zu Berlin, no. 27 (Berlin, 1948).

Cassirer and Panofsky were associated with the Warburg Institute in Hamburg. Aby Warburg himself had been a student of the cultural historian Karl Lamprecht, whose methods aroused the ire of orthodox German historians in the 1890s. The library that Cassirer and Panofsky worked in was not arranged according to disciplinary boundaries.[46] Much of the intellectual vitality in Weimar flourished in institutes where experimentation and iconoclasm were the norm. Thus, apart from the specific study of the history of Germany, the major impact of the émigré historians may have been in Renaissance studies, where their training in *Geistesgeschichte*, their skill in paleography, and the model of Burckhardt, who eschewed chronology in his magnum opus, meshed neatly with the approaches of humanist scholars who were zeroing in on northern Italy from other disciplines that were more comfortable with theory. The combination was and is a fruitful one.

Goethe begins his poem "Den Vereinigten Staaten" (The United States), written in 1827, with the lines "Amerika, Du hast es besser als unser Kontinent, das alte, hast keine verfallene Schlösser und keine Basalte." The émigrés did indeed find life better on this side of the Atlantic, and they served to introduce several generations of young Americans, including me, to the *verfallene Schlösser* and *Basalte* that we lacked.

---

46 On Lamprecht, see Georg Iggers, *The German Conception of History*. On the Warburg Institute, see the Yale dissertation of Carl Landauer, "The Survival of Antiquity: The German Years of the Warburg Institute" (1984).

12

The Americanization of Hajo Holborn

OTTO P. PFLANZE

Hajo Holborn was born in 1902 in Charlottenburg, a suburb of Berlin, to an academic family of Frisian-Hanoverian origin. He studied at the University of Berlin under Friedrich Meinecke, Karl Holl, Adolf von Harnack, and Ernst Troeltsch. His progress in the German historical profession can only be described as meteoric. He received the Ph.D. in 1924 with a dissertation entitled "Deutschland und die Türkei, 1878–1890," subsequently published in 1926. *Habilitation* came in 1930 with the publication of his study *Ulrich von Hutten*. Meanwhile other publications had appeared: He edited *Aufzeichnungen und Erinnerungen* of Josef Maria von Radowitz (2 vols.) and wrote *Bismarcks Europäische Politik zu Beginn der siebziger Jahre und die Mission Radowitz* and also produced various essays on Hutten and modern diplomatic history. His journeyman years as university lecturer were spent at Heidelberg (1926–31). In 1931 Holborn was appointed Carnegie Professor of History and International Relations at the Deutsche Hochschule für Politik in Berlin and, simultaneously, to a lectureship in history at the University of Berlin. He was only twenty-nine.[1]

The Hochschule für Politik appointment was extraordinary, to say the least. Holborn became the first permanent occupant of a new chair endowed by the Carnegie Foundation at a German institute founded in 1920 for the study of international relations. In announcing the appointment, the *Vossische Zeitung* reported, "Holborn is one of our youngest and most promising historians."[2] But not everyone applauded. Evidently the appointment aroused a feeling of resent-

I thank Frederick Holborn and Karen Greenberg for their assistance on some factual details in the writing of this essay. Unless otherwise indicated, all translations are by the author.
1 For Holborn's bibliography, see "Hajo Holborn's Works," *Central European History* 3 (1970):176–86, and "Bibliography: Hajo Holborn," in Inter Nationes, ed., *Hajo Holborn, Inter Nationes Prize 1969* (Bad Godesberg, 1969), 182–6.
2 Hajo Holborn Papers, Manuscripts and Archives, Yale University Library.

ment among some of Holborn's peers that neither the passage of time nor his subsequent achievements fully dissipated. The attitude is still evident in a memoir that Alfred Vagts wrote for inclusion – apparently unsolicited – in Holborn's papers at Yale after his death: "Among historians before 1933 he was considered something of a *Wunderkind* and also careerist, having found in Friedrich Meinecke a powerful protector in academic politics."[3]

Holborn's political orientation was that of a democratic liberal,[4] which put him out of step with most other German historians. In Weimar's superheated political environment, political commitment and historical interpretation were closely linked. In 1931, the year he was called to Berlin, Holborn published in *Historische Zeitschrift* a scorching indictment of the German historical profession.

The profound transformations experienced in all areas of intellectual, political, and social life as a consequence of the world war have as yet scarcely touched the core of scholarly historical studies. The influence of old academic traditions and institutions has had the effect of making criticism of the customary methods, directions, and objectives of historical research and writing extremely rare. More frequently expressed, perhaps, is a certain pride in how few of our inherited ideals have to be sacrificed. To swim against the stream of time could be taken as heroism. Insofar as these inclinations amount to a kind of professional "Nibelungen loyalty," which is basically just self-satisfaction, they can be seen as symptomatic of a lack of scholarly awareness and of a methodological thoughtlessness that threaten to be dangerous to our craft.[5]

As the denouement of 1933 approached, Holborn spoke out in the forums open to him. At Leipzig, on October 25, 1932, he delivered an address to the Weimar Kreis der Deutschen Hochschullehrer in which he declared that only a free state (*freier Rechtsstaat*) could guarantee free scholarship. "Both are today exposed to the greatest danger." Disenchanted with Weimar's multiparty system, more than half of the German population had become advocates of a one-party state, whether in the form of a class or classless dictatorship. The inadequacies they saw in the structure and practice of Weimar politics, Holborn explained, were historically conditioned. Bismarck's "balance system" had consigned German political parties to a nega-

3 "Memoir by Alfred Vagts – 1976?" Holborn Papers.
4 Historically this political position, once called *Linksliberalismus*, or *entschiedener Liberalismus*, implied no specific party affiliation. Frederick Holborn recalls that his father voted for the Social Democratic party in Prussian, but not in national, elections.
5 "Protestantismus und Politische Ideengeschichte, Kritische Bemerkungen aus Anlass des Buches von O. Westphal 'Feinde Bismarcks,' " *Historische Zeitschrift* 144 (1931):15–30.

tive role in the governmental process that had left them unprepared for the assumption of power in 1918. Twelve years of experience with parliamentary government during the Weimar period had not sufficed to overcome the effects of a historical development that had lasted three-quarters of a century. Apparently the presidential dictatorship of Franz von Papen was bent upon restoring the "old authoritarian state" that had failed to train political parties for the responsibility of governing. The Papen regime could justify itself, Holborn warned, only by preparing the way, through constitutional reform, for a resumption of parliamentary democracy in more effective form.[6] This contention was both courageous and rare among German historians at the time. The German academic profession in general had few supporters of parliamentary democracy during the Weimar period.[7]

The Nazi assumption of power in March 1933 made Holborn's position in Germany untenable. He left the country at the end of the summer semester, ostensibly on leave but actually to seek employment abroad. His subsequent dismissals from the Hochschule für Politik and the University of Berlin were superfluous. He had already committed himself and had no intention of returning to Germany.

When he took the train for London, Holborn left his wife Annemarie and two children, Hanna and Friedrich, behind in Charlottenburg. He was fortunate financially in that the Carnegie Foundation continued to pay his salary. His only hope of continuing his academic career lay not in Britain but in the United States. From September 1933 until February 1934, Holborn marked time in London, striving to perfect his command of spoken English and afflicted by the inevitable fear of exile with an uncertain future. On January 31, 1934, he discussed his situation with the director of the Emergency Committee in Aid of Displaced Foreign Scholars, then in London, and afterward reported to Vagts that he would soon sail to New York in search of a position. "In private," he added, "I fear – without, of course, being able to prove it in any way – that I will experience

---

6 *Weimarer Reichsverfassung und Freiheit der Wissenschaft* (Leipzig, 1933), in the series Neues Deutschland, 32 pages; see also "Historische Voraussetzungen der weimarer Verfassung und ihrer Reform," *Reichsverwaltungsblatt und Preussisches Verwaltungsblatt* 53 (1932):921–24, and "Die geschichtlichen Grundlagen der deutschen Verfassungspolitik und Reichsreform," *Deutsche Juristenzeitung* 38 (January, 1933):3–8.
7 "Holborn belonged to the few convinced supporters of parliamentary government among historians." Bernd Faulenbach, *Ideologie des deutschen Weges. Die deutsche Geschichte in der Historiographie zwischen Kaiserreich und Nationalsozialismus* (Munich, 1980), 264.

from that side [Carnegie Foundation and Emergency Committee] more good advice than assistance." And so he sought help from Vagts and Charles A. Beard, Vagt's father-in-law. "Naturally, I am as good as completely ignorant about American conditions and hence would be most grateful to you for any advice." According to Vagts, there was little that either could do to help him.[8]

On February 27, Holborn reached New York, after a fierce storm in the Atlantic that caused his liner, the *Majestic*, to collide with the Nantucket lightship, an event that must have accentuated the *Götterdämmerung* mood of the émigré. But the sun shone brighter on the western side of the Atlantic. At the end of March he was invited to Harvard for an interview, reporting back to Vagts that he had gotten on well with Sidney Fay but not at all with William L. Langer. "Personally I couldn't get off the ground with him." In May he enjoyed a pleasant week at Yale. "Everyone was truly charming to me." Without waiting for Harvard to act, he accepted Yale's offer – a two-year visiting assistant professorship. One-half of his salary was paid by the Rockefeller Foundation.[9]

Holborn's subsequent career in the United States can be summarized briefly: promoted to associate professor at Yale, 1938; to full professor, 1940; to Townsend Professor, 1948; to Sterling Professor, 1959. From 1936 to 1942 he held a concurrent professorship at the Fletcher School of Law and Diplomacy. During the war he took leave from Yale to serve in the Research and Analysis Branch of the Office of Strategic Services (1943–5); for three critical years (1946–8) after his return to the university he was a consultant to Gen. John Hilldring, assistant secretary of state, charged with the formulation and coordination of American policy in the occupied areas of Germany and Japan. Over the years he was a guest professor at numerous universities (among them Harvard, Stanford, Columbia, and Vienna), received honorary degrees from the University of Chicago and the Free University of Berlin, and was given two decorations (elevating him to the Knight Commander's Cross) by the West German government. In 1967 Holborn's status in the historical profession was recognized by his election to the presidency of the American Historical Association, making him one of only two foreign-born and -educated scholars to be accorded that honor.

Undoubtedly his displacement to the United States exacted a

8 Holborn to Alfred Vagts, February 5, 1934 (2 letters). Holborn Papers.
9 Holborn to Vagts, April 3 and 30 and May 21, 1934. Holborn Papers.

heavy toll on Holborn the scholar. In 1929 he had been selected by the Historische Reichskommission to write a history of the origins of the Weimar constitution, a project for which he was given free access to government archives. Several published essays testify to his progress on the project by 1933. Today the manuscript division of the Yale University library possesses an extensive collection of papers – notes, manuscripts, pamphlets, committee minutes, and other papers dealing with the drafting of the constitution and other contemporaneous events – that his wife, Annemarie, brought out with family possessions in late 1934. But Holborn appears to have done no serious work on the project in America. A work that might have strengthened the Weimar republic by clarifying the motives and purposes of its founders no longer seemed so pressing after the republic's collapse. The books he wrote in the immediate postwar years dealt with other subjects: *American Military Government: Its Organization and Policies* (1947) and *The Political Collapse of Europe* (1951). But he also published in this period many illuminating essays on diplomatic, military, and intellectual history, particularly on the philosophy of history, a subject of enduring interest for him since his student days. About 1950 Holborn began what was to become his magnum opus, *A History of Modern Germany*, in three volumes (1959–69).

From my observation, the greatest influences on Holborn as a historian were Ranke and Dilthey – Meinecke only secondarily. What Holborn saw in Ranke (and in a few respects, also in Thucydides) was, first, not the founder of what has ambiguously come to be called "scientific history" but rather the historian of scientific temperament, guided more by the spirit – and ethic – of objective inquiry than by any putative scientific method; and, second, the universal historian, to whom German history was inseparable from European history as a whole. What he saw in Dilthey was the earnest, inventive, yet failed searcher for a critique of historical reason capable of bridging the gulf between subjective and objective through the discovery of the "I in the thou"; or, more precisely, the humanistic philosopher, to whom the breadth and intensity of personal experience and commitment in contemporary life provide significant clues for an understanding of past human conduct.[10]

10 See "The Science of History," in Joseph R. Strayer, ed., *The Interpretation of History* (Princeton, 1943), 59–83; "History and the Humanities," *Journal of the History of Ideas* 9 (1948):65–9; "Wilhelm Dilthey and the Critique of Historical Reason," *Journal of the History of Ideas* 11 (1950):93–118; "The History of Ideas," *American Historical Review* 73 (1968):683–95; introduction to *History of Modern Germany*, 3 vols. (New York, 1959–69), 1:vii–xii.

The influence of Meinecke on Holborn was, I judge, more personal than philosophical. Like so many others, Holborn was impressed by Meinecke's command of the history of ideas and valued the inspiration and training he received in Meinecke's seminar. And yet Holborn's works do not bear the imprint of Meinecke's style of intellectual history, either in form or content. When Holborn wrote in 1968 of Dilthey as "the greatest historian of ideas," he obviously intended to place Meinecke on a lower plane.[11] Holborn advanced beyond both Dilthey and Meinecke methodologically, however, in his appreciation of the necessity for relating the history of ideas to social history within the context of general history. The essay he published in the Meinecke *Festschrift* of 1953 on the social foundations of German idealism demonstrates the point. Meinecke wrote in the tradition of German idealism, depicting the migration and evolution of ideas as autonomous forces in history; Holborn reinterpreted German idealism in the light of its social foundations, gaining thereby a better understanding of its political limitations.[12] "Social history," he once wrote, "is the necessary complement to the history of ideas."[13] Any careful examination of his history of Germany will show how important that orientation was to Holborn. There he extended his approach to the entire range of German history, from the Reformation to the present.

Holborn had a strong impact upon his American students and, beyond that, a widespread influence on the American profession at large. What we saw was a quiet, amiable man with a cavernous memory, penetrating intellect, wide learning, and balanced judgment – all of this with no hint of personal or intellectual arrogance. Vagts held it against Holborn that he did not recognize the "brilliance" of fellow émigré Eckart Kehr. I never heard Holborn discuss

The journal essays were republished in Hajo Holborn, *History and the Humanities* (New York, 1972). Leonard Krieger's introduction to this volume is the best synthesis of Holborn's historical thought. Holborn's interest in the philosophy of history led him back, in the 1940s, to the Greeks, producing illuminating essays on Thucydides and his influence on Ranke. See "History and the Study of the Classics," "Introducing Thucydides," and "Greek and Modern Concepts of History," in *History and the Humanities*, 11–74.

11 "History of Ideas," 689.

12 "Der deutsche Idealismus in sozial-geschichtlicher Beleuchtung," *Historische Zeitschrift*, 174 (1952):359–84. See also "The Social Basis of the German Reformation," in *History and the Humanities*, 168–78. Holborn and Meinecke conferred at Basel in 1938 and resumed their relationship after 1945, but Holborn publicly contested the view that his former teacher advanced in a U.S.-sponsored journal – that the Bismarckian *Machtstaat* had been a geopolitical necessity for Germany. Friedrich Meinecke, "Irrwege in unserer Geschichte?" *Der Monat* 2 (1949–50):3–6, with replies by Holborn and Geoffrey Barraclough, 531–8.

13 "History of Ideas," 692.

Kehr, but Frederick Holborn relates that Kehr's *Schlachtflottenbau* was the first historical work in German that his father urged him to read. Kehr's iconoclasm must certainly have appealed to the author of the *Historische Zeitschrift* article of 1931,[14] but Kehr's polemicism was alien to Holborn's personal and scholarly temperament, and I doubt that it appealed to him.

In June 1934 Meinecke responded to the news of Holborn's appointment at Yale with great relief.

God be praised that you have now found a safe harbor. But you are right . . . that an abyss lies behind you that will take a lifetime to overcome. I have confidence that you possess the inner elasticity to do justice to all of the internal and external demands of your new existence, and the seedlings of German scholarship that you transplant over there will soon bear fruit. And your heart will remain German above all, and it is also in the German character to spin spiritual threads between different nations and cultures. [15]

Holborn made the transition from Germany to America with surprising ease and completeness. In Roosevelt's New Deal he found an effective political leadership and an agenda for social reform within the democratic process that corresponded to his own political convictions. He adapted quickly to the demands of the American teaching and scholarly profession. Holborn was not given to disparaging comparisons of the American and German educational systems or, for that matter, of American and German culture in general. I saw no evidence in his courses, which ranged far beyond German history, that he regarded himself as a missionary for German *Wissenschaft* on American soil. On the contrary, his American experience influenced his views on Germany. "My transformation into an American," he wrote in the introduction to his *History of Modern Germany*, "has given me a much broader perspective on all things German."[16]

In accepting the Inter Nationes Prize in 1969, he remarked, "The question of the relation between law and power has occupied me throughout my career." It was the German conception of historical or organic law and the French and Anglo-Saxon conception of natu-

---

14 Holborn once told me that it was on his insistence ("If you don't, I will") that Egmont Zechlin published documents he had found in state archives revealing the extent of the planning in 1890–4 for a coup against the German constitution. See Egmont Zechlin, *Staatsstreichpläne Bismarcks und Wilhelms II. 1890–1894* (Stuttgart, 1929).

15 Meinecke to Holborn, June 12, 1934, in Friedrich Meinecke, *Werke*, 7 vols., ed. Hans Herzfeld, Carl Hinrichs and Walter Hofer (Stuttgart, 1957–68). vol. 6, *Ausgewählter Briefwechsel*, 143–4.

16 *History of Modern Germany*, 1:x.

ral law – and the virtues and shortcomings of each in legitimizing the use of power – that absorbed him. "For me the pure formulation is not enough; implementation in action is the only respectable thing to do with philosophical problems. . . . In such matters, looking backward, I see no real difference between my life in Germany and in America." As a young man he had told himself that once he had gained a measure of security in his profession he would get involved politically. "The year 1933 saw to it that this political commitment came to me, and it has never since left me. In that sense, I only kept doing what I started out to do."[17]

In 1946 Meinecke expressed the hope that Holborn would return to Germany to assist in rebuilding the historical profession. But Holborn had to respond that his experiences on this side of the Atlantic had converted him into an American.[18] He had no desire to abandon the satisfying position he had achieved in American academic and public life. At the time, in fact, he had reached a new level of political involvement. As adviser to the State Department on occupation affairs, he had an important role in the formation and execution of postwar American policy toward Germany.

In what ways Holborn may have influenced the American occupation of Germany, during those frequent three-hour lunches with General Hilldring, is impossible to say without further research. But Holborn does appear to have advocated, in the era of the "Morgenthau plan," a more realistic and humane policy than some in government service were inclined to promote. After lunch in New Haven one day (was it early 1948 or late 1949?), when I was still a graduate student, Holborn startled me by asking whether I could think of any good candidate for the new post of U.S. high commissioner in West Germany. I could not – and lost my chance to influence the course of German history. The candidate whom Holborn had in mind at the moment, it turned out, was Ellis Arnall. Arnall had achieved national recognition as an able governor of Georgia. A Southerner, Holborn explained, would know how to govern a conquered people with understanding and compassion. The appointment ultimately went to John J. McCloy, who certainly fulfilled Holborn's expectations.

During the first years of the Bonn republic, Holborn also per-

17 "Response and Acceptance," *Inter Nationes Prize*, 19–21.
18 Meinecke to Holborn, March 19 and December 1, 1946, in Meinecke, *Briefwechsel*, 247, 262–3.

formed an unofficial mediatory role between Bonn and Washington on several visits to both cities, capitalizing on personal contacts, both old and new, within the West German government and reaching out to prominent figures in the major political parties. His early experiences under the Weimar republic had left him deeply skeptical about the stability and durability of the Bonn system. I remember discussing with him in 1959 the merits of a book by journalist Fritz Alleman, *Bonn ist nicht Weimar* (1956), whose thesis is evident from the title. He found the work "too optimistic." In 1961 Holborn organized a colloquium in which twelve Yale professors met with their counterparts in the social sciences at Munich, and he came away reassured. "The war is over," he told Frederick Holborn.

In June 1969, Holborn, shortly after his sixty-seventh birthday, undertook a trip to Germany. Although only recently recovered from a severe illness, he wished to participate in the annual meeting at Bonn of the advisory board to the series Documents on German Foreign Policy, of which he had been a member since 1946. Shortly before takeoff at Kennedy Airport, a representative of Alfred Knopf at Random House arrived to present him with the first copy off the press of the third and final volume of his *History of Modern Germany*. On June 19, the twentieth anniversary of the founding of the Federal Republic of Germany, Holborn received the first Inter Nationes Prize. This award was designed by the organization's members to "distinguish a man or a woman whose lifetime has linked the world's peoples more closely together in deeper mutual understanding."[19] During the night that followed his acceptance speech, Holborn died peacefully in his sleep.[20] It was what Germans call "ein schönes Tod."

Holborn lives on in my memory as an irenic scholar vitally interested in contemporary affairs. He was generous and open-minded toward people of other convictions, yet firm in the expression of his own. His democratic social and political beliefs were grounded in an instinctive humanism, informed and fortified by his historical researches. From classical humanism, the Italian humanists of the Renaissance, the Christian humanists of northern Europe (with his wife he edited the Christian philosophical works of Erasmus), and

19 Günter Diehl, "Bestowal of 1969 Inter Nationes Prize," in *Inter Nationes Prize*, 17–18.
20 Death prevented Holborn from completing two projects that he had contemplated for many years: a study in the philosophy of history that would have incorporated and extended the many articles he had written on this subject, and a volume tentatively titled "The United States and Germany," commissioned for the American Foreign Policy Library series.

the humanistic side of German idealism came the influences that molded his attitude toward his profession and toward life itself. Holborn could not fulfill Meinecke's hope of 1934 that he would remain "a German at heart." (Personally I doubt that he would ever have expressed himself in that way at any time in his life.) The human values he cherished were exclusive neither to Germany nor America. They transcended national frontiers. To those who knew him well, who studied under him, who worked with him, and who turned to him for advice, he demonstrated in his person the civilizing effect that can be derived from the study of history by those who know how to evaluate what they read.

13

Explaining History: Hans Rosenberg

HANNA SCHISSLER

In the works which consider refugee historians, Hans Rosenberg usually commands special attention. From the very beginning of his career he belonged to that illustrious group, the students of Friedrich Meinecke. Later in his career he was honored with two *Festschriften* in West Germany, one edited by Gerhard A. Ritter in 1970, the other edited by Hans-Ulrich Wehler in 1974.[1] The authors who have contributed to these commemorative volumes and who have been influenced by Hans Rosenberg in one way or another constitute an outstanding group of scholars in their own countries. They hold chairs mainly in the United States and West Germany but also in Israel, Canada, and Austria.

In this essay I will comment briefly upon three subjects: I shall consider, first, major aspects of Rosenberg's scholarly work; second, his position as a German-American refugee historian; and third, Hans Rosenberg as teacher and mentor of younger colleagues and students.

From its beginnings in the Meinecke school, Rosenberg's intellectual path toward the kind of social history for which he became well known was long and adventurous.[2] Even in his early works on

I thank Catherine Epstein for her help with the English in this chapter and Kenneth Ledford for editorial help.

Unless otherwise indicated, all translations are by the author.

1 Gerhard A. Ritter, ed., *Entstehung und Wandel der modernen Gesellschaft. Festschrift für Hans Rosenberg zum 65. Geburtstag* (Berlin, 1970); Hans-Ulrich Wehler, ed., *Sozialgeschichte Heute. Festschrift für Hans Rosenberg zum 70. Geburtstag* (Göttingen, 1974).

2 See Rosenberg's own retrospective on his professional life, given when he received an honorary doctorate at the University of Bielefeld in 1977: "Rückblick auf ein Historikerleben zwischen zwei Kulturen," in Wehler, ed., *Sozialgeschichte*, 11–23; his intellectual and personal development is best described by Wehler in the preface to the same work, 9–21; and Heinrich-August Winkler, "Ein Erneuerer der Geschichtswissenschaft. Hans Rosenberg 1904–1988," *Historische Zeitschrift* 248 (1989):529–55; on his being driven out of the University of Cologne and his final refusal to return to Cologne after the war, see Otto Dann, "Hans Rosenberg und die Universität zu Köln. Ein Nachruf," *Kölner Universität Journal* 18

liberalism, he began to free himself from elitist views of *Geistesge-schichte* and take a more "democratic" view of history. Instead of focusing upon how ideas of liberalism influenced leading figures, he examined how group mentalities shaped historical events.[3]

In 1966 Barrington Moore published his book *Social Origins of Dictatorship and Democracy*, which traced the foundations of the social and political structure of twentieth-century societies back to their preindustrial, agrarian origins. At this time Hans Rosenberg's works on the Prussian bureaucracy and on the Junkers were still relatively unknown.[4] For years, Rosenberg had pointed to the power structures and social relations in Prussian agrarian society as a source of the undemocratic and authoritarian tendencies in German society. He had outlined the burden that the continued existence of the East-Elbian agrarian elite constituted for the process of democratization and industrialization of German society.

Following Max Weber and Otto Hintze, he showed the enormous importance of bureaucratic rule and pointed out the way in which social groups imposed their specific group interests by saturating the bureaucracy. More importantly, he also showed that the process of absorption into the bureaucracy, in turn, had the capacity to trans-form those particular group interests and at times allowed the emer-gence of a specific professional ethos within the state bureaucracy. Rosenberg's most famous expressions of these themes are his article "Pseudodemocratization of the Prussian Junkers" and his books *Bu-reaucracy, Aristocracy, and Autocracy in Prussia* and *Grosse Depression und*

(1988):13–15. On Rosenberg's personality and intellectual profile, compare also Kenneth Barkin's contribution to this volume (Chapter 11) and Gerhard A. Ritter, "Hans Rosenberg, 1904–1988," *Geschichte und Gesellschaft* 15 (1989):282–302.

3 *Rudolf Haym und die Anfänge des klassischen Liberalismus* (Munich, 1933) and his collected essays from the years 1927–30, *Politische Denkströmungen im deutschen Vormärz* (Göttingen, 1972).

4 *Bureaucracy, Aristocracy and Autocracy: The Prussian Experience, 1660–1815* (Cambridge, Mass., 1958; reprint, 1966, 1968; paperback ed.: Boston, 1968); "Die Demokratisierung der Ritter-gutsbesitzerklasse," in Withelm Berges, ed., *Festgabe für Hans Herzfeld* (Berlin, 1958), 459–86, revised under the title "Die Pseudodemokratisierung der Rittergutsbesitzerklasse," in Hans Rosenberg, *Probleme der deutschen Sozialgeschichte* (Frankfurt, 1969), 7–49; also in Hans Rosenberg, *Machteliten und Wirtschaftskonjunkturen* (Göttingen, 1978), 83–101; available in English as "The Pseudo-Democratization of the Junker Class," in Georg Iggers, ed., *The Social History of Politics* (Leamington Spa, U.K., 1985), 81–112; compare also Rosenberg, "Deutsche Agrargeschichte in alter und neuer Sicht," in idem, *Probleme*, 81–147; also in idem, *Machteliten*, 118–49; Rosenberg, "Zur sozialen Funktion der Agrarpolitik im Zweiten Reich," *Probleme*, 51–80, and *Machteliten*, 102–17; Rosenberg, "The Rise of the Junkers in Brandenburg-Prussia, 1410–1653," *American Historical Review* 49 (1943):1–22, 228–42, re-vised as "Die Ausprägung der Junkerherrschaft in Brandenburg-Preussen, 1410–1418," *Machteliten*, 24–82.

Bismarckzeit.[5] Although Rosenberg always stressed political and social responsibility in history, he was also aware of structures and forces in history which were not easily shaped or even understood by individuals. *Grosse Depression und Bismarckzeit* and his previous works concerning economic influences upon political decision making reflect this awareness.[6] But Rosenberg thought that it was the responsibility of the historian not merely to describe but to explain historical developments by looking beyond the motives and intentions of the actors.

In analyzing twentieth-century German history, Rosenberg never sought refuge in the helplessness of the "great catastrophe" – the dominant explanation advanced by the *Historikerzunft* after 1945 – but instead insisted that there were understandable explanations to be found in group interests and in specific political, economic, and social structures for what had happened.[7] Instead of expanding upon prevailing vague historical explanations, he helped to create categories which clearly distinguished causes and effects in history. Although Rosenberg used the term "totalitarianism" in the 1950s, he was not content with notions such as the idea that the masses simply "fell for" Hitler. His scholarly work contributed to avoiding the pitfalls of the dominant historiographic approach, an approach produced by historians who threw up their hands, in helplessness and despair, after 1945.[8] In retrospect, the audacity of Rosenberg's theses and his new approaches, his willingness to learn from related disciplines, his incorruptibility, and his frankness are all striking, although his analyses were initially questioned by the majority of historians.[9]

5 Hans Rosenberg, *Grosse Depression und Bismarckzeit. Wirtschaftsablauf, Gesellschaft und Politik in Mitteleuropa* (Berlin, 1967); for the other titles, see n. 4, this chapter.

6 See *Die Weltwirtschaftskrise von 1857–1859* (Stuttgart, 1934; reprint: Göttingen, 1974); "Die zoll- und handelspolitischen Auswirkungen der Weltwirtschaftskrisis, 1857–1859," *Weltwirtschaftliches Archiv* 38 (1933):368–83 (also *Machteliten*, 150–60); Rosenberg, "Political and Social Consequences of the Great Depression of 1873–1896 in Central Europe," *Economic History Review* 13 (1943):58–73; also *Machteliten*, 161–72; Rosenberg, "Wirtschaftskonjunktur, Gesellschaft und Politik in Mitteleuropa, 1873–1896," *Machteliten*, 173–97.

7 Compare the passages on Rosenberg in Volker Berghahn, "Deutschlandbilder 1945–1965. Angloamerikanische Historiker und moderne deutsche Geschichte," in Ernst Schulin, ed., *Deutsche Geschichtswissenschaft nach dem Zweiten Weltkrieg (1945–1965)* (Munich, 1969), 239–72.

8 This is especially true of Friedrich Meinecke's *Die deutsche Katastrophe*, which first appeared in Germany in 1946 and was translated into English as *The German Catastrophe* (Cambridge, Mass., 1950).

9 Berghahn shows that Rosenberg was criticized not only by his conservative German colleagues but also by his American colleagues. Berghahn explicitly refers to criticism by Fritz Stern and Gordon Craig, "Deutschlandbilder," 271–2. On the historiographic situation in Germany, compare Georg G. Iggers, *The German Conception of History: The National Tradition*

Some critics strongly reproached Rosenberg for his willingness to draw political conclusions from history. Gerhard Ritter succeeded in preventing the publication of a German translation of *Bureaucracy, Aristocracy, and Autocracy*.[10] Rosenberg remained convinced that it was the task of historians living through contemporary twentieth-century history to face the consequences of historical developments and to question historiographic traditions and viewpoints.

For a historical researcher . . . there are . . . certain intersections of development which call and oblige him to the service of the historical, political, and moral clarification of consciousness, to take a clear and unmistakable position with regard to the real facts which he has verified and to the historical pictures and legends that are bound up with them. Despite desperate efforts and endless discussions, there has been as yet not a single successful theoretical attempt to draw an incontestable dividing line between objectivity and partisanship . . . in the humanities. I do not hesitate to confess that I, in any case, am not inclined to confuse historical objectivity with indifference, agnostic neutrality, or refusal to make a judgment.[11]

This quotation illustrates very precisely his scholarly ethos as well as his attitude toward the political responsibilities of scholarly work. That same ethos and attitude affected how Rosenberg adapted to his new homeland.

Franz Neumann distinguished three ways in which intellectuals dealt with the fate of forced emigration. He distinguished among those who abandoned their previously held national positions, trying to adapt as fast as possible to the new circumstances of their lives, in part by adopting the intellectual framework of their host countries; those who attempted to cling to their previously held convictions under all circumstances, either trying to be missionaries or withdrawing from the American intellectual scene with contempt; and finally those who attempted to integrate old and new experiences intellectually. This last position was the most difficult but also the most rewarding one.[12] It was always fascinating to see how Hans Rosenberg met the challenge of reconciling his German academic training with the demands of being an American professor obliged to explain German history to American students. Rosenberg had been socialized within the German university and even after many

of Historical Thought from Herder to the Present, rev. ed. (Middletown, Conn., 1983), 229–68, esp. 253.

10 Berghahn, "Deutschlandbilder," 244; Wehler, *Vorwort*, 17; Winkler, "Ein Erneuerer," 544.
11 *Rutckblick*, 19.
12 Lewis A. Coser, *Refugee Scholars in America: Their Impact and Their Experiences* (New Haven, 1984), 12.

years of living and teaching in the United States still displayed many of the typical traits of a German professor. But he was also very critical of certain characteristics of the German university system, especially its hierarchical structure, on which he placed the blame for much of the intellectual cowardice of German historians. He never learned to accept the help of a secretary, and he never had *Assistenten* in the sense of the German university system. He thus never enjoyed the narcissistic opportunities of having others work for him. He was very critical of his colleagues' habit of claiming all credit for themselves rather than giving due credit to others.[13]

Hans Rosenberg had an enormous impact, not only as a scholar who touched upon difficult and – for the time being – unrewarding topics, but also as a teacher. Many who have written about him argue that it was a shame that his energies were taken up by teaching undergraduates for twenty-three years at Brooklyn College and that he did not have a chance to work with graduate students earlier. Hans Rosenberg himself judged his teaching experiences at Brooklyn College much more favorably and said that it saved him from the intellectual provincialism of professional overspecialization.[14]

Rosenberg, who held the prestigious Shepard Chair at the University of California at Berkeley from 1959 to 1972, was very demanding as a teacher. His comments could be harsh and at times even discouraging. His critiques were stern and severe, and it was not always much of a consolation to his students that he applied the same relentless standards to his own research. Rosenberg would not give credit in advance but rather would judge a person with whom he decided to work according to what she or he had actually accomplished. He used to say awful things to his students, occasionally suggesting that their papers were total nonsense. If he respected the person involved, Rosenberg would then go on to say that were it not for this special respect, he would not even deign to criticize his or her work. Although this was perhaps a strange way to encourage young people, it was effective. Whoever worked with him had the feeling that he or she owed him much. And in this peculiar sense, Hans Rosenberg was a great mentor.[15]

The impact of his teaching for more than twenty years at Brooklyn College is difficult to trace. More obvious was the impact of his

13 This became most clear in personal conversations with Hans Rosenberg.
14 *Rückblick*, 17.
15 See also Barkin (this volume, Chapter 11) on this point.

guest professorships in Berlin and Marburg in 1949–50 and 1955, when he trained and influenced a whole group of German scholars who would later contribute decisively to changing German historiographic traditions and establishing new standards of historical research.[16] Hans-Ulrich Wehler has reclaimed Rosenberg as the father of modern *Gesellschaftsgeschichte* in Germany.[17]

In spite of the better-established tradition of social and economic history in the United States, Rosenberg remained an outsider in this country.[18] He was especially an outsider among the refugee historians, and he was the one who most decisively broke with the historiographic tradition in which great men were seen as decisive in the course of history – and ideas, difficult to describe, imposed themselves on the fate of humankind. As a social and economic historian, as a German-American scholar, and as a person who could never reconcile himself to what he thought was his inability to express himself adequately in either language,[19] Hans Rosenberg sat between all possible chairs, which may indeed be the only worthy place for a true intellectual.

Because of his Jewish origins, something which could not have been less important to him, Hans Rosenberg left his country in 1933. Helene Rosenberg, his wife, came with him. She was a pianist and gave up her career in Germany.[20] Rosenberg felt deeply obligated to the United States, the country that had offered him refuge after he was no longer allowed to teach in Cologne and had to leave Germany. After the war, he turned down a call to go back to the University of Cologne, not least because he was of the opinion that his professional colleagues in Germany had missed the chance to understand adequately the German past.[21] Rosenberg conceived of his life's

16 Compare Wolfgang J. Mommsen, "Gegenwärtige Tendenzen in der Geschichtsschreibung der Bundesrepublik," *Geschichte und Gesellschaft* 7 (1981):149–88; see also Mommsen's contribution of this volume (chapter 2).

17 Wehler, *Sozialgeschichte heute*, "Vorwort," 20.

18 Berghahn, "Deutschlandbilder," 270–2; Rosenberg's role as an economic historian is stressed by Gerald D. Feldman, "German Economic History," *Central European History* 19 (1986):174–85.

19 Eva Hoffmann provides fascinating insights into the process of acculturation and the difficulty of living in two languages in her autobiographic book *Lost in Translation: A Life in a New Language* (New York, 1989).

20 While Helene Rosenberg's role and her own sacrifices for the emigration of her husband are usually thoroughly neglected, Winkler, "Ein Erneuerer," pays her adequate attention.

21 The story of the attempts to bring Hans Rosenberg back to Cologne are mentioned in all biographical notes. How Rosenberg was driven out of Cologne University as a young lecturer and the fatal role that his Cologne colleagues played in this story is best told by Otto Dann, "Hans Rosenberg." Reasons for emigrants not returning to Germany are given

work as the passing on of his standards for the explanation of German history to young American, as well as to German, scholars. He felt that the United States was a better place to do this than Germany, where nationalistic views of the German past remained essentially unchallenged until the Fischer controversy.

What made him return to Germany in his old age? All of his friends advised him to stay in Berkeley, where he had spent the happiest years of his professional life, and where he enjoyed respect and friendship. It was definitely not homesickness or the wish to close the circle, at the end of his life, by returning to his homeland. As always, major decisions in life do not have one single reason. Among other reasons, Rosenberg felt much more at ease with West Germany during the social democratic–liberal coalition than under previous and subsequent governments. He enjoyed seeing that his way of looking at history had shaped part of German historiography during the 1960s and 1970s.[22] As important as these factors might have been, the decisive reason for his leaving the mild and always sunny Berkeley in exchange for a small village near Freiburg, where it does, after all, rain quite often, was personal.

When Helene decided to marry Hans Rosenberg, her very rich bourgeois family in Cologne disinherited her. When the Rosenbergs left the country and came, via England, Cuba, and Canada, to the United States, she worked as a cleaning woman to support both of them.[23] Hans returned to Germany because of his wife. "She came back with me when the Nazis drove me out of Germany, and I came back because of her." Helene Rosenberg felt much less at home in the United States than her husband and wanted to live near her son and grandchildren in Germany as she grew older. She also became more and more aware of the sacrifice of her own professional career and suffered from this sacrifice at a time when it could no longer be made good. She belonged to a generation of women who had much less choice than women today in whether they wished to pursue their own profession or give it up because of their husbands' needs. The fact that Hans was forced to emigrate did not make this aspect of her life any easier.[24]

by Iggers, *German Conception*, 270.

22 See the works of Gerhard A. Ritter, Gerhard Schulz, Hans-Ulrich Wehler, Volker Berghahn, Jürgen Kocka, Gustav Schmidt, Hans-Jürgen Puhle, Heinrich August Winkler, Reinhard Rürup, and Hartmut Kaelble; Otto Büsch was especially influenced by Rosenberg. See his *Militärsystem und Sozialleben im Alten Preussen* (Berlin, 1962).

23 Compare Sibylle Quack's contribution in this volume (Chapter 6). Her observations apply precisely to the Rosenbergs.

24 This became very clear in personal conversations with both Hans and Helene Rosenberg.

Given the time when Hans Rosenberg wrote his major contributions on the burning questions of German history, they were progressive and daring undertakings. He influenced many scholars who later picked up his initiatives in their approach to German history, not least by his example of openness to the incorporation of findings and methods from related disciplines. Well-known historians of Germany in the United States and West Germany have followed his lead. Students of Hans Rosenberg are proud of the influence that he exerted upon their scholarly work and on their views of history and social reality.[25] In particular, when it comes to criticizing major assumptions about the way social history conceptualizes social inequality, it is an invaluable asset to have received the historical training Rosenberg had to offer.

Until his old age, Hans Rosenberg maintained strong human and intellectual bonds. He was invited to the conference from which this volume arose, and when I last saw him he expressed deep joy that, with the establishment of the German Historical Institute in the United States, others could step into the role which he and other émigré historians had filled: connecting American and German historical scholarship. He died on June 26, 1988, at the age of eighty-four.

---

25 This also is true for the author of this article. My own work on Prussian history was strongly influenced by Rosenberg. See Hanna Schissler, *Preussische Agrargesellschaft im Wandel* (Göttingen, 1978); Schissler, "The Junkers: Notes on the Social and Historical Significance of the Agrarian Elite in Prussia," in Robert R. Moeller, ed., *Peasants and Lords in Modern Germany* (Boston, 1986), 24–51; Schissler, "Preussische Finanzpolitik 1806–1820," introduction to Eckart Kehr, *Preussische Finanzpolitik 1806–1810. Quellen zur Verwaltung der Ministerien Stein und Altenstein*, ed. Hanna Schissler and Hans-Ulrich Wehler (Göttingen, 1984), 13–64.

14

Ernst Kantorowicz
and Theodor E. Mommsen

ROBERT E. LERNER

Kantorowicz and Mommsen, "Eka" and "Ted," so different in so many ways, were nevertheless close friends and linked as two German émigré medievalists who both had a deep influence on the study of history in the United States. While the story of their friendship is well worth telling, there is no room for that here. Instead, I will treat some main features of their work in the Old World and the New and attempt to estimate how their New World careers helped enrich American scholarship.

Access to Ernst Kantorowicz's historiographic position before his emigration can be gained by viewing the *Mythenschau* controversy of 1929–30, probably the liveliest *Historikerstreit* of Weimar. Kantorowicz, who received his Ph.D. in 1921 in political economy (*Nationalökonomie*), was self-educated as a medieval historian, for he almost certainly never took a university course in the medieval field.[1] Thus

Support and splendid working environments were provided by the Institute for Advanced Study in Princeton and the Rockefeller Foundation Study Center in Bellagio. I am grateful to Dr. Eckhart Grünewald and Martha Ripley for reading the manuscript and saving me from error.

Unless otherwise indicated, all translations are by the author.

1 Where not otherwise specified, I draw for biographical data concerning Kantorowicz's preemigration career upon the indispensable monograph of Eckhart Grünewald, *Ernst Kantorowicz und Stefan George: Beiträge zur Biographie des Historikers bis zum Jahre 1938 und zu seinem Jugendwerk "Kaiser Friedrich der Zweite"* (Wiesbaden, 1982), hereafter *Grünewald*. In lieu of narrative, the following data may be offered. *1895*: born in Posen / Poznan of wealthy Jewish family engaged in liquor manufacturing. *1913–14: Abitur*, training for career in family firm. *1914–18*: wartime military service – Iron Cross, Second Class (1915), wounded at Verdun (1916), attaché to Turkish railway-repair unit in Asia Minor and Syria (1917). *1919* (winter and spring): free-corps fighter against Poles in Poznan, Spartacists in Berlin, Bavarian Soviet Republic in Munich. *1919–29*: study and residence in Heidelberg – gains doctorate with dissertation on Muslim artisan guilds (1921), member of *George-Kreis*, publishes *Kaiser Friedrich der Zweite* (1927). *1929–33*: residence in Berlin and Frankfurt – *Mythenschau* controversy; publishes supplement to *Friedrich II.* (1931); Honorary Professor, Frankfurt (1930); Full Professor, Frankfurt (1932). *1933–4*: conflict with Nazis about professorial chair – takes leave for summer semester of 1933; forced by Nazi demonstrations to break

his first book, his biography of the thirteenth-century German Emperor Frederick II, was not an outgrowth of his academic training but rather an exposition of the ideals of the poet Stefan George. At the time when Kantorowicz was writing his *Kaiser Friedrich der Zweite*, he revered George as *Meister* (master), for, as a member of George's tightly knit circle (the *George-Kreis*) from about 1920 until the poet's death in 1933, the young Kantorowicz adhered to George, intellectually and personally, in the most devout discipleship.[2] Since George's ideals were notoriously opposed to those of the academic "guild" (*Zunft*), it was inevitable that when Kantorowicz's *Friedrich II.* appeared in 1927 (without footnotes) it would be regarded as a provocation to academia. Probably goaded by the fact that the book had become an immediate public success, Albert Brackmann, then professor of medieval history at the University of Berlin, took up the challenge in an address to the Prussian Academy of Sciences of 1929 entitled "Kaiser Friedrich II. in 'mythischer Schau.'" When the newspaper *Vossische Zeitung* trumpeted "Akademie gegen Mythenschau," and Kantorowicz fought back with gusto in two different presentations of 1930, the battle was joined.[3]

off teaching in December 1933; New College, Oxford (winter and spring, 1934), becomes "emeritus professor" (fall, 1934). *1934–8*: private scholar with base in Berlin, flees Germany (December 1938). *1939–50*: faculty member, University of California at Berkeley – Lecturer (1939), Full Professor (1945); helps lead faculty resistance to loyalty oath (1949–50). *1950–1*: research fellowship at Byzantine Studies Center, Dumbarton Oaks. *1951–63*: Professor, Institute for Advanced Study, Princeton – publishes *The King's Two Bodies* (1957). A bibliography of Kantorowicz's publications appears in Kantorowicz, *Selected Studies* (Locust Valley, N.Y., 1965), xi–xiv.

2 Kantorowicz's appellation of Frederick II as "der grösste Friedrich" – see his *Kaiser Friedrich der Zweite* (Berlin, 1927), hereafter *FZ*, 632 – was an implicit quotation from George's poem "Die Gräber in Speier": "Der Grösste Friedrich – wahren volkes sehnen." For the poem, Grünewald, 60, and for examples of Kantorowicz's deferential apostrophes to George, ibid., 65, 89. A bibliography of works on George and the *George-Kreis* through 1976 is Georg Peter Landmann, *Stefan George und Sein Kreis*, 2nd ed. (Hamburg, 1976). Titles in English are E. K. Bennett, *Stefan George* (New Haven, 1954); Michael M. and Erika A. Metzger, *Stefan George* (New York, 1972); and Andrew L. Yarrow, "Humanism and *Deutschtum*: The Origins, Development, and Consequences of Poetry in the *George-Kreis*," *Germanic Review* 58 (1983):1–11. (Dr. E. Grünewald kindly called my attention to the last title, which concentrates on Kantorowicz but is not always accurate.) I found particularly helpful Erich von Kahler, "Stefan George. Grösse und Tragik," in von Kahler, *Untergang und Übergang* (Munich, 1970), 228–49.

3 For basic data and expert analysis of the *Mythenschau* controversy, see Grünewald, 86–7, 90–101. Brackmann's address of 1929, Kantorowicz's rejoinder, and Brackmann's rejoinder to Kantorowicz's rejoinder, all of which originally appeared in *Historische Zeitschrift* 140–1 (1929–30), are conveniently reprinted in G. Wolf, ed., *Stupor Mundi: Zur Geschichte Friedrichs II. von Hohenstaufen* (Darmstadt, 1966), hereafter *Wolf*. Wolf also reprints extended contemporary reviews of Kantorowicz's work by the medievalists Baethgen and Hampe that should also be regarded as statements in the controversy. He does not reprint Kantorowicz's separate statement regarding methodological issues presented to the Deutsche Historikertag in

The debate between the guild and the *George-Kreis*, Brackmann and Kantorowicz, was widely understood at the time to be a debate about "positivism," fought largely along generational lines. Indeed, Brackmann himself emphasized the generational nature of the cleft at the onset of his attack: "Here the younger generation has certainly created a work that far outstrips anything the older generation has produced, in terms of its effect. But just because we of the older generation must plainly recognize this success, . . . we must also express our deep reservations."[4] Brackmann and "the older generation" were primarily concerned with three methodological issues: Kantorowicz's emotive literary style; his unabashed tendentiousness; and his use of "nonpositivistic" sources. Kantorowicz's style raised questions about the proper relationship between research and presentation, *Forschung* and *Darstellung*. As a member of a literary/ideological circle, he had aimed to inspire as well as edify his readers. The final lines of his biography of Frederick II will serve as an illustration: "The greatest Frederick is not yet redeemed, him his people knew not and sufficed not. 'Lives and lives not,' the Sibyl's word is not for the Emperor, but for the German people."[5]

The literary qualities of Kantorowicz's biography were appreciated by the nonspecialist public; in 1931 his book was "canonized" by inclusion in the standard German encyclopedia, *Der Grosse Brockhaus*, which referred to its "artistic empathy" (*künstlerisches Einfühlungsvermögen*).[6] Yet Kantorowicz's literary effusions were distrusted by the *Fachleute* who thought that his ardent mode of expression was so rhetorical that it stood in the way of telling the truth. Brackmann expressed concern about Kantorowicz's penchant for *Aesthetik*, and

---

1930, "Über Grenzen, Möglichkeiten und Darstellung mittelalterlicher Geschichte," but this is expertly summarized and excerpted by Grünewald. Kantorowicz's enthusiasm for pursuing the controversy publicly appears from a letter of his to George of July 8, 1929, as Grünewald, 87, to which I can offer as a supplement Kantorowicz to Brackmann in a letter of September 15, 1929, now in Rep. 92, Brackmann (Mappe Nr. 16, S. 34), Geheimes Staatsarchiv, Preussischer Kulturbesitz, Berlin: "Zudem ist unser Streit . . . von zu prinzipieller Bedeutung, als dass er der Öffentlichkeit vorenthalten werden dürfte."

4 Wolf, 5: "Die jüngere Generation hat mit dieser Biographie zweifellos ein Werk geschaffen, mit dem sich keins der älteren Generation hinsichtlich der Wirkung vergleichen kann. Aber gerade weil wir von der älteren Generation diesen Erfolg rundweg anerkennen . . . müssen wir doch unsere schweren Bedenken äussern."

5 Kaiser Friedrich der Zweite Berlin, 1927 (hereafter *FZ*), 632: "Doch der grösste Friedrich ist bis heute nicht erlöst, den sein Volk weder fasste noch füllte. 'Er lebt und lebt nicht' . . . nicht mehr den Kaiser: des Kaisers Volk meint der Spruch der Sibylle." The English translation is from Kantorowicz, *Frederick the Second*, 1194–1250, trans. E. O. Lorimer (London, 1931), 689, hereafter *FS*.

6 Grünewald, 85.

the Heidelberg medievalist Karl Hampe later raised more sustained objections to his "poetic constructions."[7] But far from backing down, Kantorowicz took the offensive regarding his style, in the more public of his responses to Brackmann, an address to the Deutsche Historikertag of 1930, by pressing for a distinction between *Forschung* and *Darstellung*: "Positivistic historical *research* becomes guilty of encroaching upon the realm of art when it attempts to force historical *writing* to bend to its rules [emphasis in original]."[8] In other words, according to him, the task of the *Geschichtsforscher* was to gather evidence and test its qualities, while that of the *Geschichtsschreiber* was to transform the evidence, by art, into art.

Directly tied to the criticism by the guild of Kantorowicz's rhetoric was its objection to his tendentiousness. The following examples will show that this trait in his biography was quite pronounced. The theme of the great emperor's special relationship with a "hidden Germany" is struck immediately in the preface, with its motto "Seinen Kaisern und Helden, das Geheime Deutschland." Although Frederick was half-German and half-Norman by birth, Kantorowicz saw him as surrounded by some "wholly German Germanic emanation." Hermann von Salza, the founder of the Teutonic Knights, was characterized by "loyalty, which since the earliest times has been possible only among Germans." But Otto IV, disadvantaged by being half-English, displayed "many an English trait: a frugality bordering on parsimony, . . . an amazing lack of education, a poverty of intellect." When Frederick II beheaded prisoners daily before the walls of Parma, "the reign of terror was no mania but frightful necessity," and when he persecuted rebels and heretics, he acted "not against their beliefs but against their unbeliefs." Opening with an evocation of the theme of "the hidden Germany," the book concludes by picturing the transfigured Frederick II in his mountain hideout: "the radiant, the merry, the ever-young, the stern and mighty judge, ... who slumbers not nor sleeps, but ponders how he can renew the Empire."[9]

7 Brackmann, as Wolf, 21; Hampe, as Wolf, 74. A list of all of Hampe's objections to Kantorowicz's inflated style is presented by Yakov Malkiel, "Ernst H. Kantorowicz," in Arthur R. Evans, ed., *On Four Modern Humanists: Hofmannsthal, Gundolf, Curtius, Kantorowicz* (Princeton, 1970), 189–90 hereafter *Malkiel.*

8 Grünewald, 91: "Die positivistische Geschichts*forschung* macht sich eines Übergriffs in das Gebiet der Kunst schuldig, wenn sie versucht, die Geschichts*schreibung* unter ihre Arbeitsregeln zu zwingen."

9 The quotations, in order, are from FS, 102 = FZ, 96: "Hier umgeistert den Staufer etwas Nur-Deutsches Germanisches"; FZ, 85: "Treue . . . wie seit Urzeiten überhaupt nur bei

Most German professors of history around 1930 would have approved of Kantorowicz's nationalistic opinions, yet, as heirs of Ranke, they were unwilling to allow that preconceived biases had any legitimate role in the writing of history.[10] (Whether they were deceiving themselves is here beside the point.) Speaking implicitly for all of them, Brackmann thus concluded his initial attack on Kantorowicz with a ringing assertion that one cannot write history "either as a George disciple, or as a Catholic, Protestant, or Marxist, but only as a truth-seeking human being."[11] His opponent, however, was not to be cowed. Answering Brackmann's call for objectivity with dripping irony at the *Historikertag*, Kantorowicz stated that "sober positivism faces the danger of becoming romantic when it argues that one can find the Blue Flower of truth without preconceptions."[12] Expressing contempt for the ideal of the "colorless, neutral type" (*farblos indifferenter Typ*) who aims to write history without convic-

Deutschen möglich"; FS, 65 = FZ, 64: "Manches englische Erbteil ist da zu erkennen: nicht minder seiner an Geiz grenzende Kargheit . . . als seine auffallend geringe Bildung und geistige Armseligkeit"; FZ, 598: "Die Schreckensherrschaft war kein Wahnsinn, sondern furchtbarste Not"; FZ, 247: "Seines Glaubens wegen hat Friedrich II. niemanden verfolgt . . . denn er hatte vollauf zu tun, Rebellen und Ketzer wegen ihres Unglaubens zu verfolgen"; FS, 689 = FZ, 632: "dem Strahlenden, Heiteren, dem Ewigungen, dem strengen kraftvollen Richter . . . der nicht schläft sondern sinnt, wie er 'das Reich erneue.' " David Abulafia, "Kantorowicz and Frederick II," *History* 62 (1977):193 is quite correct in saying that "[Kantorowicz's] view of Frederick II went far deeper than purely ethnic praise; he wrote at length of Frederick's Italian blood, his 'Mediterranean qualities' [etc.]." Nonetheless the tendentious German nationalism in Kantorowicz's biography is obviously overwhelming; indeed, even in the less rhetorical supplementary volume – Kantorowicz, *Kaiser Friedrich der Zweite. Ergänzungsband* (Berlin, 1931) – one can find such asides as this, (156) concerning Frederick II's *Book of Falconry*: "Nach wie vor bleibt es jedoch beschämend, dass sich in Deutschland zwar Bearbeiter und Verleger für Alttibetansiche Hochzeitsgesänge und Feuerländische Kleinplastik finden, aber nicht für dieses stofflich wie geistesgeschichtlich ungemein interessante Werk des schliesslich bedeutendsten Monarchen des deutschen Mittelalters."

10 Brackmann himself was in fact a dedicated German nationalist, active, in his nonscholarly capacity, in the political and propagandistic arena. See on this Kaspar Elm, "Mittelalterforschung in Berlin: Dauer und Wandel" (typescript; to be published in 1990), 14: "[Er war] parteipolitisch stark engagiert. . . . [S]chon früh, . . . hatte er es sich zur Aufgabe gemacht, die Bedeutung des Ostens für Deutschland und das Reich ins Bewusstsein der Öffentlichkeit zu rufen." (I wish to thank Professor Elm for showing me a copy of this article.)

11 Wolf, 22: "[W]eder als George-Schüler noch als Katholik oder als Protestant oder als Marxist . . . sondern nur als wahrheitsuchender Mensch." The fact that the line took on immediate resonance can be seen from a private response to Brackmann written by another George disciple, Wolfram von den Steinen, in a letter of November 26, 1929, in Rep. 92, Brackmann (Mappe no. 34, S. 174), Geheimes Staatsarchiv, Preussischer Kulturbesitz, Berlin: "[W]ahrheitsuchende Menschen sind wir doch alle!" Von den Steinen's hitherto unnoticed private response to Brackmann is worth separate consideration.

12 Grünewald, 92: "Der nüchterne Positivismus somit Gefahr lüuft, heute romantisch zu werden, indem er meint, ohne Voraussetzungen . . . die Blaue Blume Wahrheit zu finden." For the two other quotations from Kantorowicz's speech I offer in this paragraph, Grünewald, 92, 96.

tions, he held forth instead as a paragon the George disciple whose enterprise is always governed by "the dogma of the worthy future and honor of the nation" (*das Dogma von der würdigen Zukunft der Nation und ihrer Ehre*).

A final area of controversy lay in Kantorowicz's selection of sources. In creating a Frederick II "who slumbers not nor sleeps," Kantorowicz had drawn heavily on manifestos, panegyrics, prophecies, anecdotes, and rumors. Although such sources were contemporaneous to the events, most professional historians considered them excessively subjective and hence intrinsically untruthful. As Brackmann insisted, "In the case of Frederick II above all it is necessary to free him from overpainting with contemporary dyes."[13] Kantorowicz's private response was a sardonic quip in a letter to George: "The contemporary dyes so readily rejected by the academic historian are at any rate more laundry-fast than the modern I. G. Farben [*Farben* = "dyes," the pun is untranslatable] with which he is associated."[14] Although Kantorowicz did not raise the issue of his sources in his *Historikertag* address, he reemphasized his commitment to "contemporary dyes" in the supplementary volume to his biography that he brought out in 1931 by expatiating on the origin and contents of the manifestos, prophecies, and rumors he had employed.[15]

Two evaluations of Kantorowicz's role in the intellectual life of

13 Wolf, 21: "Gerade bei Friedrich II. . . . wäre die Aufgabe gewesen, das wahre Bild von der Übermalung mit diesen zeitgenössischen Farben zu befreien."

14 Grünewald, 87: "[D]ie vom zünftigen Historiker so gern verworfenen 'zeitgenössischen Farben' immer noch waschechter als die von ihm verwandten modernen I.G. – Farben seien." As Grünewald observes, the punning reference to I.G. – Farben alludes to the *George-Kreis*'s criticism of the German economic regime exemplified by the I. G. Farben cartel.

15 Oswald Holder-Egger, the "positivist" editor of the prophecy of the Erythrean Sibyl on which Kantorowicz later drew heavily, had apologized as follows for concerning himself with it: "An sich bietet dieser Text ein sehr geringes Interesse, und es ist mir recht wenig erfreulich, mich mit ihm zu beschäftigen, war ich doch nur durch die Ausgabe von Salimbene's Chronik . . . gezwungen, diese herauszugeben, nicht durch eigene Neigung diesen abstrusen Dingen zugeführt"; the quotation is from *Neues Archiv der Gesellschaft für ältere deutsche Geschichtskunde* 30 (1904–5):323. It would be going too far to suggest that Kantorowicz was alone in drawing on "nonpositivistic" sources; other Germans of his generation who did so were Percy Schramm, in numerous works beginning with "Das Herrscherbild in der Kunst des Mittelalters," *Vorträge der Bibliothek Warburg 1922–3*, 1 (1924); Herbert Grundmann in "Die Papstprophetien des Mittelalters," *Archiv für Kulturgeschichte* 19 (1929):77–138, and "Liber de Flore," *Historisches Jahrbuch* 49 (1929):33–91; and Carl Erdmann, in "Endkaiserglaube und Kreuzzugsgedanke im 11. Jahrhundert," *Zeitschrift für Kirchengeschichte* 51 (1932):384–414, "Der Heidenkrieg in der Liturgie und die Kaiserkrönung Ottos I.," *Mitteilungen des österreichischen Instituts für Geschichtsforschung* 46 (1932):129–42, and "Kaiserliche und päpstliche Fahnen im hohen Mittelalter," *Quellen und Forschungen aus italienischen Archiven und Bibliotheken* 25 (1933):1–48. Yet Kantorowicz's use of such sources was the boldest, because he used them continuously for a sustained narrative.

Weimar help put the *Historikerstreit* of 1930 into perspective. Felix Gilbert has recently emphasized Kantorowicz's liberating influence: "Kantorowicz's work on Emperor Frederick II . . . demonstrated that a different kind of medieval history, one that revealed the ideas and values that motivated the rulers of the Middle Ages, was possible and might have a wide appeal. Even if one did not share the political and literary views and values of Kantorowicz, who was a member of the elitist circle around the poet Stefan George, one admired his book for overcoming the rigidification that had set in in medieval history because of an overemphasis on historical techniques."[16]

A somewhat different angle, however, appeared in a commentary on Kantorowicz's *Historikertag* address in the cultural supplement of the *Berliner Börsenzeitung* of May 3, 1930: "Here we see how the breach in our current society is manifested in the field of historical studies: the alienation of the younger generation from the positivism of the nineteenth century, itself an inheritance of the Enlightenment, and the quest for a new legitimation of 'cultural privilege' in the eyes of the nation."[17] As I interpret this remark, it shows that Kantorowicz's methodology and his world view were taken to be inseparable – that as liberating as his methodology might have seemed to those who did not share his political or cultural ideals, it was part of a general onslaught against Enlightenment norms that might have taken as its motto either the "Seinen Kaisern und Helden, das geheime Deutschland" of the *George-Kreis* or the "Ich hasse dieses sanfte Heidelberg" of the younger Goebbels.[18]

A remark by Brackmann provides a transition for pursuing Kantorowicz's later historiographic career. Holding out an olive branch at the end of his reply to Kantorowicz's response in the pages of *Historische Zeitschrift*, Brackmann stated that his opponent was known to be working in the library of the *Monumenta Germaniae historica*. (In fact Kantorowicz was then gathering data for his supplementary volume.) Since the *Monumenta*, then under the direction of that master of diplomatics, Paul Fridolin Kehr, was the research institution that most fully stood for the ideal of technically sound scholarship,

16 Felix Gilbert, *A European Past: Memoirs, 1905–1945* (New York, 1988), 106–7.
17 Grünewald, 91: "Hier wurde deutlich der Bruch unserer gegenwärtigen Gesellschaftsverfassung im Gebiete der Geschichtswissenschaft sichtbar: die Abwendung der Jugend vom Positivismus des 19. Jahrhunderts, der selbst ein Erbe der Aufklärung ist, und das Suchen nach einer neuen Rechtfertigung des 'Bildungsprivilegs' vor der Nation."
18 Joseph Goebbels, *Michael. Ein deutsches Schicksal in Tagebuchblättern* (Munich, 1929), 185, as cited by Grünewald, 36, n. 28.

Brackmann could conclude, "There is something of a 'positivist' in Kantorowicz, . . . [who] has given evidence of a silent love for the environment of the *Monumenta Germaniae historica*; it remains therefore to be seen whether at the end of his development he will be standing with Stefan George or with Paul Kehr."[19]

How did it turn out? To begin, Kantorowicz's regret for having helped pave the road to National Socialism with his *Friedrich II.* was profound. (As a prominent *Volljude* he barely escaped arrest in the roundups after Kristallnacht, yet incredibly his biography of Frederick II was reprinted in 1936 and recognized as approved Nazi party reading, the *Führer* himself claiming to have read it twice.)[20] Pressed by his German publisher and friend, Helmut Küpper, to authorize a reprinting of *Friedrich II.* in Germany at the war's end, Kantorowicz refused, on the grounds that the book was now *fehl am Platz* and "might reinvigorate antiquated nationalisms."[21] After numerous appeals, he finally acceded to the pleas of Küpper's widow in 1962, with the proviso that the preface with the invocation of "geheimes Deutschland" be removed. But when he received congratulations about the reprinting from NATO commander Gen. Hans Speidel, a former adjutant of Rommel's, who referred to the "marvelous, always deeply-moving work about the great Hohenstaufen" (*einmaliges, uns immer erneut tief bewegendes Werk über den grossen Staufer*), he wrote to Frau Küpper, "This is of course just the element that held me back from approving a new printing for so long. One really ought to let a book fall into oblivion that once lay on Himmler's night table and that Göring sent as a gift, with his inscription, to Mussolini. . . . The recently hanged Herr Eichmann would probably have rejoiced just as much."[22]

19 Wolf, 48: "Denn in Kantorowicz steckt doch zugleich ein 'Positivist,' der sein Buch durch gründliches Quellenstudium unterbaut hat und der seit geraumer Zeit eine stille Liebe zu dem Arbeitskreis der *Monumenta Germaniae historica* bekundet, so dass noch gar nicht abzusehen ist, ob er am Ende seiner Entwicklung bei Stefan George oder bei Paul Kehr stehen wird."

20 On Hitler and *Friedrich II.*, see Grünewald, 165, n. 36. Kantorowicz's mother died in Theresienstadt in 1943 or 1944; see Grünewald, 4, n. 2.

21 Edgar Salin, *Ernst Kantorowicz, 1895–1963* (private printing, n.p., 1963), 9. (Mrs. Alice Kahler kindly gave me a copy of this memoir by one of Kantorowicz's intimates from the *George-Kreis*.)

22 Grünewald, 165: "Dies ist natürlich genau die Schicht, deretwegen ich so lange zurückhielt mit einem Wiederdruck. Man sollte halt ein Buch, das bei Himmler auf dem Nachttisch lag und das Göring an Mussolini mit Widmung verschenkte, in völlige Vergessenheit geraten lassen. . . . Wahrscheinlich hätte sich der mittlerweile zum Glück gehängte Herr Eichmann genauso gefreut . . . und gerade um dieses Beifalls wegen hatte ich so lange gezögert, offenbar nicht lange genug." Grünewald, 158–67, treats the entire correspondence between Kantorowicz and den Küppers about the postwar reprinting of *Friedrich II.*

In the American phase of his career, Kantorowicz's revulsion about the effects of his biography kept him from embracing any form of nationalism. Indeed, much of his postwar scholarship consisted of clinical analyses of the pathology of nationalism, as in his "*Pro patria mori* in Medieval Political Thought" and "Zu den Rechtsgrundlagung der Kaisersage" (the latter, perhaps not accidentally, published in German in Germany),[23] as well as in much of his *King's Two Bodies*. Yet in his American phase he held back from polemics and took the stance of scientific nonpartisanship. In the preface to *The King's Two Bodies* he was most explicit about this. There he disavowed treating medieval political myths "merely on account of the horrifying experience of our time in which whole nations . . . fell prey to the weirdest dogmas" (Did he remember his own words about *das Dogma von der würdigen Zukunft der Nation und ihrer Ehre?*), adding that "the fascination emanating as usual from the historical material itself prevailed over any desire of practical or moral application."[24] Apparently, then, in his later years Kantorowicz joined Brackmann and the "positivists" in seeking to write history "only as a truth-seeking human being."

This, however, by no means implies that he forsook his dedication to the privileged role of *Darstellung*. *Darstellung* was still privileged, but now it was of an entirely different nature – studied, precise, sprinkled with technical terms, and replete with quotations in Latin and Greek, in short *nur für Kenner*. Kantorowicz had a term for what he sought: the *Kabinettstück*, by which he meant a perfectly crafted gem, dazzling to the connoisseur but too subtle, in its austere beauty, to be appreciated by the uninitiated.[25] All the articles he wrote in his American phase fit this model, and I think that his scholarly masterpiece, *The King's Two Bodies*, fits it too, inasmuch as that book can be viewed as an anthology of *Kabinettstücke*. To see how obsessed the author of *The King's Two Bodies* was with having everything in

23 The articles were published respectively in *American Historical Review* 61 (1951):472–92, and *Deutsches Archiv für Erforschung des Mittelalters* 13 (1957):115–50 (the latter journal being – *nota bene* – the house organ of the *Monumenta*), and are reprinted in Kantorowicz, *Selected Studies*, 308–24, 284–307.

24 *The King's Two Bodies: A Study in Mediaeval Political Theology* (Princeton, 1957) (hereafter *KTB*), viii. Of course the alert reader may find asides with contemporary relevance in his footnotes; see at least KTB, 301, n. 62, where the author, writing at the height of McCarthyism, notes that "[Petrarch's] readiness to call anyone disagreeing with him an 'Averroist' has its equivalent in modern habits."

25 For a fuller consideration of the *Kabinettstück* ideal *chez* Kantorowicz, see Malkiel, 212–19. Although Malkiel occasionally overstates matters, his estimation of Kantorowicz's stress on "filigree precision" is very insightful.

its place, note the following in the published list of corrigenda: "For hermetic, read Hermetic."[26] Most likely Kantorowicz's motivation for abandoning magniloquent rhetoric for the austerity of the *Kabinettstück* was to be sure that no new work of his would end up on the next Himmler's night table. Whatever the case, the historian who cared so much about whether "hermetic" should appear with a large or small letter came very close to being hermetic himself.

If Kantorowicz's rejection of tendentiousness and his adoption of the *Kabinettstück* manner were both sharp reactions against his *George-Kreis* past, his palette of sources in his American phase displays continuity. As we have seen, *Friedrich II.* drew heavily on manifestos, prophecies, and legends, and the supplementary volume reemphasized the value of such material. Kantorowicz's second book, *Laudes regiae*, begun in Germany and completed in the United States, went farther by drawing on the evidence of ecclesiastical litanies for the study of ruler worship, and *The King's Two Bodies* went farther still by drawing on the evidence of legal maxims, art, and literature, as well as on all the other kinds of "nonpositivistic" sources he had used before. The choice of sources and the choice of subject matter in *The King's Two Bodies* in fact are inextricable; had Kantorowicz not begun to draw on prophecies and legends while seeking to create a superhuman Frederick II, in the service of Stefan George, he might never have become the author of *The King's Two Bodies*, his landmark study of "Medieval political theology."

Because Kantorowicz exerted his greatest influence on American academia with *The King's Two Bodies*, a few words about that influence are in order. No more than modest sales of the book were foreseen in 1955 when the director of Princeton University Press, Herbert Bailey, wrote, "I think it is reasonable to suppose that fifteen hundred copies . . . can be sold over a period of perhaps ten years."[27] In fact the book has remained in print since it was published in 1957 and has sold a total of seventy-five hundred copies as of May 1, 1989.[28] In the library of the Institute for Advanced Study, which has relatively little traffic, three copies have been checked out for an

---

26 KTB (first printing), 568.

27 Herbert S. Bailey, Jr., to J. Robert Oppenheimer, October 14, 1955, Kantorowicz File, Archives, Historical Studies–Social Science Library, Institute for Advanced Study, Princeton. (By permission of the Librarian.) Bailey was writing to Oppenheimer concerning a subvention from the institute for the book's publication.

28 My thanks to Joanna Hitchcock of Princeton University Press for this information. A Spanish translation of the book was published in 1985, and French and German translation were scheduled to appear in 1989.

aggregate of one hundred times. Clifford Geertz has called the work "extraordinary," "magisterial," and "seminal"; Michael Walzer writes of its "brilliance"; Michael Paul Rogin has paid it the compliment of title borrowing in his article "The King's Two Bodies: Lincoln, Wilson, Nixon, and Presidential Self-Sacrifice"; Natalie Davis has done likewise in her "History's Two Body's"; and, yes, there is also a *Queen's Two Bodies.*[29]

Kantorowicz himself was by no means aiming for a best seller (he had had one already), for he knew quite well that his book was uncompromisingly difficult. I recall as a graduate student hearing my professor, Joseph Strayer, say that he had urged "Eka" to streamline his oversized manuscript by trimming the footnotes, pruning the Latin, and cutting the chapters on Shakespeare's *Richard II* and Dante – all to no avail. Thus today's graduate student may be somewhat bewildered on taking up one of those "seminal books" he is supposed to have mastered for his qualifying exams to find allusions to "Baudelaire's Albatross," "Breughel's *Icarus*" (corrected to Brueghel in the corrigenda), and rabbinic lore about the androgyny of the phoenix.[30] In addition there are sentences like this:

Dante, too, carried Aristotelianism to (what seemed to him) the logical ends when he emphasized, time and again, that the actuation of the total human intellect was a task which could be performed collectively only by the greatest of all possible communities, the *universitas generis humani* organized in the Roman world-monarchy – as it were, the body corporate of Man as distinguished from the body natural of each individual man.[31]

Since the sentences always parse and the persistent reader with small French and no Latin can garner the sense of most of the foreign terms and phrases if he attends closely, the most frustrating quality about *The King's Two Bodies* must ultimately be its lack of a sustained argument. I know of commentators who presume to identify the books' thesis, but I know of no two who seem to agree on what it is.[32] Nor do I find this surprising when the author himself defines

29 Geertz, "Centers, Kings, and Charisma," in Sean Wilentz, ed., *Rites of Power: Symbolism, Ritual and Politics since the Middle Ages* (Philadelphia, 1985), 14–15, 34; Walzer, *Regicide and Revolution* (Cambridge, U.K., 1974), 13; Rogin, *Ronald Reagan, the Movie, and Other Episodes in Political Demonology* (Berkeley, 1987), 81–114; Davis, "Presidential Address," *American Historical Review* 93 (1988):1–30; Marie Axton, *The Queen's Two Bodies: Drama and the Elizabethan Succession* (London, 1977).
30 KTB, 3, 33, 395.
31 Ibid., 480.
32 Ralph Giesey offers the best gloss on the work's finite contribution to the historical literature when he stresses its emphasis on the role of "Romano-canonical jurists and Catholic theologians" in the shaping of early-modern legal and political belief. See Giesey, "Ernst

his aim to be studying "the fiction of the King's Two Bodies, [in] its transformations, implications, and radiations." Here, then, we have an author who delights in leading his readers on a leisurely tour through highways and byways of the past without arguing much about why the roads were built or warning about where they lead.

If *The King's Two Bodies* is difficult, elusive, and perhaps somewhat Shandyesque, how might one account for its enormous success? Putting aside the fact that some readers have a taste for that sort of thing, the answers must lie in the book's subject matter and its sources. Although "political theology" was a neglected subject when Kantorowicz wrote, the disciplines of history, anthropology, and political science meanwhile have paid much greater attention to it. Thus *The King's Two Bodies* now ranks as one of the classic pathfinding analyses of the fashioning of symbolic aspects of power, as well as a point of departure for further work. (Cassirer's *Myth of the State* and Bloch's *Thaumaturgical Kings* are other titles in this category.[33]) Kantorowicz's very display of dispassionate learning and gingerliness in referring to current events – "the author was not unaware of the later aberrations"[34] – serve him excellently in such a context, because moving from *rex supra legem* to Reagan is known to be tricky, and it rests upon the Michael Paul Rogins of this world to tell us what "the King's Two Bodies" has to do with Lincoln, Wilson, and Nixon.

Interrelated with the model learning in *The King's Two Bodies* is its sophisticated use of an enormous range of sources. Had Kantorowicz

H. Kantorowicz: Scholarly Triumphs and Academic Travails in Weimar Germany and the United States," *Yearbook of the Leo Baeck Institute* 30 (1985):191–202 (at 196).

33 See Geertz, "Centers," 34. In 1961 Kantorowicz wrote a charming letter to the *Times Literary Supplement* apropos of a review of the English translation of Bloch's *Feudal Society*, in order to set the record straight on questions of influence. The relevant part is worth reproducing: "I was slightly puzzled, though greatly honoured, by the fact that from among hundreds of scholars upon whom Marc Bloch exercised considerable influence, your reviewer saw fit to single me out by mentioning my name. It is perfectly true that I was greatly impressed by his *Rois thaumaturges*. I actually met Marc Bloch in Oxford, dining with him, in 1934, at Oriel, and talked with him until far into the small hours after our kind host, Sir Maurice Powicke, had left us alone with a good supply of Bordeaux and Whisky. Both of us got so excited in the course of our conversation that we did not sit down but stood in front of the fireplace to exchange our arguments and places and quotations about any relevant subject. I, too, felt that his historical scholarship was 'unmistakably lit from an inward individual fire' so often absent from the works of historians. But exactly this was a quality which, alas, I could not borrow from him. I am sure there are many others who were far more dependent on him than I was, though it be far from me to deny the great impression his studies and his personality made upon me." Kantorowicz to Editor, *Times Literary Supplement*, July 7, 1961, Kantorowicz File, Archives, Historical Studies – Social Science Library, Institute for Advanced Study, Princeton.

34 KTB, viii.

taken Strayer's advice and excised the book's disquisitions on Shake-speare and Dante, the work might have become more fluent and accessible. But then perhaps it might not have gained as many read-ers, for surely one of its attractions is that it offers a "cornucopia of interpretation," to borrow a phrase from Natalie Davis. Reading through it allows one to see how a masterful intellect can glean meaning about "political mysticism" from law reports, Elizabethan drama, pamphlets from the Investiture Controversy, medieval manuscript illuminations, poetry, coins, and tombs, to offer an in-complete list. Assuming that Kantorowicz's penchant for breadth of sources stemmed from his years in the *George-Kreis*, this may count as the most fruitful heritage of his early engagement in *Mythenschau*.

In 1930, while Kantorowicz was working in the library of the *Monumenta* in Berlin, he became friends with a young medievalist, Theodor E. Mommsen, who had just received an appointment with the *Monumenta* as a full-time researcher.[35] The two had previously inhabited very different worlds. Kantorowicz, born of a rich Jewish manufacturing family, was a member of a famous poetic circle and a notorious critic of the academy. Mommsen, on the other hand, could have been born in an academic seminar room: his grandfather was *the* Theodor Mommsen, and his maternal uncle Max Weber. Furthermore, almost as if the differences had been scripted, none other than Albert Brackmann had been Mommsen's thesis director. Although Kantorowicz was ostensibly moving toward the academy by working in the *Monumenta* and by having just accepted a professo-rial position at Frankfurt, Mommsen, nine years younger, certainly looked up to the well-known author and controversialist and felt apologetic about the traditional "positivistic" labors on which he himself was engaged. All of which is to say that while Kantorowicz was moving somewhere "between Stefan George and Paul Kehr," Mommsen was moving between Kehr and Kantorowicz.

---

35 For biographical data on Mommsen, see the necrology by Helene Wieruszowski in *Histori-sche Zeitschrift* 187 (1959):481–2, and the introduction by F. G. Marcham to Theodor E. Mommsen, *Selected Studies* (Ithaca, 1959). A bibliography of Mommsen's publications ap-pears in the latter volume, 349–53. Mommsen's curriculum vitae is as follows. *1905*: born in Berlin. *1923–9*: studies in Heidelberg, Vienna, and Berlin. *1929*: Gains Ph.D. in Berlin with dissertation on ideas behind Saxon and Salian foreign policy ("Ideengehalt der deutschen Aussenpolitik im Zeitalter der Ottonen und Salier"); *1929–36: Assistent, Monu-menta Germaniae historica*; research and writing in this capacity in Berlin and Italy; *1936*: leaves Germany on political grounds (no "racial" necessity). *1936–7*: Research Fellowship, Johns Hopkins. *1937–42*: Instructor, Yale University. *1942–46*: Instructor, Groton School. *1946–54*: Associate Professor, Princeton University. *1954–8*: Professor, Cornell Univer-sity; takes his own life, *July 18, 1958*.

Evidence of Mommsen's sense of ambivalence comes from a greeting he wrote on an offprint of his article "Zur Freisinger Urkunden-Überlieferung" that he sent to Kantorowicz in 1932. The article was a product of Mommsen's research for the *Monumenta*, and the greeting read as follows: "Sedative sample. Dosage: one to two pages weekly! Warning! Do not exceed! Otherwise danger of lethal yawning seizure."[36] Felix Gilbert, a lifelong friend of Mommsen's, recalls that "in the years when Theodor and I studied history, there had developed among younger scholars a resistance to the prevailing emphasis on editing and publishing sources at the expense of interpretation, although too much criticism of the historical establishment was hardly advisable for those aiming at a scholarly career in medieval history."[37] Since Kantorowicz was the very person who, as Gilbert said, had "demonstrated that a different kind of medieval history was possible," Mommsen's self-deprecating irony in presenting to Kantorowicz the purest piece of *Monumenta*-style source criticism reflects his ambivalence about publishing sources at the expense of interpretation.

Did Mommsen ever come any closer to Kantorowicz in his scholarship? Certainly he never wrote a "big book," either for a popular audience or for an academic one. (Mommsen used to say that he was "an article man; not a book man."[38]) And certainly he never repudiated his technical labors for the *Monumenta*. Indeed, having made progress, in the early 1930s, on an edition of Italian documents pertaining to the reign of Ludwig the Bavarian, he completed this project and published it in a *Monumenta* series after the war.[39] But Mommsen's most important publications after leaving Germany

36 "Schlafmittel Probe! Dosierung: je 1–2 Seiten wöchentlich. Vorsicht! Nicht mehr! Sonst Gefahr eines letalen Gähnkrampfs." The offprint from *Zeitschrift für Bayerische Landesgeschichte* 5 (1932):129–39, is now in the collection of Kantorowicz's offprints, library of the Institute for Advanced Study, Princeton.

37 Gilbert, *European Past*, 105. Gilbert also states that the *Monumenta*, under the direction of Paul Kehr, "dominated the field of medieval studies more than ever before." Note also that according to Gerd Tellenbach, "Das Preussische Historische Institut," *Quellen und Forschungen aus italienischen Archiven und Bibliotheken* 50 (1971):395–6, the "Monumentists" under Kehr had their own jingle: "So man dieses eifrig tut–kriegt man Geld und hat es gut." (A translation, with some liberty, might be: "So long as we just toe the line–We get money and have it fine.")

38 Gilbert, *European Past*, 107. It is remarkable how often Mommsen must have repeated this. I remember E. Harris Harbison quoting Mommsen to the same effect in 1961, and a different version of the formula appears in Marcham, "Introduction," xi: "To him [his work] lacked . . . volume."

39 *Italienische Analekten zur Reichsgeschichte des 14. Jahrhunderts*, Monumenta Germaniae historica, Schriftenreihe 11 (Hannover, 1952). Mommsen's only other book-length publication was his edition of Petrarch's *Testament* (Ithaca, 1957).

were studies in the history of ideas, a genre aptly described by Ernst Schulin, in Chapter 1 of this volume, as the major "counterweight to positivism" in traditional German historiography.[40] Thus it appears that pursuing *Geistesgeschichte* was as far as Mommsen could go in moving beyond Paul Kehr and his own academic heritage.

Although opinions will differ, for the present author Mommsen's best studies are "Petrarch's Conception of the Dark Ages" (1942, in *Speculum*), and "St. Augustine and the Christian Idea of Progress" (1951, in the *Journal of the History of Ideas*). Both articles interpret the positions of highly influential intellectual figures in terms of an appropriate "problematic," both present model close readings of texts, and both offer important contributions to larger issues, respectively about humanist periodization and patristic attitudes toward change. Granted that these articles, and others by Mommsen, lack the dazzle of *Kabinettstücke* by Kantorowicz, they display magisterial control over their subject matters. And in offering tangible contributions to a collective historiographic enterprise, they accomplish a quotidian usefulness that was not Kantorowicz's forte.[41]

Mommsen's contributions to the American historiographic scene lie equally in his articles and in his role as a teacher of graduate students. Accounts of Mommsen's teaching at Princeton and Cornell paint the same picture of boundless dedication. "Mommsen," Helene

---

40 Gilbert, *European Past*, 107, reports that when Mommsen was working in Italy, in the mid-1930s, he became a favorite of Robert Davidsohn, the author of the virtually definitive multivolume narrative history of medieval Florence; indeed, "Davidsohn handed over to Theodor his papers so that he might continue and complete Davidsohn's lifework." Further light on this episode is cast by a letter of February 19, 1936, written by Mommsen from Florence to his former thesis director, Albert Brackmann, in Rep. 92, Brackmann (Mappe 22, S. 71-3), Geheimes Staatsarchiv, Preussischer Kulturbesitz, Berlin. Herein Mommsen requests a recommendation from Brackmann to support Mommsen's application for a Sterling Fellowship from Yale and encloses a description of his project–"The History of the City of Florence during the Years 1330-1378." As Mommsen's proposal explains, "I regard this work as a trial to the continuation of Robert Davidsohn's *Geschichte von Florenz*. I therefore begin my researches where the book ends, in 1330. Also in method I should like to follow the model of this work, because it is generally valued as a standard type of such a monograph." Mommsen did not receive the Sterling Fellowship and apparently never made any headway with his planned continuation of Davidsohn; had he done so, his scholarship might have evolved very differently, albeit not necessarily any less "positivistically."

41 If Mommsen never matched Kantorowicz in his own writing, moreover, he made a signal contribution to Kantorowicz's own work when the two were both living in Princeton between 1951 and 1956. Kantorowicz's acknowledgment of Mommsen's contribution to the writing of *The King's Two Bodies* in that work's preface (p. xii) speaks for itself: "[T]he author's gratitude is due, above all, to Professor Theodor E. Mommsen, who loyally read the whole manuscript as – chapter by chapter – it emerged from the typewriter, who never withheld his opinion, and who gave the author a chance to discuss with him on many evenings the broader problems as well as countless details."

Wieruszowski wrote, was a great teacher. . . . [U]ntil his last day nothing was so close to his heart as the education and advancement of his students," and Frederick Marcham said virtually the same: "[h]e was a noteworthy teacher throughout his career in the United States . . . [His] graduate students were his special care; their training had first call upon his time."[42] To complement these public statements with a private one, C. H. Coster, writing to Bernard Berenson, made the same point: "As a teacher he was really inspiring and won the lasting devotion of his pupils."[43]

Marcham's account of Mommsen's teaching is worth quoting further because it tells of one of the gifts Mommsen brought from Germany to American academia, the old-fashioned "seminar method":

From term to term he chose a few documents . . . and led his students through a microscopic examination of them. They searched step by step, discussing here perhaps the phrases by which a pope described his authority . . . there a seemingly innocent word which suggested a new turn of thought in the relations of church and state. Together Mommsen and his students put before one another . . . the fruits of the studies each had made in preparation for the discussion, and in this exchange of knowledge and opinions they worked until, to use his phrase, they had "squeezed the sources dry". . . . So intense was his concentration that all felt the effects, not least Mommsen. He had prepared as assiduously as his students; he had guided and stimulated the conversation from idea to idea and called into play the whole range of his knowledge. The end of the week's seminar . . . left all exhausted. Mommsen repaired the ravages of the afternoon by leading the group . . . to dinner at the Faculty Club, where the rule was that no one should talk history.[44]

Helene Wieruszowski's 1959 necrology stated that "a number of [Mommsen's students] already teach medieval history in [America's] colleges and graduate schools." Today this is all the more true. Among those who earned a doctorate at Princeton after working entirely or substantially with Mommsen are Howard Adelson of City College in New York; Robert Benson of UCLA; Thomas Bis-

42 Wieruszowski, necrology, 482; Marcham, "Introduction," x.
43 Coster to Berenson, September 19, 1958, a letter containing extensive reflections on Mommsen's suicide. The Berenson–Coster correspondence will soon be published by Giles Constable. I am grateful to Elizabeth Beatson for calling my attention to this material.
44 Marcham, "Introduction," x–xi. Professor Karl Morrison, one of Mommsen's graduate students at Cornell, reports to me that Mommsen confessed to having "butterflies in his stomach" before teaching any class. Thus he prepared for every seminar more than his students, even when the subject was the Investiture Controversy, which, as Professor Morrison states, "he could have taught backwards."

son of Harvard; William Bowsky of UCLA at Davis; Gene Brucker of Berkeley; and Norman Cantor of NYU; among those who studied with him at Cornell (where he taught for only two years before his death) are Karl Morrison of Rutgers; William Percy of the University of Massachusetts at Boston; and Richard Rouse of UCLA. No fewer than six of Mommsen's students are fellows of the Medieval Academy of America – quite a progeny for a man who taught at the graduate level for only twelve years.

Theodor Mommsen took his own life at age fifty-four, at the height of his activity as a scholar and teacher. Who knows how much more he might have accomplished had he lived? As Erich Kahler wrote at the time, *Ein grosser Jammer*.

APPENDIX

Even though the foregoing account has paid scant attention to biography, it seems appropriate to publish here a vignette of Theodor Mommsen written by Erich Kahler. This vignette is taken from the first part of a letter sent by Kahler – philosopher, historian, and man of letters – to his cousin, Edith von Kahler, on July 24, 1958, six days after Mommsen's suicide. (Kahler had been close to Mommsen at both Princeton and Cornell.) I am grateful to Mrs. Alice Kahler for showing me this letter, for elucidating a Yiddishism, and for giving me permission to publish. I am also grateful to Prof. Knut Nörr for extensive paleographical aid.

My dear Edithlein,

Thanks for your lovely, detailed report. From here I must send a sad and shocking one: Dr. Ted Mommsen has killed himself. In fact I expected he would do that some day, depressive as he was, and burdened with a terrible inferiority complex. But just now I was not worried. In recent months, when I was with him almost daily, he was cheerful and sociable as I had hardly ever seen him before; he would chat at parties without inhibition, and he felt so much better there [at Ithaca] than at Princeton. He had great plans for trips. And what fine evenings I had with him, with wine, good conversation, music. Right now he was supposed to be visiting Princeton for two weeks. And suddenly it caught him again. He was very sensitive [*unvital*], burdened with the degenerative inheritance of his great-grandfather and of his equally mighty two uncles, Max and Alfred Weber. But such a dear, intelligent, and noble person! And such a friend! A great pity.

[Mein liebes Edithlein,

Danke für schönen, ausführlichen Bericht! Von hier muss ich einen traurigen, erschütternden geben: Dr. Ted Mommsen hat sich umgebracht. Ich habs ja erwartet, dass er [es] einmal tun wird, depressiv wie er immer war und mit einem schrecklichen Minderwertigkeitsgefühl behaftet. Aber grad jetzt war ich gar nicht in Sorge. Er war die letzten Monate, in denen ich ja fast täglich mit ihm zusammen war, so heiter und gesellig wie ich ihn kaum je vorher gesehen habe, is[t] dauernd in parties herumgeplauscht, ohne Hemmungen, und hat sich dort [Ithaca] so viel wohler gefühlt als in Princeton. Hat grosse Pläne gemacht für Reisen. Und so gute Abende hab ich mit ihm gehabt mit Wein, schönen Gesprächen, Musik. Grad sollt er für zwei Wochen nach Princeton kommen zu Besuch. Und plötzlich hats ihn wieder erwischt. Er war sehr unvital, belastet von der degenerativen Erbschaft seines grossen Grossvaters und seiner ebenso gevurösen [*gevüre* = Yiddish for "strength," "charisma"] zwei Onkeln Max und Alfred Weber. Aber so ein lieber, gescheiter und nobler Mensch! Und so ein Freund! Ein grosser Jammer.]

15

Refugee Historians and the German Historical Profession between 1950 and 1970

WINFRIED SCHULZE

In Munich, on September 14, 1949, nearly two hundred German historians from east and west met for the first time since World War II to discuss officially the state of German historical scholarship. All participants were delighted to hear the keynote speaker at the meeting. He was Hans Rothfels, a converted Jew and one of the leading historians of Weimar Germany, who had not left Germany until 1939. He had returned for the first time in 1949 and enjoyed a very successful semester at the university in Göttingen, and now he was delivering a lecture entitled "Bismarck and the Nineteenth Century." His prominence on the program seemed to represent some compensation, in the eyes of his fellow historians and in his own, for the man who had last addressed the profession on the topic "Bismarck and the East" in 1932, when German historians had met in Göttingen for the last time before the Nazi seizure of power. Both times, Rothfels gave a very sympathetic evaluation of Bismarck's policy. Most importantly, in 1949 he denied all connection between Bismarck and the Third Reich; in his view, Bismarck's Second Empire stood in sharp contrast and opposition to all that the Third Reich had propagated and done. It was no wonder that the audience felt strong relief when the formerly persecuted emigrant who had returned finished his speech. He brought down the house. For many participants, the lasting applause for Rothfels was the strongest impression of the Munich meeting, and they have treasured its memory up to the present. Rothfels himself was deeply impressed. He felt at home again.[1]

Unless otherwise stated, all translations are by the author.
1 Rothfels' paper is reprinted in L. Gall, ed., *Das Bismarck-Problem in der Geschichtsschreibung nach 1945* (Cologne, 1971), 84–96. For Rothfels' impression of his "success," see the report on his journey to Germany in 1949 in "Nachlass [hereafter *NL*] Rothfels," Bundesarchiv Koblenz (hereafter *BAK*): NL 213, no. 59.

Nevertheless, if one considered only this moving scene in Munich in 1949 and Rothfels' own feelings about his success, it would convey the wrong picture of the complicated relations between German historians and their émigré colleagues after the end of World War II. When Ernst Schulin asked me to write a paper for his conference on German historiography between 1945 and 1965, I had only very scanty ideas about these relations. Naturally I knew about Hans Rothfels, Hans-Joachim Schoeps, and Golo Mann, about Dietrich Gerhard and Hans Rosenberg, but I could not venture to give a serious and well-documented judgment about the difficult problems of "re-migration" of historians after 1945. Had a genuine effort really been made in those times to attract the emigrants back to Germany, or had history faculties tried to keep them out? During the last two years, I have tried to find out something about this question, and I am very glad to present here some of the results, which are treated at greater length in my book *The German Historical Profession after 1945*, published at the beginning of 1989.[2]

This essay will concentrate on three subjects:

I. The situation at German universities immediately after the Second World War and the question of what was done to bring the emigrants home;

II. The personal fate of Hans Rosenberg and the negotiations at Cologne University to call him back, as one example of the personal choices facing emigrants when confronted with the chance to go back; and

III. A rough assessment of the effects of both remigration and permanent emigration on German historiography in the 1950s and 1960s.

I

The plight of the history faculties at the universities in postwar Germany was indeed chaotic. In Cologne, Peter Rassow was the only historian, after two of his colleagues were suspended from office. In Göttingen, the dean of the philosophical faculty reported that only octogenarian historian Karl Brandi could teach, because all other faculty members were ill, had been dismissed, or remained prisoners

2 Winfried Schulze, *Deutsche Geschichtswissenschaft nach 1945*. Supplement to *Historische Zeitschrift* 10), (Munich, 1989).

of war (for example, medievalist Percy Ernst Schramm was working at Versailles for the U.S. Army Historical Division, reconstructing Germany's last western campaign). History faculties at other universities did not fare much better, especially when some professors suffered temporary dismissal.

These obvious difficulties caused by postwar staff deficiencies in German universities provoked public discussion about the return of émigré scholars to Germany. Much of the German public strongly demanded such a return. Various state ministries of cultural affairs found it necessary – especially after press campaigns attacked them on the issue – to publish the records of their efforts to entice back some of the émigré professors permanently, or at least to invite them to give guest lectures. The Göttingen university newspaper published a detailed account of the fate of those professors who had left their positions in Göttingen for political reasons after 1933.[3]

As early as February 1946, the presidents of the universities of the British zone decided at a meeting in Goslar to demand special funding to support the reintegration of émigré professors. This decision amplified an earlier agreement of September 1945, which had been a very general recommendation that all emigrants should be called back but advanced no concrete plan to offer them jobs. Interestingly, the background to this maneuver was a press campaign in Great Britain, where influential newspapers, reporting about the reopening of German universities, criticized the fact that only a few German emigrants had so far left Britain. The Society for the Protection of Science and Learning (SPSL) had already contacted the relevant branches of the British military government to facilitate a quick return of those emigrants who wanted to go back: "It is hoped," wrote the SPSL, "that the universities will invite many of these scholars to return, but their freedom of appointment is recognized and safeguarded by the plans that have been made."[4] But newspaper articles were not so tolerant. On the contrary, their agitation to protect the English job market from undesired competitors provoked harsh initiatives toward German university presidents by British officers in charge of university life. The presidents, however, proved capable of defending themselves by raising innumerable practical obstacles

3 *Göttinger Universitäts-Zeitung*, vol. 2, no. 16, p. 16.
4 Gerhard Hirschfeld, "The defence of learning and science . . . Der Academic Assistance Council in Grossbritannien und die wissenschaftliche Emigration aus Nazi-Deutschland," *Exilforschung – Ein Internationales Jahrbuch* 6 (1988):28–43.

to discovering the names of those German scholars who were willing and able to return. So the SPSL initiative received no answer from German universities nor from the North-West German Conference of University Presidents.[5]

Josef Kroll, rector of Cologne University, reported to the Ministry of Cultural Affairs that out of twenty-nine colleagues who had left his university during the Third Reich, four had already returned to Cologne and that three more had been contacted. Some had died, and the addresses of most of the rest were unknown to the university.[6] In Bonn, the philosophical faculty had tried in vain to entice medievalist Wilhelm Levison back from his British exile. In the catalog for the summer semester of 1946, he was listed with the remark "Called back, but not yet arrived." Nevertheless Levison remained in close and friendly contact with his old university. For instance, he reestablished contact with the writer Thomas Mann, in order to arrange for the university to reconfer Mann's honorary degree, which had been revoked in 1936. Levison even bequeathed his personal library to the Historical Institute and the university library, as a sign of his goodwill and his long-standing connection with his "old *alma mater Bonnensis.*"[7]

At the beginning of 1947, the nonconformist magazine of the "younger generation," *Der Ruf*, addressed the problem of the remigration of scholars. The specific occasion for the first article in *Der Ruf* was the removal of thirty-three professors from the University of Munich because of denazification and the openly expressed suspicion of German scholars that the military government wanted to lower the quality of German universities. The article listed the names of forty-two German professors who had emigrated (including such luminaries as Theodor E. Mommsen, Hans Rothfels, and Veit Valentin) and demanded that the military government and the responsible ministries arrange for the "homecoming of this huge and true Ger-

---

5 My report follows the documents found in Hauptstaatsarchiv Düsseldorf (hereafter *HSTAD*), NW 25, no. 84 ("Protokoll der Rektorenkonferenz vom 25./27.2. 1946 at Goslar"). The Northwest German Conference of Rectors, which met in September 1946 in Göttingen, again described the restoration of the rights of the émigré university teachers and their recall to teaching positions (or, rather, adequate provision for them) as a "joint duty of honor for all universities." Compare Rolf Neuhaus, ed., *Dokumente zur Hochschulreform, 1945–1959* (Wiesbaden, 1961), 16.
6 The report in HSTAD, NW 25, no. 227, January 4, 1946.
7 P. E. Hübinger, "Wilhelm Levison," in *150 Jahre Rheinische Friedrich-Wilhelm-Universität zu Bonn 1818–1968. Bonner Gelehrte. Beiträge zur Geschichte der Wissenschaften in Bonn. Geschichtswissenschaften* (Bonn, 1968), 328.

man academy" from abroad. Moreover, the author of the article made it quite clear that he considered it the moral duty of the emigrants to return to Germany now.[8]

The reaction which *Der Ruf* evoked from the United States military government makes this controversy interesting for our purposes. *Neue Zeitung*, which was published by U.S. military authorities, found the appeal important enough to reprint and to respond to extensively. Even OMGUS (Office of the Military Government of the United States) reacted. Its response made it clear that the U.S. military government would not assume the right to force particular scholars upon German universities. The selection of professors was the responsibility of the universities and the relevant ministries. The OMGUS article also referred sympathetically to those emigrants who were unwilling to return to Germany. If they had top positions at institutions in the United States, if they had employment contracts for longer periods, or if they were too old, one could not expect them to return to bombed-out German cities. Moreover, this article emphasized the tendency of the Germans to criticize the emigrants, as had Bavarian Minister-President Hoegner. The author, Dolf Sternberger, speculated how "unimaginably efficacious" it would have been if university students had demanded, unanimously and publicly, the return of the émigré scholars. He encapsulated the situation of these years when he called it a shame for the German universities that this initiative came from students and not from the professors, the faculties, or the university administrations. A subsequent article in *Neue Zeitung* revealed that the Bavarian Ministry of Cultural Affairs had contacted about fifty emigrants.[9] Despite this effort, and others, difficulties were manifest. The uncertainties of the risky return to Germany and the emotional commitment of emigrants to their new universities made it a very difficult job for the German side to entice them back.[10]

Even progress made in identifying refugee scholars could not eliminate all concern. In February 1948, the North-Rhine-Westphalian minister for social affairs complained that too few emigrants had

8 "The Future of German Universities," *Der Ruf*, no. 10, January 1, 1947.

9 *Neue Zeitung*, no. 12, February 9, 1947. The same article also quotes Alfred Weber, who had described the recall of the emigrants as the "moral and political duty of all faculties."

10 The account here is taken from Jerome Vaillant, *Der Ruf. Unabhängige Blätter der jungen Generation* (Munich, 1978), 109–13. The article which began the debate was reprinted with commentary in *Neue Zeitung* on January 4, and the response of the military government in *Neue Zeitung* on January 6.

been called back. The responsible ministry official stressed, in reply, that it was a matter of course to consider for appointments those persons who had been persecuted for political and racial reasons. However, in many cases the efforts had been in vain, because the emigrants now had outstanding positions and did not want to return to Germany. She highlighted a crucial point of such efforts when she reminded the ministry that not every emigrant would meet the requirements for a professional position.[11] Nevertheless, in 1950 the West-German Conference of University Presidents – confronted by steady attacks in the press – felt obliged to collect data from the different universities to prove that they had made all possible efforts to recall emigrant professors. Unfortunately the answers from the universities arrived so late that the staff could not compile the results in time for the conference session of 1950.[12] Later on, the question apparently was forgotten. I have been unable to locate the file in the Westdeutsche Rektorenkonferenz Archive at Bad Godesberg.[13]

The University of Frankfurt even felt obliged to take a spectacular step into the realm of public relations after the Hessian minister for cultural affairs, Dr. Stein, in a speech to the Landtag, harshly criticized the university's policy with regard to bringing back emigrants. Dr. Stein accused the university of resenting the pressure to call back the emigrants and of making only token efforts to attract them. The university thereupon published a report to prove that immediately after its reopening it had contacted jurists like Erich Kaufmann, Rudolf Smend, and Otto Kirchheimer, that it had reinstated Kurt Riezler to his position of honorary professor,[14] and that it had granted *Habilitation* to ancient historian Hermann Strasburger, which had previously been denied for political reasons. The university had already negotiated with Max Horkheimer and Paul Tillich to join the faculty. It had also welcomed economic historian Ernst D. Fraenkel and political scientist Arnold Bergsträsser as guest professors. Nev-

---

11 Referentin Dr. Auburtin to Sozialminister, March 2, 1948, HSTAD, NW 25, no. 227.
12 Universitätsarchiv Köln (Cologne University archives, hereafter *UA Köln*) 471/44 of May 10, 1950, with reference to the decision of the Nineteenth West German Rectors' Conference in Hannover in March of that year.
13 Protokoll of the Twentieth WRK (38) of August 1950 in Bonn, in WRK Archiv. Unfortunately, the responses which were received from the universities cannot be found in the archive of the WRK. I wish to thank Dr. Horst Kalischer for his friendly assistance.
14 Diplomat Kurt Riezler (1882–1955), who had been a close aide to imperial chancellor Bethmann-Hollweg between 1915–17 and had been honorary professor of philosophy at the University of Frankfurt since 1928, emigrated to the United States in 1938 and taught until 1952 at the New School for Social Research in New York.

ertheless, Dr. Stein singled out the University of Frankfurt because of its bad reputation.[15] At Heidelberg the balance sheet was also unfavorable, because out of thirty-four emigrants only four had come back.[16]

Despite these indisputable efforts, one cannot exclude the possibility that negotiations with emigrants were sometimes conducted only to impress the military government. For example, when Otto Vossler recommended to Peter Rassow, dean of the Cologne philosophical faculty, that Golo Mann be invited back to Germany, Vossler concluded, "If he rejects the invitation, you will be in the good books of the men of power and you will have shown good will."[17]

In an important step, the president of the German Research Council (Deutsche Forschungsgemeinschaft, or DFG) in December 1951 asked the chairmen of various professional organizations whether they knew of any émigré colleagues who lacked pensions. He referred to plans under consideration in the Federal Home Office to appoint these men to German "foreign" professorships, in order to provide them pensions. Gerhard Ritter, at that time chairman of the Verband der Historiker Deutschlands, named eleven historians, who, he thought, met the conditions of this plan: Viktor Ehrenberg (formerly of Prague, now of London); Fritz Epstein (*Privatdozent* Hamburg/Stanford); Gerhard Masur (*Privatdozent* Berlin/Virginia); Dietrich Gerhard (*Privatdozent* Berlin/St. Louis); Hans Baron (Newberry Library, Chicago); Hans Rosenberg (*Privatdozent* Cologne/Brooklyn College, New York); Richard Koebner (Professor, Breslau/Jerusalem); Hajo Holborn (*Privatdozent* Heidelberg/Yale); Ernst Kantorowicz (Princeton); Martin Weinbaum (*Privatdozent* Freiburg/Queens College, N.Y.); and Frances L. Carsten (*Privatdozent* Danzig/London).[18] In fact this initiative from the Bonn Home Office led to a

15 I have selected here only several examples from the extensive "Response of the Johann-Wolfgang-Goethe-University in Frankfurt am Main to the Speech to the Landtag by Minister of Cultural Affairs Dr. Erwin Stein on July 28, 1948," which selected proceedings to call faculty members predominately from the legal faculty (NL Mommsen), BAK. Stein's declaration also caused further reactions. The public debate illustrated the conflicting arguments of those who entrusted a fundamental reform to the autonomy of the universities and those politicians who regarded the universities as unsuited to pursue such a policy.

16 These figures are drawn from the excellent investigation by E. Wolgast, "Die Universität Heidelberg im Dritten Reich," in Ruprecht-Karls-Universität Heidelberg, ed., *Die Geschichte der Universität Heidelberg. Vorträge Während des Wintersemesters 1985/86* (Heidelberg, 1986), 186–216, 191.

17 UA Köln, 197/39.

18 About the last of these Ritter clearly made a mistake. F. L. Carsten, who left Germany for political reasons, received his Ph.D. in London only *after* the war. Ritter also indicated that Martin Weinbaum was at Manchester University in England; actually he taught at Queens College in New York City.

number of professional appointments for these men.[19] Expert opinions determined theoretical dates when they would have been appointed to tenured positions in Germany, thus providing a basis for the amount of the pensions to be paid under this law. It is interesting to note that this law, which provided restitution for National Socialist injustice to emigrants, was adopted and published on the same day as the law regulating the reintegration of Nazi officials into the civil service of the Federal Republic, the so-called 131 Law, was adopted.

The law of restitution was a most ambivalent measure. On the one hand, it provided at least some sort of financial justice for the men whom the Nazis had driven from their country; it tried to offer compensation for lost chances in life. On the other hand, it had an effect, surely unintentional, on the question of re-migration. The finances of the recipients of these pensions now were improved, because the émigrés now had a double income: the salary they earned abroad and the pension. Under these conditions, it would have been against all financial common sense to return to Germany and to give up this favorable treatment. I mention this problem with some trepidation, but after discussions with some older German colleagues who had personal contacts with emigrants, I think it is worthy of consideration.

We know only too well that there was no significant return of emigrants which might have effected a new orientation of historical writing in the Federal Republic of Germany. The very few returnees of the first postwar years[20] were Hans-Joachim Schoeps (to Erlangen), Ernst D. Fraenkel (to Frankfurt), Walter Mohr (to Saarbrücken), and Hans Rothfels (to Tübingen). Rothfels had already received several offers of university chairs before his impressive performance at the first postwar meeting of German historians.[21] He considered his return to Germany to be a "return to a position given

---

19 The basis for this was the Law to Regulate the Reparation for National Socialist Injustice to Members of the Public Service, of May 11, 1951 (*Bundesgesetzblatt,* pt. 1 (1951):291–6). The 131-Law dates from the same day.

20 Of 134 historian-emigrants, only 21 returned to the two German states during the first two decades after the end of the war. This data comes from *Biographischen Handbuch der deutschsprachigen Emigration nach 1933,* edited by the Institut für Zeitgeschichte and by the Research Foundation for Jewish Immigration (Munich, 1980–3). I heartily thank Lothar Mertens, M. A. (Bochum) for preparing these data. The presentation by Horst Möller, *Exodus der Kultur. Schriftsteller, Wissenschaftler und Künstler in der Emigration nach 1933* (München, 1984), esp. 102–18, is also based upon this material.

21 In the summer of 1947, he received offers from Erlangen and Heidelberg. In 1951, he accepted the offer from Tübingen. For a biography of Rothfels, see the obituary by Werner Conze in *Historische Zeitschrift* 237 (1983):311–60, 347.

by nature."[22] Golo Mann did not come back until 1958. In 1947, he was not yet interested in returning, and later it took several attempts for him to obtain a professorship in the Federal Republic, over the opposition of conservative faculties. Dietrich Gerhard also came back in the 1950s. In 1954, he took a chair in American history at Cologne University, but he retained his American post in St. Louis even after he moved to the Max-Planck-Institute for history in Göttingen in 1961. Several attempts by Fritz Epstein, a specialist in Eastern European history who worked in the United States as a librarian, to return to a German university or research institution failed. In 1955, when he theoretically had a chance to receive an offer from Cologne University (after the first man on the list had declined), the ministry in Düsseldorf passed him over, for reasons which were very difficult to explain to Epstein. German colleagues blamed financial considerations, but Epstein was nevertheless deeply hurt. Three years later, when he sought appointment as director of the Munich Institut für Zeitgeschichte, Hans Rothfels had to tell him that this appointment would tarnish the institute by giving it the reputation of a "Morgenthau-Institute."[23]

Other emigrants who belonged to the liberal school of Friedrich Meinecke – in spite of Meinecke's personal intervention with Hajo Holborn and Hans Rosenberg – remained in the United States and came back to Germany only as guest professors.[24] By returning to serve as part-time teachers at German universities, they highlighted for the German academic world the changes that could have occurred in Germany had more emigrants gone back permanently, for they tried to demonstrate in their books and articles the fatal influence of certain continuities in German history, based upon serious research. More important was the fact that they returned to Germany only temporarily, too late, or not at all.[25] Because the emigrant historians

---

22 Thus in a letter to Kaehler (1951), mentioned in Meinecke, *Werke*, 7 vols. (Stuttgart, 1957–68), ed. by Hans Herzfeld, Carl Hinrichs, and Walter Hofer: vol. 6, *Ausgewählter Briefwechsel*, 565. On the position of Rothfels among the emigrants, see Georg Iggers, "The Decline of the Classical National Tradition of German Historiography," *History and Theory* 6 (1967): 382–412, 393.

23 Rothfels to Epstein, December 30, 1958, NL Epstein, no. 82, Schieder–Epstein Correspondence, BAK.

24 Meinecke, *Ausgewählter Briefwechsel*, 247, where Meinecke spoke of the lack of good forces. In a letter to Rassow on February 19, 1947, Meinecke spoke of the rising generation in modern history as a "ruin" (UA Köln 197/39). Hajo Holborn was in Germany in the fall of 1947 merely in the service of the American government, in order to prepare a report on the progress of democratization.

25 Compare B. Faulenbach, "Der 'deutsche Weg' aus der Sicht des Exils. Zum Urteil emi-

remained abroad, the German historical profession failed to under-
take the much-promised and much-debated revision of historical
thinking that was needed after 1948–9. Even Friedrich Meinecke,
who had sharply attacked Prussian militarism in 1946, retreated in
1949. He spoke not of "guilt" but of "tragedy," for Germany, he
stated, had acted in legitimate self-defense. Hajo Holborn never hesi-
tated to criticize his teacher for this change of mind.[26]

II

All these observations attempt to sketch the total picture, and of
necessity they neglect the personal situations of emigrants who were
confronted with the question of an eventual return. Before I risk
some general remarks about the personal plight of emigrant historians, I would like to examine the special fate of Hans Rosenberg. It
seems to be a good example to illustrate both the difficulties posed
for German faculties that sought to entice an emigrant back and the
problems of the emigrants themselves.

There is no need to give a biography of Hans Rosenberg, from
his Cologne *Habilitation* in 1932 up to his teaching career at Brooklyn
College in New York, which began in 1938. In 1944 he became a
citizen of the United States.[27] As early as March 1946, Peter Rassow
addressed an appeal to him, as well as to all other émigré faculty
members, in response to a formal order of the British Military Government. Rassow wrote:

After Nazi domination has been abolished, all regulations by which members of the faculty have been excluded for racial or political reasons have
become obsolete. The philosophical faculty begs you to return to our community and to take again the place you once had. Certainly it is a very
difficult undertaking to come back to Cologne, a city for the most part
destroyed, and to take root here again. Just as intensively as we shall work

grierter Historiker," *Exilforschung. Ein Internationales Jahrbuch* 3 (1985):11–30.

26 The articles by Meinecke and Holborn were printed in *Der Monat*: Meinecke, "Irrwege in
unserer Geschichte?" *Der Monat* 2 (1949): 3–6; Holborn and Geoffrey Barraclough,
"Irrwege in unserer Geschichte? Zwei ausländische Historiker kommentieren Friedrich
Meineckes Aufsatz," *Der Monat* 2 (1950): 531–5.

27 H. Rosenberg, "Rückblick aud ein Historikerleben zwischen zwei Kulturen," in idem,
*Machteliten und Wirtschaftskonjunkturen. Studien zur neueren deutschen Sozial-und Wirtschaftsge-
schichte* (Göttingen, 1978), 11–23, deals only very briefly with his personal fate. Of course
it became quite clear to what degree Rosenberg's historical works were influenced by the
question after the ultimate success of National Socialism in "secular sight." See H. A.
Winkler, "Ein Erneuerer der Geschichtswissenschaft. Hans Rosenberg 1904–1988," *Historische Zeitschrift* 248 (1989): 529–55.

to reconstruct our university, so vigorously shall we do everything possible to help you become reestablished.[28]

Rosenberg rejected this general offer, which was not connected with any definite job and which all university faculties were required to send to their émigré members in 1946. But he declined it politely, even deeply moved, pointing out his possession of a secure job in New York, saying nothing definite about a possible return to Germany.

Negotiations began in Cologne to fill the chair vacated by liberal historian Johannes Ziekursch, whose pupil Rosenberg had once been. Rosenberg was a serious candidate from the beginning; Meinecke himself had recommended him in a letter to Rassow. Discussions very soon narrowed the list to Theodor Schieder, Hans Rosenberg, Hans Herzfeld, and Carl Hinrichs, in that order, the last two names placed *ex aequo* in third place. The reasons for this order became much clearer when the dean sent a "supplement" to the list to the board of curators. This supplement was occasioned by a letter from Rosenberg detailing his latest publications and – above all – his interesting plans for teaching in the next five years.[29] Thereafter the philosophical faculty emphasized its desire to persuade Rosenberg to accept the chair: "If the information had arrived earlier in Cologne, the faculty undoubtedly would have put Hans Rosenberg at the top of the list," wrote the dean to the chairman of the board of curators. "The faculty refrains from changing the list only because this could be seen as a discourtesy toward Professor Schieder, who was kind enough to agree to substitute for the chairholder in the next semester, if he has been denazified by that time." The dean proposed this resolution in a session of the board at which the mayor of Cologne, Robert Görlinger, who had been an emigrant too, showed his personal interest in Hans Rosenberg.

Since Rosenberg's readiness to come to Cologne was uncertain,

28 UA Köln, 197/39.
29 Rosenberg's plans are of special interest precisely because of the relatively unchanged course offerings of the historical seminars. He described to the Cologne faculty ten main thematic points which he wished to treat in lectures and seminars ("What is to be expected and not to be expected of me"): history of dictatorship from the Renaissance to the present; world history since 1914; general history of early capitalism (1200–1750); general history of high capitalism and the planned economy; comparative constitutional and administration history of Europe and North America in the modern era; German history from the Reformation to the French Revolution; German history since 1815; Russian history; history of political theory and social philosophy from the Middle Ages to the present.

the board left the list formally unchanged but directed Dean Fritz Schalk to inquire immediately about Rosenberg's plans. "If Rosenberg shows an interest, we are going to demand the appointment of Rosenberg from the ministry." That meant that the continuation of the proceedings now depended upon Rosenberg's answer.

Rosenberg found himself in a difficult situation after he received Dean Schalk's letter, compounded by the fact that the British university officer indicated his personal interest, in a postscript to the same letter. At that moment, Rosenberg recognized that he had raised expectations too high in Cologne by sending his letters, his list of books and articles, and his teaching plans. As early as the middle of September 1947, he had been puzzled that Cologne expected an answer to the question " 'When,' although the question of 'If' is not yet clear to me," he wrote. In letters to Cologne, he stressed that good friends had warned him against returning to bombed-out Cologne, posed questions about the status of Cologne libraries, and once more underlined his obligations to Brooklyn College and to his wife. Also he wanted greater clarity about the psychic and political climate in Cologne, especially about the problem of anti-Semitism.

Rosenberg's answer illustrates the difficult decision facing emigrants when they were confronted, in that very early postwar period, with the question of suddenly leaving the secure and rich United States. "There are too many uncertainties, complexities, and imponderables in the picture," Rosenberg wrote back to Cologne on November 27. "I cannot accept a permanent professorship at Cologne University." From my impression of the records and my conversations with Rosenberg in the last year of his life, it was respect for his wife, who had seen her destroyed hometown in the summer of 1947, which made Rosenberg reject the offer from Cologne. Had he been alone, I am sure he would have been ready to go back to Germany.

Subsequently the board of Cologne University did not have to proceed as it would have had Rosenberg answered positively. Theodor Schieder, who already was serving as substitute professor in Cologne, could now be appointed to a permanent position, and he began his remarkable and important teaching career there. In the case of Hans Rosenberg, the faculty had taken all possible steps – insofar as I can judge the case from the records of the faculty, the board, and the personal papers of Rosenberg himself – to attract back an émigré colleague. I did not find any hint of personal resentment against Rosenberg or other emigrants.[30]

But Cologne was not the only faculty which would have liked to make Rosenberg a colleague. Even though the Free University of Berlin was not as ambitious in this regard as was Cologne, there can be no doubt that Meinecke urged Rosenberg strongly to return to Germany, for he appointed him guest lecturer in Berlin in December 1948. Meinecke reported to Siegfried A. Kaehler at the end of May 1949 that after "the failure to keep the extremely successful Rosenberg in Berlin," the faculty planned to think seriously of Hans Herzfeld.[31]

III

Even after this presentation of a well-documented single case, it seems very difficult to make a final judgment about the intensity and seriousness of the efforts to call back émigré historians. If one considers the inner resistance developed by emigrants against Germany during the years of National Socialism, the extremely insecure conditions of life in occupied postwar Germany, and the relatively low number of men who had a high enough scholarly profile to be appointed to a professorship, one must finally conclude that, under the given circumstances, one could not have tried very much harder. One must emphasize Meinecke's tone of regret when he pointed out in a letter to Hajo Holborn the general difficulty of finding capable candidates for modern history chairs in postwar Germany.[32]

Even Hans Rothfels, who usually is described as immediately ready to return after the war, found himself in a dilemma in October 1950, when he had to decide between a history chair at Tübingen and a guest professorship in Berlin. The main question, he wrote to

---

30 The circumstances of the appointment, which without a doubt indicated the direction of the postwar German historical profession, is recounted here on the basis of Cologne appointment records, the protocol of the Kuratorium (UA Köln 197 / 39 and 471 / 44), and supplementary documents in the private possession of Hans Rosenberg.

31 A review of the pertinent documents in the archive of the Free University of Berlin revealed this (Hochschularchiv FUB: Rektorat, Akte 2 / 2500 / 1 [Phil. Fak., Dek., 1949–60] vom 8. Dez. 1948), for which I heartily thank Michael Erbe. Meinecke's statement is here quoted from G. A. Ritter, "Hans Herzfeld. Persönlichkeit und Werk," *Jahrbuch für die Geschichte Mittel-und Ostdeutschlands* 32 (1983):13–91, 60.

32 Meinecke to Holborn, March 19, 1946, in Meinecke, *Ausgewählter Briefwechsel*, 247.

Fritz Epstein, was whether to return to Germany at all, and he asked Epstein for his opinion on this central issue. Epstein's answer not only shows the personal difficulties of the emigrants in general, but it may also explain the impossibility of coming to a final judgment on this question. The problem, Epstein replied, was that on a decision of such consequence, no one was able to speak for another: "You know very well about the advantages of an eventual return, and I feel like you. In my opinion it is decisive whether you have true friends, whether you have found professional and personal response or will find it sometime." The ages of his children certainly played a role for him, and maybe – so he reasoned, to encourage himself – one could do something from the United States for scholarly cooperation with Germany. Concerning the last question in Rothfels' letter, Epstein could only report good news. After his visit to Berlin, he felt convinced that the present generation of students was not going to forget in the future the harm that the persecution of Jews had done to the German name.[33]

Naturally one cannot generalize this exchange between Rothfels and Epstein to all émigré historians, but it highlighted the most important aspects of the discussion on the subject. We may take it for granted, however, that the decision of an emigrant family to return depended more decisively upon their specific personal and professional perspective on life in the United States than upon a political evaluation of German conditions before and after the war. A scholar whose children were still attending college saw no immediate reason to return, nor did colleagues who for good reasons felt deeply obligated to their American friends, who had helped them out in the most difficult situation of their lives.

The balance sheet cannot be drawn solely from the mere number of historians who went back to Germany to live and work. We must also consider historians who periodically returned to Germany as guest professors, such as Rosenberg, Dietrich Gerhard, Fritz Epstein, and Gerhard Masur.[34] Theodor Mommsen, Ernst Kantorowicz, Hajo Holborn, and Felix Gilbert, all of whom had decided to remain in the United States, discussed these guest professorships many times. They regarded it as their special duty to intensify scholarly exchange between the United States and the western part of Germany, and

33 NL Epstein, no. 102, Briefwechsel Epstein–Rothfels, BAK.
34 Horst Möller, *Exodus der Kultur*, 105–6, has correctly called attention to this point.

they sought to establish a new attitude of cooperation toward Germany at their American universities.[35]

Viewed from the perspective of the 1990s, we must emphasize that there was – as Friedrich Meinecke observed in 1949 – no form of *emigrantisches ressentiment* among the emigrants.[36] It was surprising how quickly the émigrés reestablished contact with Germany, through the exchange of letters and regards and – more importantly – parcels, and through requests for books which had been published in Germany during the war. I was somewhat astonished, even shocked, to find that the return to normality in this regard came about as quickly as the return to business as usual within the German historical profession. Hans Rosenberg demonstrated that he knew very well how to differentiate between qualified, personally honest, and politically harmless former party members and several "denazified Nazis" who had to be watched, when he remarked upon the development of the Free University of Berlin, with its different categories of politically charged professors.[37]

Hans Rothfels also emphasized, in his report about a journey he made to Germany in 1949 under the auspices of the so-called reorientation program, the astonishing ease of relations with colleagues who all "had been affiliated with the Nazi setup in one way or another."[38] I could not discover any examples of a breakdown in personal relations. The intensity of exchange programs everywhere demonstrates the quickly restored willingness to cooperate. This seems to be a remarkable phenomenon which may have some significance for the strength of the historical guild and its professional values, its "team spirit," and the close ties of the emigrants to the cultural system of Germany and Europe. When I read the letters exchanged between some refugee scholars and their German colleagues just after the war, I was very astonished to find that they attributed only minor significance to the Holocaust and to the problem of "guilt," a fact that cannot be explained solely by a low level of awareness of the terrible dimensions of the "final solution."[39]

---

35 I base this point upon a letter from Felix Gilbert, for which I am most grateful to him.
36 Meinecke to Dehio, July 21, 1947, in Meinecke, *Ausgewählter Briefwechsel*, 281.
37 Thus in a letter to Howard Johnson of September 24, 1949 (private possession of Hans Rosenberg).
38 NL Rothfels, no. 59, BAK. It is interesting to note in this connection that in 1933 Eckart Kehr had described Hans Rothfels as "the first Fascist among German historians" (quoted from Joachim F. Radkau, *Die deutsche Emigration in den USA. Ihr Einfluss auf die amerikanische Europapolitik 1933–1945* [Düsseldorf, 1971], 308, n. 254).
39 On several aspects of this problem, compare Walter Laqueur, *The Terrible Secret: Suppression*

The close ties between refugee historians and their colleagues in Germany seem to form a remarkable contrast to the fact that only a few scholars found their way back to Germany. Veit Valentin, who evidently was willing to return, died not long after his first visit to Frankfurt in January 1947.[40] A man like Hajo Holborn, who had gone into emigration in 1933 under the guise of beginning a "journey for studies" and had hoped that the journey would end one day at home, refused to respond to the earnest entreaties of his old teacher Friedrich Meinecke.[41]

I wish to add one more observation to this puzzle of impressions about the postwar period in the German historical profession. There not only was an emigration to the United States and other secure countries; there was also a kind of inner emigration in Germany. I do not include here those German historians who had been consciously silent during the Third Reich or had even been in contact with the resistance movement (like Fritz Kern, Gerhard Ritter, Friedrich Baethgen, or Peter Rassow). Instead I want to mention a man who had lived in obscurity as a *Vierteljude,* as he described himself in his curriculum vitae for the U.S. Military Government in 1946, Ludwig Dehio (the son of the famous art historian Georg Dehio), who had survived the Nazi regime as an archivist at the Prussian archive at Berlin-Charlottenburg.

In 1946, Friedrich Meinecke, who had come into closer contact with Dehio during the war, recommended him for the position of editor-in-chief of *Historische Zeitschrift.* After some hesitation, Dehio accepted this job, which gave him a key position in the German historical guild. His work for this first-rank scholarly journal offered him the chance to press for a revision of German history, which seemed indispensable to him. He did not want to return to business as usual, but he instead looked searchingly for new insights into his troubled times by means of historical investigation. It was his firm intention to include in each issue of the journal some great article by a leading historian, discussing the changes in German political life since the catastrophe. However, his policy could not triumph over the "terrible urge for normalcy." When he could not quickly find

---

of the Truth about Hitler's "Final Solution" (London, 1980).

40 Compare Peter Th. Walther, "Emigrierte deutsche Historiker in den USA," *Berichte zur Wissenschaftsgeschichte* 7 (1984):41–52, 49.

41 The quotation comes from a letter from Holborn to Dietrich Gerhard in September 1933, Dietrich Gerhard, "Hajo Holborn: Reminiscences," *Central European History* 3 (1969): 9–48, 14.

the path-breaking articles he sought, his publisher could delay publication no longer. Dehio wanted to bring out the first postwar number of *Historische Zeitschrift* with at least a new foreword – more critical, more committed – but the publisher did not want to open the new series with Dehio's bitter prose, which deplored the "improverishment of our science as a consequence of forbidding free discussion, of separation from foreign countries, of emigration, . . . and of the sheer misery after the catastrophe." According to the publisher, these clear words did not suit the situation of 1949.[42]

During my research I found only relatively few historians who were clearly willing to return to Germany without first arranging for a position. Helmut Hirsch, who taught at Roosevelt College in Chicago, wrote to Gerhard Ritter in 1952 to express the wish "not only to visit my old *Heimat* but to try to find a job in Germany, in spite of the enormous difficulties." Six years later, he wrote to Hans Rothfels that he wanted to go back to Germany because he saw no professional future for himself in the United States. He was able to return only in 1961, when he found a position at the Verwaltungs- und Wirtschaftsakademie in Düsseldorf, where he taught until 1969.[43] As far as I know, Gerhard Masur, Fritz Epstein, and George Wolfgang Hallgarten were willing to go back to Germany but could not find a satisfactory tenured position.[44] They had to content themselves with guest lectures and other forms of scholarly cooperation. It is too difficult to make a judgment about the relative professional reputations of these very different scholars, but I learned from discussions among the emigrants themselves that there were important differences which were known both in the United States and in Germany.

It seems, then, that to be fair one must recognize that much was done to bring the émigré historians back to the German universities and that problem cases do not prove the existence of a general policy

---

42 This sentence was part of an introductory article by Dehio, intended for the first issue of *Historische Zeitschrift* but never published. The text may now be found in Schulze, *Deutsche Geschichtswissenschaft*, 101–4.

43 Letter to Ritter, dated March 3, 1952, in Archiv des Verbandes der Historiker Deutschlands, Max-Planck-Institut für Geschichte, Göttingen, and a similar letter to E. W. Zeeden from 1957. The letter to Rothfels, dated November 18, 1957, is from NL Rothfels, no. 1, BAK. Hirsch first returned to the Federal Republic in 1958. He taught at the Administrative and Economic Academy in Düsseldorf from 1962 to 1969 and as honorary professor at the Comprehensive University at Duisburg from 1973 to 1977. I am grateful to Helmut Hirsch (Düsseldorf) for this supplementary information.

44 Compare also Walther, "Emigrierte deutsche Historiker."

of keeping them out of Germany. The remarkable influence that guest professors like Hans Rosenberg exercised in Germany also tends to disprove any policy of exclusion. But the attitude of the professional organization of German historians was quite different. When German historians met for the first time after World War II at Munich, Gerhard Ritter assumed the role of natural spokesman of German historians, a position of eminence recognized much more in the United States, than in Germany itself. Ritter found no reason for a general reorientation of historical scholarship in Germany. He even felt obliged to criticize voices from the United States that warned about the traditional and even *völkische* character of some historical dissertations produced in Germany.[45] This meeting of German historians, which on the one hand welcomed Hans Rothfels warmly, on the other hand said nothing about the émigré historians. Those who had expected some expression of regret, not to mention an admission of guilt, from Gerhard Ritter, who had helped to draft the Stuttgart "confession of guilt" of the Protestant churches, must have been disappointed after his opening speech. He complained about the loss of libraries and archives and about the difficulty of arranging scholarly exchanges between the occupation zones, but he neither found a word of regret for the loss of the émigré scholars nor voiced any sense of obligation to attempt to reestablish relations with his colleagues abroad. He found it necessary, however, to attack Felix Gilbert for his critiques of some postwar dissertations which seemed, by their choice of concepts, to prolong the Nazi era in the field of historical research.[46]

It would give a false picture to exaggerate the influence exercised by the émigré scholars after their return or during their visiting professorships, but their role was significant. Hans Rothfels was politically indistinguishable from his conservative German colleagues, but he nonetheless established the new branch of contemporary history in Germany, introduced systematic approaches from political science into history, and sharply attacked the traditional paradigm of objectivity. Hans Rosenberg influenced a generation of Berlin students like Otto Büsch, Friedrich Zunkel, Gerhard A. Ritter, and

---

45 In his speech at the first meeting after World War II at Munich; cf. "Gegenwärtige Lage und Zukunftsaufgaben deutscher Geschichtswissenschaft," *Historische Zeitschrift* 170 (1950):1–22, where he criticized Felix Gilbert.
46 Felix Gilbert, "German Historiography during the Second World War," *American Historical Review* 53 (1947–8):50–8.

later Hans-Ulrich Wehler. On the other hand we must recognize that the important development of "modern German social history" during the 1950s did not stem from the traditions of Karl Lamprecht or Otto Hintze but from a special sort of history that I would like to call a "denazified *Volksgeschichte,*" propagated by men like Otto Brunner, Hans Freyer, Gunter Ipsen, and Werner Conze and going back to the "discovery" of the *Volk* in the early Weimar republic. Of necessity, the writing of history had changed under the experience of National Socialism. Only after the war did the many ruptures in German society from the middle of the nineteenth century find their way into the conceptual system of German history, a process which had been completed much earlier in other European countries.[47] Only after the experience of National Socialism did the "history of mankind," as it was proposed vaguely by Friedrich Meinecke, become possible "as a great historical duty of the future."[48] Meinecke's insights could not come to fruition all at once. The concept was first discussed by Werner Conze and Theodor Schieder, when Conze criticized the traditional historical method as inadequate to the modern world and when Schieder tried to define the role of "man in history." Schieder, especially, tried to create a kind of history consciously oriented toward man, who was to be found in the "social constructs" built by human beings, thus reconciling the fruitless polarization of individualism and collectivism.

But this method of *Volksgeschichte,* which was rebaptized "social history" or "structural history" and organized, above all, in Conze's "Working Group for Modern Social History" after 1957, was only one form of innovation within the German historical profession. A second and weaker influence came from the liberal wing of the Weimar historians, who, for example, explored the relation between the foreign policy and the domestic policy of states; the sociohistorical foundation of the military organizations of states; or the social conditions of the production and reception of ideas.

This partial recourse to the conceptual discussions of the Weimar periods unites – at least in my essay – these two methodological approaches. Hans Rosenberg profited from his first postwar contacts with Germany, obtaining the collected essays of Otto Hintze, which had been published during the war. Felix Gilbert and Fritz Epstein

---

47 I discuss this point in Chapter 16 of my *Deutsche Geschichtswissenschaft.*
48 Meinecke to S. A. Kaehler, January 29, 1945, in Meinecke, *Ausgewählter Briefwechsel,* 514.

were already convinced in 1948 that "Otto Hintze will more and more be recognized as one of the greatest German historians in modern times."[49] When Theodor Schieder praised the new edition of Hintze's collected essays in 1963, the two directions were brought together, and a broader basis for further development of German historical writing was established.

49 Epstein to J. Dow about a remark made by Gilbert in an article in *American Historical Review* (NL Epstein, no. 59, BAK).

Conclusion

JAMES J. SHEEHAN

In 1959, philosopher Karl Löwith offered these reflections on his experiences as a refugee and on his homecoming:

After an absence of eighteen years I returned to Germany in 1952 and found that, despite all that had happened in the meantime, the situation in the universities was remarkably unchanged. Only later did I realize how little the emigration to a foreign country, the experience with other ways of thought, the destiny of history itself could change the character of an adult or of a nation. To be sure, one learned something and could not view the remains of old Europe as if one had never left. But one did not become a different person, even though one did not simply stay the same; one became what one is and within the limits of what one can be.[1]

To what extent does Löwith's assessment hold true for the refugees to whom this book is devoted and to the historical profession to which some of them returned?

The first thing to be said about this question is that it has no single answer. As many of the preceding essays have shown, the character and fate of the refugees, their experience in America, and their relationship to Germany were all extremely diverse. A man like Hans Rothfels, probably the best-established of the refugees before 1933, stayed in Germany as long as he could and returned as soon as possible. His address to the meeting of German historians in 1949, which is described in Winfried Schulze's essay, was an expression of continuity rather than conversion. Rothfels was, as Schulze put it, "at home again." Few other refugees found it so easy to go home again. The practical difficulties of making a life in Germany during the postwar years were formidable. Moreover, many of the refugees had developed new personal and professional ties that they were

---

1 Karl Löwith, *Mein Leben in Deutschland vor und nach 1933* (Frankfurt, 1989), 151. (My translation)

226

reluctant to abandon. Finally, how welcome they would be in their old universities was, at best, an open question: While there is no evidence of systematic discrimination against refugees, there were also few signs that the German profession was prepared to confront the moral and practical implications of the refugees' fate.

The German historical profession that so vigorously applauded Rothfels in 1949 probably corresponded rather closely to the picture of German academic life that Löwith drew ten years later. Coming to terms with their own recent history – what came to be called "mastering the past" – would take time, both for professional historians and their society. Thus Ludwig Dehio's attempt to begin his editorship of *Historische Zeitschrift* with a critical confrontation with the Nazi past was defeated by a widespread desire to get on with the pressing concerns of the postwar present. For the first decade or so of its existence, the Federal Republic's historical profession sought an odd kind of normalcy: No one apologized for the crimes of nazism, but few believed that their primary task was to explain nazism's place in German history.

During the 1960s, a different climate of opinion developed among German historians. A series of dramatic historiographic controversies – most significantly, those surrounding Fritz Fischer's work on the origins of the First World War – raised important questions about nazism's historical origins and significance. By the end of the decade, a new generation of scholars, their careers greatly aided by the expansion of the German university system, began to publish work that was highly critical of German historical traditions and historiographic conventions. Of course, not everyone, even among the younger generation, shared these views. It was not long before the "critical historiography" most closely associated with the work of Hans-Ulrich Wehler came under attack from a number of directions. German historiography soon became – and has remained – a highly contentious enterprise. However one might feel about these polemics, there seems no doubt that they are a sign of vitality and engagement, clear indications of the transformation that has occurred in the German historical profession during the past twenty years.

A number of refugee historians played a role in this transformation. In their writing and, more significantly, through the personal contacts they made in Germany as visiting professors, scholars like Hans Rosenberg and Hajo Holborn helped German historians find alternative foundations upon which to build their own, critical vision of the German past. Once again, the refugees functioned as ambassadors, in part from the New World, in part from those sectors of prewar German thought that had been repressed under nazism. Through the refugees, German historians were reintroduced to Eckart Kehr, Veit Valentin, Johannes Ziekursch, and other democratically engaged scholars from the Weimar era. Of course the refugees' relationship to the new Germany was sometimes strained, their attitudes ambivalent, their connections overlaid with new loyalties and commitments. Nevertheless, it is very likely that their influence was most significant and will prove most enduring in their native land. In this sense, the refugees returned to their origins and picked up again the political and intellectuals threads that had been severed in 1933.

Name Index

229